Feminist Sociology

BSA *New Horizons in Sociology*

The British Sociological Association is publishing a series of books to review the state of the discipline at the beginning of the millenium. New Horizons in Sociology also seeks to locate the contribution of British scholarship to the wider development of sociology. Sociology is taught in all the major institutions of higher education in the United Kingdom as well as throughout North America and the Europe of the former western bloc. Sociology is now establishing itself in the former eastern bloc. But it was only in the second half of the twentieth century that sociology moved from the fringes of UK academic life into the mainstream. British sociology has also provided a home for movements that have renewed and challenged the discipline; the revival of academic Marxism, the renaissance in feminist theory, the rise of cultural studies, for example. Some of these developments have become sub-disciplines whilst yet others have challenged the very basis of the sociological enterprise. Each has left their mark. Now therefore is a good time both to take stock and to scan the horizon, looking back and looking forward.

Recent volumes include:

Nationalism and Social Theory
Gerard Delanty and Patrick O'Mahoney

Interactionism
Paul Atkinson and William Housley

Feminist Sociology

Sara Delamont

SAGE Publications
London ▪ Thousand Oaks ▪ New Delhi

First published 2003

SAGE Publications Ltd
6 Bonhill Street
London EC2A 4PU

SAGE Publications Inc
2455 Teller Road
Thousand Oaks, California 91320

SAGE Publications India Pvt Ltd
32, M-Block Market
Greater Kailash - I
New Delhi 110 - 017

British Library Cataloguing in Publication data

A catalogue record for this book is available from the British Library

ISBN 0 7619 7254 4 Cb
ISBN 0 7619 7255 2 PB

Library of Congress Control Number Available

Printed and bound in Great Britain by TJ International Ltd, Padstow, Cornwall

contents

acknowledgements

I am grateful to Robert Moore for encouraging me to write this book. Paul Atkinson has allowed me to rehearse all the ideas in here many times and as he has actually read *Breaking Out* he also understands them. Rosemary Bartle Jones and Karen Chivers word-processed this book for me, and I am very grateful. The ideas in this book have been clarified over thirty years of argument with women and men, from Margo Harding (then Galloway) in Edinburgh, and Lorna Duffin and Irene Jones in Leicester, to Teresa Rees and Amanda Coffey in Cardiff. I dedicate it to Ginnie Olesen who is always an inspiration.

introduction

of silverbacks and tree houses

When struggling to write this book I wondered why I had asked to do so. On hearing about the series I wrote to the editor Robert Moore and asked who was writing the gender/feminism volume. In part this was to ensure that feminist, and gender issues were included in the series: the price of feminist inclusion is often eternal vigilance. Had I been told that volumes had already been commissioned on women and/or on feminism and/or on gender, I would have rejoiced and got on with other projects. When Robert Moore told me that he had yet to organise any book on gender or 'women and men' or feminism or queer theory or men's studies I stepped forward and said I was available as an author if that would suit him, even though writing a book like this is a poisoned chalice. However, I did also want to write it, because I had finished an introductory textbook on gender in modern Britain (Delamont, 2001) and that had led me to revisit and rethink where I stood on a whole range of topics in feminist sociology which I had not been addressing since I had finished *Knowledgeable Women* (Delamont, 1989b). Robert Moore and I discussed how gender, feminism, queer theory, and the new men's studies might or might not figure in the series, and settled on the structure and perspective of this book. I got the contract, cleared the desk (metaphorically) and started to write, to read and reread, and to think and rethink. Writing a book on feminist sociology is not a recipe for a quiet or an apolaustic life: only for serious struggle. There have been six problems. These dilemmas are not unique to me, of course: most are old favourites. I have confessed to each, and to my solution, below. They are: (1) demarcating feminist sociology from feminist perspectives in other disciplines; (2) distinguishing feminist sociology from the sociology of women and/or of gender; (3) dealing with the malestream of sociology; (4) the temptation of messy texts and fictions; (5) the fear of rejection by my sisters; (6) and the lure of detective stories.

The biggest problem is the large, and rapidly expanding literature on feminism, on gender studies and on lesbian and gay studies. Not only is it hard to keep up with that literature (there were three collections of feminist science studies published by one firm in 2001 and many many more in fields like cultural studies or literary criticism), there is also a definitional problem. How far is this work *sociology*? Take, for example, Ahmed et al.'s (2000) collection *Transformations: Thinking through Feminism*, which frames a book series of the same title. Is the book a contribution to sociology? Is the series? There are sociologists in the volume, but there are also scholars in other fields such as English and Philosophy. Oxford University Press have a series: Oxford Readings in Feminism Studies with 12 titles. There is no book on Feminism and Sociology, but many of the titles that do exist address themes central to sociology (the public and the private, science, race, cultural studies). *A Glossary of Feminist Theory* by Andermahr et al. (2000) is, similarly, a collaboration between two sociologists and a literary theorist: is it sociology or not? Deciding to exclude feminist work because it is not primarily sociological seems petty, yet the book is for a British Sociological Association (BSA) series, and is meant to be about sociology. The distinction is not trivial. Much of the dispute in Allen and Howard's (2000) collection is between political scientists (Hekman, 2000) and sociologists (Smith, 2000), and focuses on feminist ideas becoming troubled at disciplinary boundaries. Smith robustly attacks Hekman: 'Susan Hekman's interpretation of my work is so systematically out to lunch it is difficult to write a response ... Apart from a lack of care and thought, what is she doing that leads to her systematic misreading?' (2000: 59).

Smith's answer to her own robust and rhetorical question lies partly in disciplinary differences. 'Speak for your own discipline, Susan', she cautions. Sticking strictly to Sociology could involve leaving out many important and exciting ideas; even if we do not entirely follow the late Carl Couch's (1997: 102) statement that 'most sociologists are as dull as turnips'. Also, I have a weakness for straying into anthropology, my original discipline, while steering away from political science, philosophy, economics or psycho-analytic theory, where I feel alien. Some of the topics I have treated as sociological overlap with other disciplines. Domestic violence is perhaps the best example. This is a social problem that has been extensively researched by criminologists, and I have drawn on that discipline in my thinking about domestic violence.

Distinguishing feminist sociology from the sociologies of women and/or of gender is a second problem. There are certainly anti-feminist writings on women and on gender, and there are publications on women and gender whose authors may not self-identify as feminists, or who may self-identify but are unrecognisable as feminists to anyone else. In the 1970s any sociological research on women or on gender was potentially feminist because all the empirical areas were only just open-ing up, and so all the research done was mutually cited and integrated. In 2002 it is possible for a sociologist to do research on, for example, women and divorce, and not be feminist at all, not to cite feminist work, and not to be integrated with any feminist sociology. For this book I have charitably assumed that anyone who wrote about women or gender from a feminist perspective, loosely defined, in the period 1960–80 'counts' as a feminist sociologist for this book. After 1980, I have narrowed the focus to include only those authors who have self-defined as feminist.

A third dilemma turns on men: should I focus on sociological work by, on, and for women, or scrutinise the impact of feminist perspectives on malestream sociology and men's responses to feminist sociology? There is no easy answer to this: the dilemma is central to Chapter 5. This dilemma is shared by many distinguished feminist sociologists. Joan Acker (1997), for example, confesses to it. Here I know that I am going to annoy many feminists, because I am committed to changing the malestream. Throughout my career I have always been an advocate of feminist ideas being incorporated into a changed malestream. My whole academic life has been spent campaigning for qualitative meth-ods and (liberal) feminist perspectives to be taken seriously by leading scholars in sociology. From this standpoint, my 30-year battle is nowhere near won. There is a continuing need to harry malestream sociologists to take feminist perspectives seriously, to cite women, to read women's work, and to confess to previous sexist sins of omission and commission. I do not see any point in creating a feminist ghetto.

ix

Here comes a diversion from the five problems. Talk of ghettos leads inevitably to thoughts of the golem (Collins and Pinch, 1993, 1998; Lichtenstein and Sinclair, 1999; Meyrink, 1915; Ripellino, 1995). Meyrink's novel tells of a rabbi in Prague who, in 1580, created a golem from mud, to be a giant shambling servant, which one Friday runs amok. Collins and Pinch (1993, 1998) use the image playfully in their popularisation of key ideas from science, technology and innova-tion studies. Lichtenstein and Sinclair invoke the mythology in their unravelling of the 'secret' of David Rodinsky's disappearance from his room over the synagogue in Princelet Street, Whitechapel. Princelet Street is only a few minutes walk from the former Fawcett, now the National Women's Library's new building in Old Castle Street, where our feminist legacy is preserved with lottery funds, both of course in the area where Jack the Ripper killed his victims. The image of the golem is a haunting one. As Lichtenstein and Sinclair evoke it:

> Now a golem can be nothing more than a heap of dust, a few unidenti-fied rags in a forgotten room. In the best fiction ... the creature is already a memory; it belongs in a fabulous but longed-for past. The

golem is that which has been banished, an atavistic cartoon. A dream companion. The ugly shape of something that has gone and cannot be recalled. A dark absence whose strange gravitational field sucks in the spectres of anxiety, paranoia, impotence. Miss Havisham is a golem. So is Mr Rochester's first wife (and her pale avatar, Daphne du Maurier's eponymous *Rebecca*). Strange how the English like to gender-bend their golems, turn them into women. The cobwebs of English romanticism are wisps of an unblooded wedding dress, *memento mori* for a mad bride in the attic. (1999: 180)

The feminist resonances are multiplex and blatant. This is the London of Sylvia Pankhurst, Annie Besant, Sarah Adler (who founded the first Yiddish Theatre in London with her husband) and Toynbee Hall, Bedlam itself. The very mention of Bedlam invokes the feminist classic Sandra Gilbert and Susan Gubar (1979) *The Madwoman in the Attic*. The thoughts of Jack the Ripper and of *fin-de-siècle* moral panics about women's changing roles conjure up J. Walkowitz's (1992) *City of Dreadful Delight*. These are potent images of the world of the First Wave feminists, and the attempts by Third Wave feminists to preserve their legacy and our own: of the violence against women, and the madhouse as a prison for women. Identifying oneself with a gender-bent golem is a strange feeling.

x   In that strange landscape where First Wave and Third Wave feminisms are multiply enfolded, modern sociological questions are raised. The spectre of the *flâneur* walks those streets, and it is here that the debate about the possibility of the *flâneuse* is contested. Ian Sinclair is, as Wilson (2000) aptly points out, the *flâneur* of modern London: the *flâneur* of the new economy of signs and space. In writing this book, the arcane dispute about whether or not there were, or ever can be, women *flâneuses* is ever present. Because the *flâneur* is a central concept in postmodernism, the possible existence or the impossibility of a *flâneuse* is important. (see Barrett, 1992; Wilson, 2000; Wolff, 1985.) It is an old idea: John Buchan (1919) has Richard Hannay apologise for mistaking a stout fellow for a *flâneur* in *Mr Standfast*, and in 1926 has a character warn a young man to take up a profession and not be a *flâneur* in *The Dancing Floor*, both very nineteenth-century novels. Parsons (2000) explores the idea of the *flâneuse* in a range of novels by women about cities in which the female characters draw their identity from the urban setting. The term has moved out of academic writing and novels. There is a Flâneur Foodhall in Clerkenwell where modern Londoners can buy gourmet specialities or eat guanaja chocolate cake with poached fruit in the restaurant. (And I do not know what guanaja is either.) This debate resurfaces in Chapter 7 but it runs throughout the book. Whatever image the sociologist has, whether *flâneur*, dull turnip, intrepid hero or deep thinker, women always have to ask: is *this* sociological identity a male only one, or is it available for women too? Clearly, women can be turnips: but can we be *flâneuses*, heroines or deep thinkers?

My career has been a continual series of meetings at which I was the only woman, or one of a handful of women, who had to stand up and say: 'You don't mean men/chaps/guys, you mean people', 'We *don't* want the best man for the job, you want the best *person*', 'That's an all-male platform party, we need a woman', 'We can't have an all-male committee/panel/team/board/collection/list: we must find some women', 'How many women have we elected?', 'Is that shortlist all men?'. The experience Lyn Lofland describes is entirely recognisable to me. She recalls attending an early meeting of the inner circle of the Society for the Study of Symbolic Interaction (SSSI) of which she was just about to become President.

> When I entered a private hotel room in New York to attend my first executive council meeting in 1980, the experience was very much that of the stranger intruding into a group of old friends; or perhaps a better analogy is of a girl wandering into the boys' locker room. Except for me, everyone in the room was male, and except for me, everyone in the room clearly knew everyone else. (1997: 136)

Of course things have got much better during my career but I am still vigilant and wary.

About four years after Lyn Lofland's presidency of the SSSI, Donna Darden became Secretary/Treasurer, a post she held for eight years. She writes:

> because of her presidency, and maybe because the world has changed a little, and because our members are mostly good people, my experiences as sometimes the only and sometimes one of the few women in a group of men were different from hers. I experienced the SSSI and its leadership not as a group of old boys with a tree house to keep me out of, but as a group of professionals. (1997: 99)

An optimist would say that Darden is reporting a real change of climate in the SSSI. A cynic would say that doing all the routine drudgery of being Secretary/Treasurer is exactly what men like women doing, and Darden's labour was welcomed because she combined two grotty jobs. I am glad that Darden felt part of a collegial group, but I wonder if they read her publications. I hope that Donna Darden also gets read and cited by the boys in the treehouse. I want to be in the treehouse, and I want the knowledge treasured in that treehouse to be suffused with feminist ideas.

The fourth dilemma concerns a temptation. For the past 15 years it has been more and more acceptable for sociology and anthropology to be written in non-academic ways, with poems, plays, dialogues, stories, and so on. I love the freedom this provides, and I have enjoyed indulging in the inclusion of fictional episodes in recent books and papers. They are useful for lightening difficult patches of hard ideas in books for students, for heightening tension, for emphasising the important passages. Dialogues are excellent for exploring places when I am ambivalent. However, I have decided to minimise fictions and poems in this book. There is one episode of dialogue in this Introduction and one in the Conclusion: and I have a few vignettes from the fictional university of Burminster which I have created to bring the changes of the past 30 years alive. I have eschewed poems altogether although I enjoy writing parody versions of poems (Delamont, 2000b).

The fifth problem which arises in writing a book on feminist sociology is the most unmentionable. I write about it here with some trepidation, but it has to be said. Writing a feminist book exposes its author to the scorn and derision of most men (if they do not ignore it altogether), anti-feminist women by definition, and many other feminist women. Feminist academic life is characterised by cliques, schools, jealousies and arcane disputes. Every sentence of this book will be received with patronising scorn and howls of derision by some other feminists. As I sat writing this book watching England lose another Ashes series to Australia I did wonder why I was exposing myself to the critical gaze of my academic sisters. To be writing the only 'feminist' volume in the BSA series is a form of masochistic self-exposure akin to being the England No. 11 facing Shane Warne. Any reader who doubts the level of scorn that one feminist deploys on another can consult the disputes between Hekman (2000), Hartsock (2000), Harding (2000) and Smith (2000) or between Felski (2000) and Braidotti (2000).

The sixth temptation concerns detective fiction, not only my leisure passion but, for me, a repository of feminist ideas. I have written elsewhere (Delamont, 1996b) about the feminist agenda in the novels of Sayers, Marsh and Allingham in the anti-feminist era of 1919–49. There is always a temptation to write about golden age or contemporary detective fiction and its feminist functions. However, I have eschewed it here. My analysis of the importance of Rachel Wallace in the novels of Robert Parker (1982, 1985), or of Rosa Gomez and Helen Soileau in those of James Lee Burke (1993, 1998) has been sidelined while I wrote this, apart from the chapter titles. I have reserved for another time my argument that in the detective story the two great patriarchal institutions, the family and the liberal professions, are routinely revealed to be not what they seem. Neither is the safe haven in which women can place their trust: rather they are institutions in which women need to be vigilant and wary.

A PERSONAL NOTE

Feminist sociology was founded in the early days of the Third Wave of the feminist movement, when the two powerful slogans were 'Sisterhood is powerful' and 'The personal is political'. Accordingly, I have concluded this chapter with a brief autobiography. I was born in 1947, went to a girls' grammar school, to Girton College Cambridge, did a PhD at Edinburgh and became an academic. My mother was a feminist, although her feminism does not map easily onto any of the current perspectives. I was a PhD student when the Third Wave broke over us, and I am an academic feminist not an activist. I have been marginally involved in a few campaigns, for nurseries, with Women's Aid, and for women's studies degrees. I did march to keep the 1967 Abortion Act, against Clause 28, and I stood outside several rugby grounds with Welsh Anti-Apartheid, but I did not go to Greenham. As a child I was a tomboy – I was a cowboy, a pirate, a sailor in Nelson's navy (we played Hornblower a lot). I did play with dolls, but mine went to school. They sat at desks and worked: their lives did not involve dressing up or having tea parties. At seven I decided to be a barrister, an ambition I only abandoned in the sixth form when all the men I knew reading law told me how bored they were and I discovered how much it would cost to be in chambers. As an adult, I dress like a 14-year-old girl's idea of a feminist, without make-up and usually in trousers. My career has also involved being the 'First Woman to' on three or four occasions. However, because I am childless (by choice) and a workaholic, I am not a useful role model for women who want to be mothers *and* bank managers.

To conclude this Introduction, there is a note on the style of the text. Some of the language used in the book is colourful: I have written about silverbacks and treehouses, about the Gorgona, poisoned chalices and turnips, golems and *flâneurs*, rapiers to the heart, stags, locker rooms, blue meanies, chilly climates and sacred groves, and Monday morning quarterbacks. I also use an ornate vocabulary, which may send some readers to the dictionary to discover what I mean by sciolism, *trivium* and apolaustic. Also, in a very sparing way, I have used fictional characters. I have invented three fictional feminists in recent publications. They are Eowyn, an educational ethnographer; Sophonisba, a feminist historian; and Zenobia who was Eowyn's PhD student. Eowyn is named for the woman warrior in *Lord of the Rings*; Sophonisba is named for the pioneer sociologist in Chicago; and Zenobia for the third-century warrior queen of Palmyra. Eowyn and Sophonisba are two aspects of my scholarly identity, Zenobia is a device: a character who only exists to have Eowyn and Sophonisba explain things to her. Hers is a dull life: she serves a purely textual function. Eowyn is an ethnographer whose main aim has been to campaign for high standards in the qualitative research done in education and sociology. She sees herself as an ally of everyone else doing qualitative work, whether male or female, and her task is to defend qualitative work against its enemies. Virginia Olesen calls positivists 'blue meanies': Eowyn fights blue meanies. When qualitative research, or sociology of education is under attack, as they were in the late 1990s by James Tooley (1998) and Chris Woodhead (1998), she defends all ethnographers and all sociologists. Inside the charmed circle she is anti-positivist and sceptical about postmodernism. Eowyn wants people to go out and get good data, because there are so many aspects of social life about which we know nothing. Many of her intellectual allies and her friends are men, and Eowyn sees herself riding into battle in a largely male army: relatively few women have been active in qualitative educational research for 30 years.

Sophonisba is an historian and a stronger feminist: her work is on girls' schools, women in universities, gender and science, feminism and sociology. These are areas in which very few men are interested, and the research is mainly of concern to a small number of feminist scholars. Sophonisba is frankly scared of postmodernism, because it threatens to sweep away all the gains of Third Wave feminism in the academy. First Wave feminism was destroyed, intellectually, by Freudianism. As the intelligentsia adopted Freudianism in the 1920s, it undermined, fatally, the moral authority and intellectual coherence of feminism. Sophonisba is worried that postmodernism could do the same to contemporary feminism, unless feminists learn to *use* its ideas and engage with them inside the frame of its discourse. Both Eowyn and Sophonisba have written this book although usually they do not write together. Eowyn writes empirical sociology and methods (e.g. Delamont, 2002a; Delamont et al., 2000a); Sophonisba writes 'pure' feminism (Delamont, 1989b, 1992a, 2002b). Hammersley (2001) has attacked my use of dialogue, I find it useful to dramatise ambivalence. Hammersley complains that an author who uses a dialogic format is hiding their own, true, evaluative voice behind a literary device, and is thus acting in bad faith by avoiding responsibility for their actions. His particular objection was to a book review where I had used a dialogue to explore one problem facing women academics. When one woman and one man are asked to write on the same topic, the women *knows* that if she does not write as a feminist, there will not be a feminist perspective. She may not want to write the feminist account, but if she does not, no one else will. This presents a dilemma between feminist duty and scholarly inclination. Hammersley attacked the device and, of course, complained that a feminist perspective was subjective and biased, while missing the point of the dialogue altogether.

Leicester: April 2002

The British Sociological Association is having its annual conference in Leicester. Sophonisba, Eowyn and Zenobia are having a curry in a restaurant opposite the station. Eowyn and Sophonisba have travelled down from Glasgow, Zenobia up from Kent. Eowyn passes the stuffed nan to Zenobia and says:

Eowyn: Please remind me to do a really systematic trawl of the publishers' exhibits: I need to find a new text to use for the gender course with the masters people. Can I have the daal?

Zenobia: Sure, here: I heard Sara Delamont was writing one in the BSA Millennial series ...

Sophonisba: I wonder why they asked her: she's not very well known as a feminist.

Zenobia: No – but then that means she's not really in one of the camps ... not a Marxist, not a radical, not a postmodernist.

Eowyn: I think she's a liberal feminist, and a symbolic interactionist. If it's out I'll look at it, it might do.

Zenobia: I'm really nervous about my paper on Wednesday ...

Eowyn: Don't be. You'll be fine – I think it's a real argument – try this lentil pasanda – it's better than the one we used to eat in Sauchiehall Street ...

Sophonisba: Are you going to the ASA in Chicago?

Eowyn: No – but I am going to Atlanta in 2003, I have promised the group from Northeastern that we'll present the stuff on chemistry technicians ...

Sophonisba: I've said I'll go to Atlanta too – the women doing the big biographical dictionary I've written for are having a bash to celebrate the centenary of Marion McLean's publication on sweat shops and asked us all to come.

Zenobia: Atlanta – in August – Yuk! – you'll melt or fry: can I have the prawns, please?

We will leave the three women in Leicester and rejoin them in the summer of 2003 at the end of the book.

one

when the patriarchy gets worried

When the patriarchy gets worried it goes into action. (Cross, 1981: 22)

T his is a book about feminist sociology. It is *not* an account of the sociological research on women. There are plenty of those (e.g. Delamont, 1980, 2001 and Pilcher, 1999). Rather it is an account of a theoretical perspective in sociology which has been important for 30 years. The central argument of the book is that the feminist sociologies are now 30 years old, are more subversive of the dominant paradigm than the other 30-year-old marginal perspectives such as ethnomethodology, conversational analysis and discourse analysis, yet they have been successfully ghettoised by the malestream. Throughout the book I will write of feminist sociolog*ies*, because the three main traditions come from different roots and occupy different positions in the discipline today. They have in common that all three are ghettoised and marginalised in sociology.

This may seem an absurd claim: certainly those who dislike, resent or fear feminist sociology see its malign influence everywhere. The American men who contributed to a symposium in *Sociological Forum* in 1994 on 'What's Wrong with Sociology?', such as James Davis (1994) share this negative perception. If, for example, a person attending the 2000 BSA conference at York strolled round the exhibition put up by the publishers and booksellers, and picked up their promotional leaflets about the titles being offered at a discount, it might seem that there were dozens of books on feminism. In fact, as Table 1.1 shows, titles on women, gender, feminism and men's studies/masculinities are still a small proportion of what publishers think they can promote at a BSA conference.

While Table 1.1 shows that there are many more books on women, on gender and on men's studies/masculinities than there would have been in 1960 or even 1980, there are relatively few titles on feminism, and some publishers have none on show at all. Once one considers that there are many varieties of feminist sociology, the exposure of any one type of feminist sociology is pretty small. To examine how sociology has reached 2002, we will use vignettes of Burminster, a fictional British university.

Publisher	Women	Gender	Feminism	Men and masculinities	Total titles on display
Macmillan	18	5	4	-	150
Sage	-	-	6	4	144
Pearson	6	2	4	2	133
Polity	1	2	1	2	133
CUP	2	1	-	-	97
Routledge	4	1	2	1	97
Continuum	6	3	1	2	91
Ashgate	5	3	-	2	69
Berg	7	2	-	1	60
Wisepress	2	1	2	-	51
OUP	2	3	1	1	47

Table 1.1: *Books showcased at the 2000 BSA Conference*

FEMINIST SOCIOLOGIES AND HISTORIES OF FEMINISM

To understand the varieties of feminist sociology it is important to know something of the history of feminism as a social movement, because the feminist sociologies are a product of a particular phase of feminism. For the purposes of the book, feminism is divided into three broad phases. First Wave feminism, from about 1848 to 1918, focused on getting women rights in public spheres, especially the vote, education and entry to middle-class jobs such as medicine. The views of these feminists, at least as they expressed them in public, were puritan about sex, alcohol, dress, and behaviour. The Second Wave, from 1918 to 1968, was concerned with social reform (such as free school meals for poor children, and health care for poor women) and 'revolution' in the private sphere: the right to contraception, the end of the sexual double standard, and so on. Third Wave feminism, from 1968 to the present, has been concerned with public issues again (equal pay, an end to sex discrimination in employment, pensions, mortgages, etc.) and with making formerly private issues (such as rape and domestic violence) matters of public concern and reform. The Third Wave has also produced a revolution in the scholarly knowledge bases of most disciplines, such as feminist sociology, which is of concern to women in education if to no one else. In this Third Wave all the humanities and social sciences have developed feminist sub-specialisms: there are feminist geographies, histories, political science, psychology, and so on. In this chapter, some of the central ideas of feminist sociology are outlined.

Both First Wave and Third Wave feminism have been concerned with political action, with improving the economic status of women, with tackling violence against women, with the education of women, with raising the status of women's and children's health, and with ensuring that female voices and experiences are treated as seriously as male. One of the major differences between First Wave and Third Wave feminisms in the English-speaking world is particularly relevant to sociology: attitudes to knowledge. In general, the First Wave feminists were concerned to open up academic secondary education, higher education and professional training to girls and women. In the first wave of feminism from 1848 to 1918, there were few challenges to the contents of academic disciplines – women wanted access to schools and universities to study subjects. In an era where only males could study algebra, Greek, Hebrew, Latin and the physical sciences, the goal of feminists was to open them up to females, and prove that women could excel at them. There were a few feminists who queried the epistemological status of the male knowledge base, but this was not a major preoccupation. When women were forbidden to learn male knowledge, it was necessary to gain access to it, and to show that women could engage successfully with it, before it could be challenged (Delamont, 1989b, 1992a). In the second phase of feminism, from 1918 to 1968, the emphasis on social reform and welfare rights also failed to generate fundamental challenges to the academic knowledge base of disciplines.

There are some ways in which sociology, and the universities in which it lives, have changed unrecognisably. Hess (1999) captures this in a book review where she comments on:

> Evi Glenn's memory of how angry she was in the 1960s that Harvard's Lamont Library was not open to female students; yet when I and my Radcliffe classmates were denied entrance when it first opened in the late 1940s, it never occurred to us to protest – we had no paradigm or vocabulary for sex discrimination. (1999: 287)

By the late 1960s, when Third Wave feminism arose, women in Britain and the USA were allowed access to most spheres of male knowledge. The Third Wave feminist movement has focused on challenging the epistemological basis, the methods, and the content, of 'mainstream' or '*male*stream' knowledge. This shows in the academic departments, degree courses and textbooks in women's studies; in the feminist publishing houses and feminist lists in the established houses; in the social science methods textbooks; and in arts and social science disciplines

3

where there are feminist journals, women's caucuses in the learned societies, and books on many feminist topics. Sociology has been a fertile ground for feminist challenges to the knowledge base. When the third wave of feminism erupted in the aftermath of the upheavals of 1968, however, the re-making of knowledge came to be one of its central, and most enduring legacies. Every arts and social science discipline developed a committee or pressure group of women scholars, many started new journals, conferences, courses and series of books. The whole 'discipline' of women's studies spread out across the Anglo-Saxon world, and 'feminist perspectives' on everything from medieval Italian to management studies grew up.

OUTLINE OF THE BOOK

This chapter introduces the book and briefly explores its place in the series. The chapter will explain the 'crisis of western sociology' in the late 1960s, to use Gouldner's (1971) phrase, and the consequent explosion of new ideas and the 'zesty disarray' that developed out of that crisis. The theoretical schools of feminism will be introduced: socialist, radical, liberal and 'black'. Their historical origins and development will be outlined. Challenges to feminist sociology will be mentioned (to be developed in later chapters). The central organising principles of the book will be (1) the interrelations between feminist sociologies and the discipline's mainstream (or, as many feminists would term it, malestream); and (2) the diversity within feminist sociology. Chapter 1 will open up both these organising principles and justify them.

Chapter 2 outlines the rise of feminist sociology in Britain and the USA since 1968, with some discussion of the French school. The development of the competing schools of feminist sociology, leading up to the socialist feminism of Michèle Barrett, the radical feminism of Sylvia Walby, the liberal feminism of many sociologists, and the 'black' feminism of bell hooks and others. The rise of the Women's Liberation Movement and its concern with remaking knowledge will be explored. Friedan's attack on Parsons, the re-discovery of de Beauvoir's ideas for sociology, and the discussions of parallels between women and African-Americans will also be covered. A brief survey of the dominant patterns of empirical work (such as the lack of data on the class position and social mobility of women) will be included.

Feminist sociology has established journals, produced many books and articles, and changed the agenda of research in many empirical areas. Chapter 3 explores those achievements. The chapter will also foreshadow the rise of feminist methods. The achievements will be explored covering theoretical ideas, empirical findings and methodological debates. Interrelations with queer theory and with the 'new men's studies' will be debated. Domestic violence is one of eight aspects of private, domestic life that have been opened up by sociology in the past 30 years. Violence, whether physical or sexual against spouses, dependent children, or the frail elderly has been studied first to prove its existence and then to try and understand it, with a clear motivation among many investigators to design preventative policies (see Dobash and Dobash, 1992). In the same period, other researchers have explored housework (Oakley, 1974; Sullivan, 1997); money (Pahl, 1990; Vogler, 1998); caring for dependants (Finch and Groves, 1983); and food choice and preparation (Charles and Kerr, 1988; Murcott, 1983). Researchers have explored marriage, divorce and remarriage using the insights gained from studies on food, money, violence and housework.

Issues of method have been at the forefront of debates about feminist sociology. In Chapter 4 three strands to the debates are explored. First, the role of feminists in disputes between quantitative and qualitative methods. Second, challenges to positivist ideas about the selection of research questions and standpoints. Third, issues of reflexivity highlighted by feminists. All these strands are drawn together with new postmodern challenges to sociological research. These are the focus of Chapter 8.

5

Chapter 5 explores the origins of feminist sociology in the Enlightenment, through Fuller, Wollstonecraft, Martineau, Beecher, Addams and the women of the Chicago School, Beatrice Webb, Barbara Wootton, and so on. The historical origins of the different schools of feminist sociology will be traced. Parallels with the role of women in the development of anthropology will also be drawn. The tensions between theorising and empirical research, between the ivory tower and political engagement, between sociology and social policy, and between the public and the private will be explored. The analysis of how the feminist pioneers of Chicago sociology were expelled from the sociology department and expunged from its history published in *Women's History Review* (Delamont, 1992a) will be developed. Parallel accounts of other key institutions will be presented. A contrast with anthropology, whose *longue durée* is more inclusive of founding mothers, is illuminating.

In 1971 the Schwendingers wrote a paper 'Sociology's founding fathers: sexists to a man?'. In 2002 that claim is a starting point for examining the contribution of feminist sociologists in general, and British feminist sociology in particular, to the work of re-evaluating the founding fathers and to future scholarship on their ideas. Chapter 6 examines how feminist sociologists have engaged with the fundamental texts of Marx, Weber, Durkheim and Mead, and with the schools of thought in sociology that have developed from those founding fathers. Then it will explore how feminists have engaged with the ideas of key twentieth-century scholars, especially Merton and Parsons, Bourdieu and Beck. Feminism's uneasy relationship with Freud will also be explained. The chapter will then explore feminist sociology's engagement with the major theoretical schools of the present day and the foreseeable future – foreshadowing Chapter 8.

Chapter 7 explores how far feminist sociology has become simply another specialist sub-field, and how far – if at all – its ideas have impacted on malestream sociological theories. This chapter focuses on the interfaces between feminist sociologies and the malestream. In some ways – such as the number of women at all ranks of the profession, on the boards of journals, active in professional associations and in the focus of empirical work – feminist sociology has changed the malestream. In others, however, nothing has changed. Books are still being written that cite no women, ignore feminism, and reproduce sexist ideas without commentary. It is possible to see feminist sociology as 'just' another sub-field, like the sociology of science or education, that is irrelevant to the big debates.

The *fin-de-siècle*, as in the equivalent eras in the 1790s and 1890s, saw moral panics about sex, gender and sexuality in capitalist society. Outwith academic sociology, some commentators argued that feminism had gone too far and was endangering male sanity, and was even destabilising society. Others produced spurious, pseudo-science to the effect that feminism was doomed to fail because it was 'against nature'. Inside academic sociology the rise of postmodernism challenged all the schools of feminist sociology by removing their essentialist categoric base(s) (class, gender, sisterhood) and challenging the 'data' beloved of Fabian sociologists and liberal feminists. Chapter 8 addresses the challenges from postfeminism and postmodernism and explores how feminist sociology has responded.

The conclusion in Chapter 9 is more speculative, as it outlines the future tasks, responsibilities and goals of feminist sociology, the parallel responsibilities of those in the malestream, and sets an agenda of theoretical, empirical and methodological priorities.

A NOTE ON SOURCES AND EXAMPLES

The potential literature which could be cited in a book such as this is overwhelming in range and in sheer amount. I have, therefore, illustrated the arguments made with examples from four empirical areas: the sociologies of education, stratification, science and medicine. These are the areas I know best in sociology. I have crossed the boundary between sociology and anthropology, rather than the boundaries with other social sciences, because anthropology is where my own roots lie. As well as academic writing I have used autobiographical essays by sociologists, especially 22 memoirs by distinguished American men, and 42 by American women, including 22 distinguished women. I have also illustrated some points with fiction, usually popular novels rather than literary ones. When, for example, I discuss the term *flâneur*, I have mentioned its use in John Buchan's thrillers rather than any novel F.R. Leavis would have approved of. I do this in the spirit of interdisciplinarity which is a characteristic of feminism.

VARIETIES OF FEMINIST SOCIOLOGY

a caveat

The account which follows is an oversimplified one, and is also contested. The material in the following seven chapters will subvert the simple schema which follows. Maynard (1995) proposed, several years ago, that the 'three schools' model which follows was not an accurate characterisation of feminist sociology in the 1990s. Paula England (1999: 263) argues that the tripartite division is 'outdated' because of postmodernism and the claims of women of colour. However, there are good reasons for starting from the model of liberal, Marxist and radical perspectives. It has been important for 30 years, it does remind us that a unitary label 'feminist' is absurdly imprecise, and it does reflect some real differences in sociological approach. Also, despite many articles arguing that the 'three schools' model is outdated and unhelpful, it is still widely used.

7

orthodoxy

There are three currents in feminist sociology which can be clearly distinguished from the early 1970s to the present day: liberal feminist sociology, Marxist feminist sociology and radical or separatist feminist sociology. In the past decade, there has also been a distinct postmodernist feminist sociology. There are other theoretical positions in *feminism* which could be the basis for a sociological theory, but which have not been developed into coherent sociological perspectives. The most important feminist position here is black feminism. There are distinguished and thought-provoking black feminists whose ideas could be developed into a coherent sociological position: bell hooks (1981), Audre Lorde (1984) and Patricia Hill Collins (2000). In Britain there is not a black feminist sociology: there is black feminism and there is feminist sociology but not a black feminist sociology. Heidi Mirza's (1997) collection shows the vitality of *Black British Feminism*, but it is not a sociological book. I have therefore said little about black feminism in this volume.

Liberal feminist sociology, Marxist feminist sociology, and radical or separatist feminist sociology are all long-standing perspectives. They are, however, differentially grounded. Liberal feminist sociologists do not necessarily share any *theory*: their common ground is a political belief in using research data to effect social reform and a faith in empirical research which is essentially *Fabian*. A liberal feminist sociology can be grounded in the scholarship of a founding father or dead white male. There is no requirement that the theory is woman-centred or that the research methods are feminist. A liberal feminist sociology could be Weberian, Durkheimian, symbolic interactionist, or even Parsonian: the common ground is a faith in the possibility of social change; in evidence, and in rational decision-making on issues of sex and gender. Liberal feminists are the most likely to believe that there *can* be objective social science: to hold on to the Enlightenment project.

Marxist and radical feminists are unlikely to be positivists; unlikely to believe in objective social science; unlikely to hold to the Enlightenment project. For Marxists, 'objectivity' is a class-based myth: the ideas of the ruling class proclaimed as universal and objective. For radical feminists, the myth of objectivity is a male one: men invented science in the seventeenth century and invented objectivity specifically to exclude women, and to valorise their own thinking. Radical and Marxist feminists have little else in common, but they do share a profound scepticism about claims to objectivity. Marxist feminist sociologists, in contrast, are united by their theoretical commitment to Marxism. They may or may not do empirical work, but they share a philosophy. At its simplest, they believe that the economic system drives the other aspects of every society such as education, the family and the mass media, and that class inequalities are paramount. The theoretical founders are Marx and Engels, and other revered theorists are also male (Althusser, Gramsci, Habermas, Adorno or Mao). Methods are also shared with male sociologists. Radical or separatist feminists share a foundational belief that sex inequality predates class inequality in human prehistory, and that patriarchy is the fundamental system of oppression. It is among radical feminists that calls for feminist theory, and feminist methods are loudest. Audre Lorde's famous dictum, that the master's tools cannot be used to demolish the master's house, is invoked.

The most important distinction between the three perspectives is best grasped by focusing on how social change takes place to improve women's status and everyday lives. For Marxist feminists the subjection and oppression of women (and of ethnic minorities), and sexism as an ideology (like racism) are consequences of capitalism. It is in the interests of the ruling class that the majority of the population is divided into groups who despise, reject and exploit other groups. So racism and sexism keep the working class divided, and help blind them to the realities of class struggle. Thus, if women's status is to improve, the capitalist social order has to be overthrown. In a socialist society it would be *possible* to have sexual (and racial) equality, in a capitalist one, it is *not* possible to have either. In this world-view, human societies can change, but the economic system determines most if not all facets of the society and most of the individual's life chances and life choices. To produce social change, and individual change, therefore, the economic system must be altered. Men could behave and think differently, if their economic conditions and accompanying social institutions were different. Campaigns therefore need to be focused on class and economic issues, and sociological research on women must always keep class and economic issues foregrounded.

Liberal feminists have faith in the plasticity of the human species and the mutability of human organisations and societies. Just as the Roman Empire embraced Christianity, or nineteenth-century Britain took to the railways, so too societies could become less sexist, and individual men could grow up less violent and more comfortable with women and with female qualities. Changing child-rearing, changing socialisation, and changing social policy can reduce, or even eliminate sexism. Liberal feminists have faith, too, in rationality. If the facts are known, people will change. Small changes are worth making, and basing change on research is always sensible. Liberal feminists use a variety of sociological theories, and may conduct research on anything.

Radical feminists have the bleakest and most pessimistic view of the human species. Because patriarchy is the oldest oppression, dating back a million years or more, it is unlikely that men can change, even if they wished to. Consequently women's best chance of safety and fulfilment lies in avoiding men, and male institutions. It is better to live in all-female groups, and try to minimise all contact with patriarchal institutions. The sociological research is frequently focused on issues where men of all classes are equally complicit in sexist practices, such as pornography, rape and domestic violence. Radical feminist sociology overlaps with gay and lesbian sociology, and with queer theory. Issues of sexuality, sexual orientation and the emotions are often central. The large collection edited by Bell and Klein (1996) contains vigorous assertions of the current state of radical feminism.

A BRIEF HISTORY OF SOCIOLOGY SINCE 1968

In parallel with the growth and diversification of feminism, the discipline of sociology was also changing. In the mid-1960s, the dominant American sociology, which therefore dominated the English-speaking world, was Parsonian structural functionalism. In 1971 Gouldner published an attack on this orthodoxy *The Coming Crisis of Western Sociology* which was savaged at the time but was prescient. As America found its complacency disturbed by labour disputes, by protests against the Vietnam War, by student unrest, by the civil rights movement and then the Black Power, Gay Liberation and Women's Liberation manifestations, the universities, and especially the social sciences were changed. In the rest of the capitalist world, similar social disturbances occurred: the events of May 1968 in France being the most famous. Internationally, the Soviet invasion of Czechoslovakia upset the balance of power which had settled uneasily since 1956: overall loomed the threat of nuclear war. Sociology began to change. Ideas from Germany (especially the humanist neo-Marxism of the Frankfurt School), from France (the anti-humanist neo-Marxism of Althusser, the poststructuralism of Bourdieu, Foucault and others), and new coinings from America itself (especially the Californian ethnomethodology), gained enthusiastic adherents. These were minority enthusiasms, but they produced a more diversified discipline. Against that background, the women's movement also grew and diversified. Marxist feminists could draw on the neo-Marxist ideas from France and Germany, as well as exploring the role of women in Mao's China, the USSR and in Eastern Europe. Separatist feminists could look at the same societies and social theories and draw the opposite message: not progress but universal patriarchy. For the Marxist feminist sociologists the new space for Marxist sociologies gave them intellectual scope, for the radical feminist sociologists the interactionist sociologies (symbolic interactionism, phenomenology and ethnomethodology), with their focus on the apparently mundane and their use of qualitative methods, created an intellectual space to gather data on women's lives and perspectives.

From 1968 through to 1989 there was more space for dissenting voices in sociology than there had been in the previous 25 years. Liberal, Marxist, and radical feminist sociologies could grow, and there was space for black feminism to develop and produce its critique of the unacknowledged and unconscious racism of the three types of white feminism and the three schools of white feminist sociology. However, just as 1968 had seen a shift in the landscape of sociology, so too did 1989. The collapse of communism, or at least of the Soviet empire and therefore of state socialism in Europe and much of Asia symbolised by the fall of the Berlin Wall in 1989 (Borneman, 1992), has led to a crisis in Marxist social science. Meanwhile the twin economic pressures of the globalisation of production (where most manufacturing is being moved to the Third World/under-developed countries where labour is exploited, expendable and therefore cheap) and the de-industrialisation of the capitalist 'industrialised' economies, have changed, and are changing rapidly, the working lives of ordinary men and women. Simultaneously, there has been globalisation of communication: with satellite and telecommunications allowing both more democratic sharing of information *and* greater control of it by the owners of the transmitters (Albrow, 1997).

Overlying all these seismic shifts was an artificial 'hysteria': millennial fervour. As the year 2000 approached for the *Christian* world (Gould, 1998) we were still in a state of expectancy: we were in the *fin-de-siècle* (Pahl, 1996; Showalter, 1996). At the ends of the eighteenth and nineteenth centuries the western world experienced political and intellectual ferments, it was not surprising to find equivalent disarray in 1998 and 1999. This sense of unease, especially disquiet about sex roles and sexuality, common at the ends of centuries, persisted although the Christian 2000 is not 2000 for Islam, Jews, or the Japanese who have different calendars, even though we all knew *rationally* that this was a date we had set for ourselves, that it is arbitrary, that it changed nothing.

11

There are four shorthand labels for the current era, espoused by different sociologists: (1) post-industrial; (2) the post-modern; (3) post-traditional reflexive modernity (Beck et al., 1994); or as Beck (1992) calls it (4) the risk society. Beck (1994: 24) has argued that conventional sociology, or as he prefers to call it 'the ageing sociology of modernisation' has to be replaced, because the economic base of modernity has gone, so too must the sociology of modernity. Scholars interested in the lives of women in Britain such as Bradley (1996) and Walby (1997) have also drawn attention to these changes in the economic base of British society, and the implications of de-industrialisation and globalisation for women. For women who used feminist sociology to explain the gender relations in a modern society, calls such as Beck's to replace the 'ageing sociology of modernisation' with a new sociology of post-traditional reflexive modernity have been particularly problematic. This is because the new postmodern sociology does not 'fit' alongside or on top of any of the popular varieties of feminist sociology, but rather undermines them. For feminists, one type of replacement sociology, creating a postmodern sociology to explain the postmodern world, is particularly problematic because it challenges feminism itself. Accordingly, postmodernism is the focus of a whole chapter (Chapter 8). Deciding where I stand on postmodern feminism, and how to explore the ideas of the movement in this book, is problematic. Bradley

(1996) captures my dilemma when she writes: 'post-modern approaches sit uneasily with study of material factors such as inequality and deprivation and those influenced by the ideas of postmodernism have tended to avoid these topics' (ibid.: 3). Bradley sets herself to 'pull together' traditional approaches to inequalities with the 'newer perspectives' (ibid.: 3). I, too, am trying to meld two approaches.

DANGEROUS IDEAS?

Amanda Cross (1981: 22) has a sympathetic character say: 'when the patriarchy gets worried, it goes into action'. The action of the patriarchy is apparent in many of the chapters, and the 'backlash' against feminism is discussed in Chapter 7. Feminism is a controversial ideology, even in sociology which is generally a broad church, tolerant of many theories and viewpoints. As I write that, however, I remember the furious anger of James Davis (1994) and Jonathan Imber (1999) who feel their discipline has been polluted by disparate perspectives, and want it purified and returned to a Parsonian 'scientific' ivory tower, to a fundamentalist creed with strong barriers around it. Many of the ideas explored in this book are unpopular. Bourdieu (1988) described *Homo Academicus* as a book for burning. For many people, this too will be a book for burning. I doubt if any BSA member will say in public or write for publication that there should not be a book on feminism in the millennial series, but it will cause dissent in private and some annoyance.

In 1987, 27 women were shot at the University of Montreal's Ecole Polytechnique. 14 of them died. All but one of the dead women were engineering students. Their killer, who committed suicide, considered himself 'a rational erudite'. He had shouted, before the first six women were killed 'You're all a bunch of feminists and I hate feminists' (Scanlon, 1998: 225). A fictional response to the massacre is depicted in Appignanesi (1999), a novel by a woman who has also written on de Beauvoir, Freud and women and postmodernism. This massacre can be seen as the work of one deranged, sick person or it can be seen as an extreme example of misogynist fear and loathing of women and/or feminists. To date, no one has massacred feminist sociologists (and one terrible irony of the Montreal event is that most women engineers are not feminists at all). However, the power of the ideas put forward by feminist sociology provokes fear, loathing and misogyny.

two

neither young, nor luscious, nor sycophantic

developments in feminist sociology 1968–2002

The Leicester sociology department in which I studied from 1967 to 1972 was large, prestigious, and had a male-dominated academic staff. (Deem, 1996: 7)

For the women who became feminist sociologists in Britain after 1965, what Deem describes at Leicester is instantly recognisable. Deem argues that the Leicester Department operated a tripartite internal market, with an applied sociology track (female-dominated, low status), a theoretical track (high status, difficult, male-dominated) and an empirical track (intermediate in difficulty, and not marked by gender). We do not have detailed data on the staffing, curricula and student enrolments of all the other sociology departments in the UK over the past 40 years, but the male-dominated staff and the prestige of 'male' theory were normal in the period from 1960 to 1980, and other women will recognise the same gender regime. Most students would have experienced the gender regimes of their alma mater in the same way as Deem, although not all of them would be as articulate and analytic about it. Let us pay our first visit to the fictional university of Burminster.

vignette 2.1

Burminster is a university in a cathedral city in middle England: a city with a county cricket ground and a soccer team that moves in and out of the Premier League. There are about 12,000 students in 2002. The university was founded in 1893, with 24 students, and admitted women from the outset. Sociology began at Burminster in a small way in the 1950s, inside Economics, and became a full department in 1964.

Burminster is a 'typical' sociology department in 1968. There are eight staff; seven men and one woman. Professor Westwater is the only professor, and is the head of department. Dr Amysfort is an 'old' senior lecturer, in his late fifties. Dr Greenslade is the rising star, a senior lecturer at only 40. The other staff are lecturers, including Miss Glynde, who lectures on social policy and welfare. The male lecturers are mostly in their 20s and 30s. One, Tom Twisdon is a neo-Marxist, who has read Althusser, Gramsci and the Frankfurt School. Another, Homer Scudder, has joined from California and is an ethnomethodologist. Both scare Professor Westwater: they are so modern. However, everyone despises Miss Glynde, who does not publish, and frets about students who get pregnant. None of the courses, except the one on 'marriage and the family' taught by Miss Glynde, mention women or gender at all. Theory is an all-male course, methods are quantitative and very 'macho', the empirical courses on work, education, developing countries, politics, social movements and religion are all delivered by men, with no women authors on the reading lists, and all valorise class. Apart from Tom Twisdon and Homer Scudder, the staff are either British 'Fabians' or draw on the American 'scientific' ideas of positivism using Talcott Parsons. There are about 60 students in the three years, roughly half of them women. One of the four PhD students is a woman, Tamzin Wrankester, who is interested in women workers in the textile industry. Her supervisor, Mr Whaddon, is nice, but clearly does not expect her to become a professional sociologist.

14

Such is our fictional university: as the feminist revolution develops, we will see Burminster change. There are three ways in which the fictional Burminster is very different from a sociology department today: it is much smaller with a more generous staff-student ratio, it is influenced by Parsons or British Fabianism, and it relies on quantitative methods. In the period from 1968 to 1976 all these changed. The discipline grew in popularity so student numbers rose and staff-student ratios began to worsen, as it has continued to do ever since. Such changes were gradual, and not immediately obvious. More noticeable was what Gouldner (1971) called the crisis of western sociology (that is of American Parsonian structural-functionalism). Briefly, the combined impact of the anti-war movement, the student protests, the Soviet invasion of Czechoslovakia, the industrial unrest and the stirrings of Black Power, Gay Liberation and Women's Liberation produced a crisis in many social sciences in the USA, including sociology. The dominant orthodoxy had not predicted any of these, and could not explain them. A range of different perspectives, backed by enthusiasm for 'new' (or rediscovered) data collection methods rapidly thrust themselves into the academic arena. Four particular types of 'new' sociology were advocated:

1 Conflict theories
2 Neo-Marxist theories
3 Interactionist theories (SI, phenomenology, ethnomethodology)
4 Sociology of knowledge

With the skills of hindsight, or as the American term has it, Monday morning quarterbacking, these were not equally successful as successor sociologies to structural functionalism and positivism. The classic American functionalism with positivist methods survived, and is still the most favoured research approach in the USA. A glance at the *AJS* or *ASR*, or at the programme of the ASA annual conference shows how well the pre-1968 paradigm has survived. Conflict theories, associated with Randall Collins, never 'took off'. Neo-Marxist ideas, drawing on the Frankfurt School for a humanist Marxism or on Althusser for an anti-humanist Marxism, or on Gramsci (with his useful term 'hegemonic') have survived but never came to dominate sociology. The three types of interactionism remain minority 'schools'. The symbolic interactionists developed the SSSI, a journal and a year book, and live on, but many of their key ideas spread unacknowledged (Atkinson and Housley, 2002; Maines, 2000). Ethnomethodology was infamous and fashionable briefly, but quickly became a small sect. Phenomenology never became widespread in sociology, and its 'method' is a travesty of both phenomenology and methods. The sociology of knowledge was not widely adopted either.

The four responses to the crisis of western sociology highlighted by Gouldner, distilled by Giddens (1973) and clearly apparent in the early 1970s (see Delamont, 1976, for an early use of Giddens's typology as an explanatory framework) were all false trails. Only SI can be seen as a clear alternative to the dominant paradigm in the USA today, and its role is that of loyal opposition. Looking back from 2002 the real, lasting challenges to the dominant paradigm have come, not from within the sociology of 1971, but from the intellectual developments which grew out of the political campaigns of 1968–73. Instead of the four responses suggested by Giddens, there are five anti-functionalist, anti-positivist sociologies which have posed a serious challenge:

1 Postmodernism
2 The cultural turn
3 Critical race theory
4 Queer theory
5 Feminist theory

There is not a massive presence of these five sociologies in *AJS* and *ASR*, but they are all highly visible in the programmes of the annual ASA conferences of the 1990s. Their absence from the *AJS* and *ASR*, paralleling the absence of the neo-Marxist and interactionist approaches of the 1970s, is more revealing about these journals than about what most sociologists find exciting. Abbott (1999: x) states that the *AJS* has metamorphosed 'into a narrow, rigid structure, unable to reach beyond

15

its fixed place', as it suffers 'intellectual sclerosis'. Abbott confesses he does not read his copy of *AJS*, shelving it unread, although he is its official historian. Other books in this series, and other sociologists deal with the successful challenges that postmodernism, the cultural turn, critical race theory, and queer theory have posed to functionalism and positivism. Alongside the rise of the five theoretical approaches there has also been a rapid growth of qualitative methods and increasingly a turn to data collection by interview with an enthusiasm for narrative (Atkinson et al., 2001; Atkinson and Silverman, 1997). Other volumes deal with this methodological concern (Atkinson et al., 2001, for example).

My concern is with the feminist theories, whose success was quite unpredicted and whose very existence was quite unsuspected by Gouldner (1971) who did not see the absence of women or sexist stereotypes as a problem endemic in western sociology and by Giddens (1973) who was totally uninterested in gender. However, the seeds of the feminist challenge had been sown by 1971, in Friedan's (1963) *The Feminine Mystique*. Friedan provided a devastating critique of two male thinkers powerful in the American intellectual landscape of the 1950s and 1960s: Freud and Parsons. Freud is discussed in Chapter 6, here the focus is on Parsons. Friedan dared to argue that Parsonian structural functionalism was a pseudo-science, describing 1950s' America as if it were the acme of human achievement, and labelling all those who felt rebellious or unhappy as ill or deviant. Friedan argued that Parsons's sociology was being taught in an over-simplified way to thousands of young women in courses on marriage and the family. This was a classic example of Fleck's (1979) ideas about the gulf between frontier science and textbook science. One such course featured in the film *Where The Boys Are*, a vehicle for Connie Francis, which included a scene from a class on marriage as part of the safe, but cold and dull world of a snowbound campus in the Mid-West, from which the heroines flee to hot, sunny Florida for spring break. Friedan's critique was particularly good at exposing how easily functionalist ideas about gender slid from description to prescription. Gouldner neither recognised the deeply ingrained sexism of sociology in the 1960s, nor queried the lack of women in the discipline, especially the lack of women in tenured posts in elite universities, and in the management of the learned societies.

Neither the topic of women, nor the existence of women as sociologists were apparent in 1968. There were some women lecturers, and a tiny number of women professors, but they were not visible in the subject. Sheila Allen (2001: 1) wrote that when she became president of the British Sociological Association: 'Barbara Wootton, President from 1959–64 was overlooked in 1975 when *Network* announced I was the first woman president and replied to my apologetic note expressing no surprise at becoming invisible in so short a time.'

The position of women is well captured by Amanda Cross (1981: 47) in the quote that provides the chapter title. The heroine, Kate Fansler, a distinguished literary scholar from Columbia, describes her reception at Harvard: 'as a woman, and a woman neither young nor luscious nor sycophantic, she was simply invisible to those who still viewed Harvard as an all-male institution'. Women were, unless they were luscious or sycophantic, simply invisible in sociology. When the three feminist perspectives, liberal, Marxist and radical, developed in the early 1970s, their proponents had to make themselves and their theories *visible*.

In the early days of feminist sociology there were eight main tasks. These could be grouped into aims for changing the profession, aims for changing the discipline's intellectual agenda, aims for changing under-graduate curricula, aims for changing the universities, and changing the learned societies. Underlying all these goals was a desire to make the subject a more accurate reflection of women's lives and careers, and make it a less chilly climate (Smith, 1999) for women studying and teaching it. The goals for changing the discipline included:

1 To develop feminist theories/adapt the dominant theories to accom-modate women.
2 To rethink research methods: to develop non-sexist or even feminist methods.
3 To point out the gaping holes in the coverage of the social world where women had not been studied and/or where topics women thought important had not been studied.
4 To get published, especially to get feminist ideas into print.
5 To get feminist work read, and then cited, and then 'mainstreamed'.

Alongside these five goals, feminists wanted to change the undergrad-uate curricula, and teach the new ideas to graduate students:

6 To get things feminists thought important into the syllabuses taught by feminists and then by all sociologists.

Part of the agenda for feminist sociologists was to change higher edu-cation, and to change the learned societies:

7 To get the learned societies to recognise women members.
8 To get jobs for feminists, both for themselves and their students.

17

This chapter deals primarily with the first and third of these eight goals. Chapter 4 is all about methods. There are briefer sections on the other goals. Some of them, such as goal 4, are returned to in Chapter 3, where I discuss how feminist sociologists founded new journals to create space for feminist sociology. These were radical, and lofty goals in 1974. They may no longer seem particularly revolutionary. Today, sociology is so different that different goals are required. For many sociologists the challenges of postmodernism loom large. These goals and challenges are addressed in Chapter 8.

GOAL 1 DEVELOPING AND ADAPTING THEORIES

Chafetz (1988) defined feminist theory in sociology with four criteria: (1) that gender is a central focus; (2) that gender is systematically related to social contradictions, inequalities and pressure points; (3) That the theory accepts that gender relations are mutable, have changed and will change; and (4) that it can be used to 'challenge, counteract or change' situations in which women are devalued or disadvantaged. Any sociological theory which met these four criteria was, in Chafetz's view, feminist. In 1997 she revisited feminist sociological theories to see how far they had developed, and if they had made any impact on the mainstream discipline. Her work is discussed in more detail in Chapter 3.

18

From the earliest years of contemporary feminism scholars have been developing theories. For example, Ruth Wallace's (1989) collection on feminist theory in sociology brings together the American sociological theory produced by feminists up to that date. However, much of the intellectual effort has gone into developing feminist theory, rather than feminist *sociological* theory. Against the one collection by Wallace there is a series of volumes on interdisciplinary feminist theory. In 1981 Bunch edited *Building Feminist Theory* based on papers published in *Quest*. This latter collection included Hartsock's (1975, 1981) early formulation of feminist standpoint theory, still being debated in Allen and Howard (2000). In 1982 Keohane, Rosaldo and Gelpi edited *Feminist Theory* drawn from early issues of *Signs*. In 2001 a specialist journal, *Feminist Theory*, was founded to provide an outlet for this theory.

In the UK the best-known feminist sociological theorising came from two women who epitomised the intellectual positions of Marxist and radical feminism: Michèle Barrett and Sylvia Walby. In Canada, Dorothy Smith (1987) blended elements of Marxism and ethnomethodology for feminist purposes. Many feminist sociologists would see Smith as one of the most creative, innovative and thought-provoking theorists in the world, with an impact far beyond Canada.

Laslett and Thorne's (1997) collection of feminist autobiographies shows the importance of Dorothy Smith as a foundational scholar for modern feminist sociology. I was very shocked to discover that a group of women PhD students in sociology of education at a conference in Seattle in 2001 had never heard of her. While Britain, Canada and the USA had indigenous feminist sociological theorists, for many feminist sociologists the main theoretical developments came from France.

There are several French women thinkers whose ideas have been influential in British and American feminist sociology. Christine Delphy's ideas were publicised in Britain by Diana Leonard from the mid-1970s onwards, from her inclusion in Barker and Allen (1976) through to Leonard and Adkins (1996). Delphy is certainly a sociologist, with a commitment to a materialist feminism. Some sociologists have been inspired by Monique Wittig (1992) especially those drawn to work on the body and/or lesbian issues. However, the most influential theorists are not sociologists: Cixous, Irigaray and Kristeva. It is a paradox that the three most influential women theorists in feminist sociology are not sociologists and indeed, are not themselves even feminists in any way that most Anglophone women would define the term. Many feminist sociologists do not have good enough French to read the work in the original, and have used translations, compilations and the exegesis by Weedon (1987) as their source. There are several features of their position in France, and several aspects of their ideas, which make them problematic as icons for feminist sociology. Judith Butler (1999: x) points out that in her 1990 edition of *Gender Trouble* she 'read together, in a syncretic vein' a number of French intellectuals who were not, in France, friends, colleagues, allies or even producers of texts for the same audience. Braidotti (2000: 94) remarks that the same theorists are 'marginal' in France, with 'barely any institutional pull'. Bourdieu (1988: xviii) reminds Anglophone readers of *Homo Academicus* that many of those lauded in the USA 'held marginal positions in the university system which often disqualified them from officially directing research'. Irigaray was sacked by Lacan in 1974 and has never held an academic post since. Cixous has been based at Vincennes/Saint Dennis, which is a marginal university in the French system. Kristeva is depressingly anti-feminist. Bourdieu bemoans the fact that in both the USA and France:

> attention and discussion focus on a few female theorists, capable of excelling in what one of their critics has called 'the race for theory', rather than on magnificent studies ... which are infinitely richer and more fertile, even from a theoretical point of view but are less in conformity with the – typically masculine – idea of 'grand theory'. (2001: 98)

19

These women, because they are central to any discussion of postmodern feminism, are discussed in more depth in Chapter 8.

GOAL 3 THE GAPING HOLES

One of the priorities in the early days of feminist sociology was drawing attention to the gaping holes in the sociological coverage of the social world where women had not been studied, and/or where topics women thought important had not been studied.

A landmark collection from the USA was Millman and Kanter (1975). This collection contained 12 chapters, on nine empirical areas. There are chapters on education, crime, urban studies, medicine, organisations, culture, work, race, and emotions, plus three discursive ones. The manifesto of the collection included six summary critiques of sociology, or more accurately, *American* sociology, 25 years ago, which epitomise the need for finding and then filling the gaping holes. These were:

1   Sociology often assumes a 'single society' with respect to men and women, in which generalisations can be made about all participants. Yet, men and women may actually inhabit different social worlds, and this possibility must be taken into account (1975: xiii).
2   In several fields of study, sex is not taken into account as a factor in behaviour, yet sex may be among the most important explanatory variables (ibid.: xiv).
3   Important areas of social inquiry have been overlooked because of the use of certain conventional field-defining models; alternative models can open new areas for examination, about both women and men (ibid.: ix).
4   Sociology has focused on public, official, visible and/or dramatic role players and definitions of the situation, yet unofficial, supportive, less dramatic, private, and invisible spheres of social life and organisation may be equally important (ibid.: x).
5   Certain methodologies (frequently quantitative) and research situations (such as having male social scientists studying worlds involving women) may systematically prevent the elicitation of certain kinds of information which may be the most important for explaining the phenomenon being studied (ibid.: xv).
6   Sociology frequently explains the status quo (and therefore helps provide rationalisations for existing power distributions) yet social science should explore social transformations and encourage a more just, humane society (ibid.: xiv).

20

The authors of the empirical chapters showed how these six flaws were common in 'their' area. One example will suffice here. A typical analytic work of spotlighting the gaping holes is summarised to show the power of the strategy. In 1975 Lyn Lofland published an analysis of the portrayal of women in American urban sociology, which she centred on the 'thereness' of women. She argued that in the classic urban sociology of the USA, women were present in the same way that the butler was ubiquitous in the English country house detective story of the golden age (see Delamont, 1996b; Watson, 1971). In such detective stories there are always servants who:

> glide in and out of rooms, providing drinks and food. They are questioned by the police or private detective. Frequently they 'discover' the body. Often they behave 'suspiciously' enough to, at least momentarily, take centre stage ... And yet, despite, or perhaps in part because of their omni-presence, they remain, by and large, merely part of the scene. They are continually perceived, but rarely perceivers. They are part of the furniture of the setting through which the plot moves. Essential to the set but largely irrelevant to the action. They are simply, there. (1975: 144–5)

Lofland went on to show how urban sociology either portrayed women as 'part of the locale or neighbourhood or area', described like the 'ecology or demography' but 'largely irrelevant to the analytic action' (ibid.: 145) or used as 'fuzzy, shadowy, background figures' to frame male action. She suggested that this was partly because male researchers had difficulty in hanging around to gather data in places where women spent time, and called for 'finely-textured, close-grained and lovingly empirical' portrayals of women in urban society. Since she wrote, the feminist movement in sociology has produced many empirical studies of women and their lives of exactly the kind she recommended. For example, Gimlin (1996) is an ethnographic account of a hairdressing salon, a setting Lofland specifically mentioned as neglected by urban sociology.

21

While the past 25 years have seen many of the gaps in the coverage of women's social world filled by empirical research, and the theoretical and methodological literatures permeated by analyses of gender, Lofland's original comments can still be applied to the historical narratives of our own discipline. In the same spirit, I demonstrated the absence of women from the sociology of science (Delamont, 1987a). Because that paper was researched a decade after the original 'gaping hole' critiques, the paper contrasted sociology of science with other empirical areas which had changed to accommodate feminist critics by the mid-1980s. My critique drew on a content analysis of four journals in the field, and over a dozen well-regarded monographs and edited collections. The neglect of gender in the four journals was exemplified by their failure to review seminal books by Margaret Rossiter (1982) and Evelyn Fox Keller (1983, 1985). Hilary Rose (1983) had earlier set an agenda for a feminist sociology of science. She divided feminist work on science into five areas: (1) naming exclusionary practices; (2) recovering lost women; (3) re-evaluating scientific work about women; (4) critiquing the epistemological bases of taken-for-granted features of western science; and (5) analysing feminist science fiction. Rose did not emphasise conducting fine-grained observational work on scientists doing science to explore how far an activity where most practitioners are men is actually constructed in a particular way. Rose's five areas for feminist work were all remedial strategies, necessary before feminist STIS could be built.

My own major sub-field, education, had been criticised from the early 1970s onwards. Sociologists of education paid little attention to gender until the 1970s. During the growth in the sociological study of education from 1945 onwards, many studies were conducted on male-only samples, and the sexual division of labour in industrialised societies was taken for granted, not treated as a topic for investigation or for theoretically informed debate. This is demonstrated (with a content analysis of major journals) for the UK by Acker (1981, 1994) who reviewed educational research in Britain from the 1950s to the 1970s. She found that gender issues were frequently ignored, and that female experiences and the outcomes of education for women were regularly left unresearched. Many highly respected studies were based on male-only samples. The 1972 social mobility study of England and Wales (Halsey et al., 1980) for example, was based on a sample of 10,000 men. Lightfoot (1975) reached a similar conclusion about American research. A content analysis of sociology of education conducted in 1988 revealed that little had changed 20 years after the beginnings of feminist sociology. I showed (Delamont, 1989b, Appendix 1: 272–3) that, of 29 published ethnographies of adolescents in UK schools, seven were of boys only, ten of girls only, and 12 of both sexes, but that the studies of girls only were much less likely to have been published in book form (only four of the ten) than those of boys only (seven of seven).

An examination of 33 textbooks and readers in sociology of education found that only eight had a section or chapter on women and girls, and only 12 indexed women or girls. Only three of the 15 textbooks indexed 'feminism' or 'sexism'. The omission of gender as a topic and feminism as a perspective is particularly striking when one considers what the authors and editors *did* find room for. Morrish (1972) found space to cover cybernetics, but not gender. The third edition of the textbook by Havighurst and Neugarten (1967) devoted more space to feral children (reared as or by wild animals) than to gender divisions in the USA. Cordasco (1970) gave more space to Inuit education than to gender.

In the 'gaping hole' phase one of the commonly pursued, and invaluable, tasks was the compilation of bibliographies, especially annotated bibliographies, of the work that was available. When research and theoretical material were rare, and badly publicised, such bibliographies not only drew attention to the scholarship that had been done, they also gave legitimacy to the new area. If an official body, such as a learned society, published a bibliography, it gave legitimacy to the area. In 1977 the British Sociological Association produced *Sociology without Sexism: A Sourcebook*. This was a 77-page, typed, annotated bibliography of 'introductory materials on sexual divisions in the various sub-fields of sociology' (1977: i). The section on Crime and Social Control was six pages long, and included, for example, the special number of *Issues in Criminology* (vol. 8, no. 2, 1973) on women, crime and criminology, and Carol Smart's (1976) book. The sections are not attributed to compilers, but I compiled the education section. In sociology of education Walker and Barton (1983) included a bibliography of work on gender and education in the USA, the UK and Europe, Australia and New Zealand which took up 40 pages out of 213 in an edited collection. Rosenberg and Bergstrom (1975) and Een and Rosenberg-Dishman (1978) were multidisciplinary bibliographies which included a lot of sociological material. Chaff (1977) produced a large bibliography on women in medicine which ran to 1,102 entries. The explosion in research is shown by a comparison of Rosenberg and Bergstrom (1975) and Een and Rosenberg-Dishman (1978) with Watson (1990a, 1990b). There were 3,600 items in the 1975 volume, with a further 2,400 in the second. By 1990 Watson's Bibliography had 7,364 entries on 1,703 pages in two volumes, while being much more selective and academic.

An immediate solution to the absence/gap problem was editing special issues of journals. Many groups of feminists persuaded the editors and boards of academic journals to have a special issue on women, gender or feminism. I have already mentioned such a number of *Issues in Criminology* (vol. 8, no. 2, 1973). In the same spirit, Huber (1973) was a reprint of vol. 78, no. 4 of the *American Journal of Sociology*. This was one of the first 'special issues' of a mainstream journal to focus on women. Abbott (1999) states that it was part of 'an exciting time' in the history of the *AJS*, when the managing editor, Florence Levinsohn, tried to make the journal more controversial and exciting. The special issue was 'immensely successful', but Levinsohn was sacked in 1974, and *AJS* has never been as exhilarating again.

Contemporary feminist sociologists have also focused on how the discipline is itself gendered. It is not sufficient that research is done on both sexes without stereotyped biases, it also has to be published, read, cited and be accepted as part of the canon for the discipline to rid itself of sexism.

23

GOAL 4 TO GET PUBLISHED

The goal of getting published was complicated by a dilemma. Feminist sociologists had to decide whether to aim their publications at existing sociological journals and get books published by existing publishing houses; to establish new journals or book series or even new publishing houses specifically for feminist sociology; or to establish and publish in the new interdisciplinary field of women's studies/feminist studies/gender studies. Later on, with the rise of gay and lesbian studies, lesbian feminist sociologists had a fourth possible 'space'. A similar dilemma arose about which conferences to present at, and so on. There are advantages and disadvantages to each location.

Feminist social scientists since 1968 have certainly chosen to create their own spaces by establishing journals. In the USA, Jessie Bernard argued, sociological feminism or feminist sociology had achieved 'recognition of the scientific legitimacy' (1987: 24). She charted the rise of periodicals (50 of them) in which women's studies and feminist sociology could be published, quoting their mission statements. The journals featured included *No More Fun and Games* (1969); *Feminist Studies* (1972), *Women's Studies* (1972); *Quest* (1974); *Women's Agenda* (1976); *Psychology of Women Quarterly* (1976); *Chrysalis* (1977), and *Signs* (1976). In 2001, one publisher, Sage, offers seven journals founded by feminist social scientists: *The European Journal of Women's Studies, Feminism and Psychology, Feminist Theory, Gender and Society, Gender Technology and Development, Sexualities*, and *Violence against Women*.

Feminist sociologists also made efforts to publish in the existing journals, and to monitor how far they were successfully encroaching into them. Ward and Grant (1985) analysed all the issues of ten leading American sociology journals from 1974 to 1983. They examined all the issues of 'ten major sociology journals' (ibid.: 144) published from 1974 to 1983 in the USA. These were the *American Journal of Sociology (AJS)*, the *American Sociological Review (ASR)*, the *Journal of Health and Social Behaviour (JHSB)*, the *Pacific Sociological Review (PSR)*, *Social Forces (SF)*, *Social Problems (SP)*, *Social Psychology Quarterly (SPQ)*, *Sociological Quarterly (SQ)*, *Sociology of Education (SOE)*, and *Work and Occupations (WO)*. These ten journals included all those published by the American Sociological Association except their review journal, and the leading journals not produced by the ASA. Ward and Grant focused on the full-length articles (3,674 of them) and ignored all the other content, such as book reviews and editorials.

Ward and Grant focused on two things: whether articles were about gender, and, if they were empirical, whether the data came from male, female or mixed samples or populations. They found that 19 per cent

(705) of the published papers were about gender. The percentage had risen from 14 per cent in 1974 to 23 per cent in 1982. There were more gender articles in *JHSB* than any other journal, but *WO*, *SPQ*, *SP* and *SOE* also carried over 20 per cent of gender articles. Ward and Grant comment that this is in line with their expectations, because more women work in the specialisms of health, education, work and social psychology. The two highest status, generic journals *ASR* and *AJS* carried less than 20 per cent of articles on gender. Ward and Grant (1985: 151) concluded that 'Women appear to have gained sociological visibility over the decade.'

Women comprised only 8 per cent of the single authors in 1974, but at least 17 per cent every year from 1975 to 1983. They were 16 per cent of 'first' authors in 1974, and at least 18 per cent every year after that till 1983. They conclude that 'there was a dramatic increase in women's participation as solo and first authors between 1974 and 1975' (ibid.: 151) but it then stabilised. Lutz (1990) conducted a parallel analysis of women's visibility in American socio-cultural anthropology from 1977 to 1986 studying *American Anthropologist*, *American Ethnologist*, *Ethnos* and *Human Organisation*. Lutz (ibid.: 612–13) reports that women authored 30 per cent of the 1,004 articles published in the four top American anthropology journals, and were 29 per cent of the authors of the 650 books published in anthropology in 1986.

GOAL 5 TO GET CITED, TO GET READ

Feminist sociologists set out to get their ideas into print. However, 'just' getting work published is not enough. The work needs to be read, to be treated seriously, and to be cited. All these three audience responses are social matters. Sociologists read sociology, treat it seriously or discard it, and decide whether or not to cite it according to the norms and values of the discipline. Citation patterns have been studied sociologically most intensively by the sociologists of science (Moravcsik, 1988). There is a paradox about citations. Scholars cite their friends and colleagues, their supporters, and some of those they are in dispute with. However, there is a pattern of citing the people with whom one's disputes are minor, and/or those one believes one can destroy utterly. Really challenging, rapier-to-the-heart critics, and those who seem to be so wrong as to be mad, do not get cited at all. If you do not cite people's work, that is a way of keeping them out of the discourse altogether. Thus, getting feminist sociology cited is not a straightforward task.

One problem which faced all women writing and publishing academic work, whether or not they were feminists, has been discussed by Tescione (1998). She argues that women's surname changes disadvantage them in citation counts. A woman who publishes under her maiden name, her married name, her divorced name, and her remarried name is very unlikely to be credited with all her publications in any bibliometric exercise, because there is no method of plotting and accumulating citations by the same person under different names. It is possible, of course, that women's work may make less impact than men's when it has appeared under several different names. In the sociology of education, for example, all of Martyn Hammersley's publications from 1976 to 2001 appear under his name. The feminist Madeleine Arnot produced her earlier work as Macdonald. The feminist anthropologist Naneke Redclift started publishing as Naneke Codd. Rayna Rapp Reiter has published as Rapp, as Reiter, and as Rapp Reiter. A feminist bibliometric project would be to compare the citations to the work of a woman who never changed her name, such as Miriam David, who is a contemporary of Madeleine Arnot, with those of Arnot.

I have explored the citation patterns among British sociologists writing about social mobility elsewhere (Delamont, 1989a). The two dominant groups, at Oxford and Cambridge, systematically failed to cite, or address the research done by A.P.M. Coxon and his colleagues (Coxon and Jones, 1978, 1979a, 1979b). In that area arguments put forward by feminist sociologists were addressed, while Coxon's much more fundamental and foundational challenge was *totally* frozen out. Often, though, feminist work is not cited, especially not by men. Male sociologists of education in contemporary Britain are systematically citing research by men, and not citing studies by women (see Delamont, 2001a and 2001b). Catherine Lutz (1990) conducted an analysis of the citation patterns in four leading American Anthropology journals from 1982 to 1986. In 446 articles there were 11,642 citations: 8,661 to males, 1,932 to women, 874 self-citations, and 175 to a person of unspecifiable gender. So 18 per cent of citations were to women. Women authors are more likely to cite women than male authors: twice as likely. Ward and Grant (1985) conducted a similar study in *American Sociology*. Many feminist papers were not cited even in future issues of the same journals. They found that papers which added material on women to debates, or called for gender-based modifications of sociological arguments were subsequently ghettoised or frequently ignored. Such 'papers were not criticised or refuted by authors' they 'simply were ignored' (Ward and Grant, 1985: 152). This omission of feminist papers was *particularly* striking in synthesising or state-of-the-art papers. Michelle Fine (1999) has published a parallel analysis of the citation patterns in American psychology journals, with essentially similar conclusions.

Ignoring counter-arguments is a good way to destroy them and their proponents by freezing them out of the discourse. At one level this sounds pretty trivial. However, there is almost no point in writing and publishing theoretical or empirical research if no one reads it. Of course, publications build up on the CV, and are used to help get jobs, tenure, promotion, and so forth. However, a long list of unread and uncited publications is not career-enhancing. Few feminists would accept the reliance on citation counts as an indicator of the quality of the research as uncritically as Cole (1979), and Cole and Cole (1973) did. However, some universities use citation counts as an indicator of esteem, as Tescione (1998) warns. In the United Kingdom, the past 20 years have seen a rapid growth of audit and accountability measures. In particular, staff in universities have been subjected to the recurrent Research Assessment Exercises, and the organisation of university vice-chancellors currently called UUK and formerly the CVCP have collected annual publication returns, so a scholar needs to be publishing to have an individual CV and to contribute to the departmental profile. However, few scholars would be happy publishing merely to build up a list of unread works.

Consequently, one of the goals of feminist sociology has been to get feminist work read, understood, appreciated and cited. Here the differences between Marxist feminists and liberal feminists, on the one hand, and radical feminists, on the other, are readily apparent. Marxist and liberal feminist sociologists see themselves as part of mixed scholarly communities, and therefore expect their male colleagues to read their work, and take it on board. Radical feminists are much more interested in an all-female audience, building up a separatist sociology. There are no Marxist or liberal feminist writings circulated only to women, but there have been radical feminist publications barred to male readers.

Of course, before our work can be cited, it needs to have been read. Many leading scholars, especially men, seem to find it difficult to read feminist work. Shirley Ardener (1975) edited a collection of feminist papers, called *Perceiving Women*. A decade later she wrote that one of her male colleagues confessed to her that he 'wanted' to read it, but 'couldn't bring himself to' (Ardener, 1985). Ruth Behar (1995) reports that when she was planning Behar and Gordon (1995) a 'kindly male anthropologist' warned her that men would dismiss her project as 'derivative', because it was a feminist response to Clifford and Marcus (1986).

27

GOAL 6 CHANGING TEACHING

There is a need for a thoroughly researched study of the changing nature of the curriculum in sociology at school, university undergraduate and postgraduate levels since 1968. We have histories of women's studies (Bird, 2001) but not of the changing nature of sociology. It is likely that the school and the university curricula have changed to incorporate feminist sociological perspectives. However, these may be compartmentalised (one lecture in the theory course, one option in the final year), or perhaps they permeate the whole curriculum. In the absence of data on this topic, I have not explored it further here.

GOAL 7 CHANGING THE LEARNED SOCIETIES

In the years after 1968 in both the UK and the USA feminist sociologists challenged their own learned societies, the BSA and the ASA. Typically there was a working party on the equality of the sexes, which later became a permanent committee. Inside the learned societies, women's caucuses tried to get women onto the important committees, elected to the high offices, to get funds to support women's topics as conference themes, and even to start journals.

The American Sociological Association had 13,055 members in 1999, and 48 per cent of them were female. The proportions of male and female full members (as opposed to student members) is roughly equal in the under-50s, but there are twice as many men as women in the 'over-50' age range. These figures on the sexual division of labour in American sociology are not surprising: in the past 30 years women have been increasingly appointed to permanent jobs, and increasingly active in the ASA. *Footnotes* (December 2001: 3–4) the newsletter of the ASA states that in 1997, 40 per cent of all sociologists under 75 with PhDs in employment were female. In 2000, women were 45 per cent of ASA's membership. Women are over-represented in the sections on sex and gender, the family, medical, and race, gender and class. Men are over-represented in the theory section, and those for political sociology and comparative/historical sociology. The other sections have men and women in the regular 55:45 per cent proportions. The path from the relative absence of women to the 2000 figures is made up of many individual careers. Some of these are recorded in publications, enabling us to empathise with the struggles of individual feminist sociologists. Dorothy Thomas, wife of W.I. had a PhD from LSE. She was the first woman President of the ASA in 1952. Subsequently Mirra Komoravsky (1973), Alice Rossi (1983), Matilda Riley (1986) and Joan Huber (1989) were. Rossi, Riley and Huber were all married to leading male sociologists active in the *ASA*. Throughout this book, an analysis of published autobiographical essays by American men and women sociologists is drawn on to humanise the statistics. The autobiographies of 42 women sociologists published in three collections (Goetting and Fenstermaker, 1995; Laslett and Thorne, 1997; Orlans and Wallace, 1994) were analysed with a parallel study of 22 male autobiographies. The samples are not equivalent, because the 42 women are not nearly as distinguished as the 22 men: some have worked in low status institutions, some have had stalled careers. The women's autobiographies differ from the men's in two obvious ways: the autobiographies are published without ASA endorsement by 'marginal' presses, and ten of the 42 women report a denial of tenure. None of the 22 men report such a denial. However, they are useful data to explore the achievements of feminist sociology.

Progress in the UK has been similar. The BSA publishes a membership register. The 1977 edition listed 1,106 members, of whom 171 were female (15.4 per cent). Some 58 of the 1,106 said they were professors, and four of these were women. Not all the members had provided entries for the register, but there is no evidence that women in general, or professorial women, had failed to return their forms disproportionately compared to men. In the register, members listed their research interests. Those who listed theory, industrial sociology and stratification were nearly all men; women were more likely to report research interests on education, health and illness, and women. In 1988 the BSA had 1,616 members, of whom 680 had completed a questionnaire, while 936 had not; 241 of the 680 members were women. Of the 1,616 members, 96 were professors, of whom 13 were women. By 1997 there were 2,600 members, of whom 79 were in Europe and 122 elsewhere in the world. Among the UK-based members 165 were professors, of whom 45 were women. In 1979 when the BSA was 28 years old, it had had only two women Presidents Barbara Wootton (1959–64) and Sheila Allen (1975–7). After 1979, Sheila Allen, Meg Stacey (1981–3), Jennifer Platt (1987–9) and Sara Arber (1999–2001) were women presidents.

29

Among the important jobs in sociology are staffing the academic journals. Ward and Grant (1985) examined the editorial boards of ten American sociology journals from 1974 to 1983. Five of the ten journals had no female editor-in-chief in that period, four had had a woman for four or more of the ten years. In 1977–8 four of the ten had a woman editor, in 1981 all ten had male editors. Four of the five journals which never had a woman editor published fewer than 20 per cent of articles on gender in that decade. All ten journals had some women on their boards or acting as assistant editors (from 10 per cent up to 37 per cent).

GOAL 8 THE BATTLE FOR JOBS

One of the goals of feminist sociologists has been, since 1970, to increase the career chances of women in the discipline at all levels from doctoral studentships to full professorships. Some of the campaigning to get women, or feminists, into jobs has been done privately inside each university. Man and women have been encouraging women to apply for posts, have been shortlisting them, insisting on equal opportunities training for interviewers, and have been making appointments. The results of this work show in the statistics, but are not discussed in public. As this campaign moved ahead over the past 30 years, several features of the occupation of university lecturer and university professor were scrutinised. As a by-product of the feminist campaigns, much more is known about the job, which turns out to be experienced very differently by men and women. In the early years of feminist sociology, women faculty were rare in elite American institutions, especially in tenured jobs, and scarce in British ones too. As women have gained a higher percentage of the posts, the ways the role are performed may be changing the discipline itself. To understand the nature of the academic labour market in sociology, it is helpful to start with the analyses of the whole occupation, which are more numerous and thoughtful than extant studies of sociology alone. Men and women perform the role differently or occupy different roles in the same occupation. There are three aspects of the job – teaching, administration, and research – but each of these has several facets.

'Teaching', for example, can include a wide range of activities from seeing a single frightened first year who cannot write an essay, or supervising a PhD project, to lecturing 700 students in a vast hall. Administration can cover being a Dean, representing a faculty of 300 staff and 8,000 students, or dealing with the pastoral care of a new student who does not know how to deal with the mice in his bedsitter. Research can mean running a research project with a multimillion pound budget employing 20 people, or spending 20 years all alone in the archives of an Austrian family and ultimately writing a book only 200 people will read in the next 20 years. The world of the full professor in science, who attracts big grants and is on many committees is quite different from that of the new lecturer in art history who will never hold research funds or lecture to more than 40 people.

The occupation of university teacher is thus a deeply segmented one (Bucher and Stelling, 1977) and the evidence we have is that men and women occupy rather different segments of it, and experience it in different ways. The American studies have found women carrying bigger teaching loads than their male colleagues, and loads made up of less prestigious teaching. In the USA women are more likely to be teaching introductory and service courses while men supervise PhD students. The research carried out by Williams et al. (1974) found that in the UK women did not carry bigger loads than men, but did do the less prestigious work. In both the USA and the UK, women in universities are frequently found to be doing more hours of teaching, especially at the lowest levels (that is, introductory and service courses rather than PhD work), more pastoral care, less administration and committee work, and less research and publication. This last area is the one where the differences between males and females in university work are most significant, because the size and prestige of research grants and the list of publications, are the two most visible, and easily measured, criteria for judging job performance. Teaching and administration are invisible, and despite lip service being paid to their importance, promotion and recognition are actually based on publications and research to a great extent because they can be quantified, compared and assessed most easily.

The first, and most significant feature of research and publication is that large numbers of people in the occupation do little of either. Although it is widely believed that in higher education one must 'publish or perish', in fact substantial numbers of men and women publish very little and do not perish (Cole and Cole, 1973: 92–3). Most people teaching in higher education are silent: men as well as women. The relative lack of publications and citations of their papers which characterises most workers in higher education is thrown into relief by a comparison with Nobel Laureates (Zuckerman, 1977). Cole and Cole looked at the published output up to 1970 of 499 matched men and women in chemistry, biology and psychology who had gained PhDs in 1957–8. They found that the average 'lifetime' output of this group was nine papers over the 12 years, and that the typical male's papers were cited 11 times a year, while the typical woman's were cited four times. The men in this sample were more productive than the women, whether married or single. Reskin (1978) also found that American women publish less than matched samples of men in the same disciplines and that what women *do* publish is cited less. In Britain Williams et al. (1974: 399) found that women published less than men in all disciplines, but that married women were more productive than single ones. In the two years before the research was done (i.e. 1967–9), more than half the single women had published nothing, while only one quarter of the married had been silent. Similarly one in six of the married women had produced six or more publications, while only one in 12 of the single ones were that productive. The impact of successive Research Assessment Exercises in the UK since 1985 may have changed this pattern and the period 1974–2002 is also one in which more women have entered the occupation. Brooks (1997) reports a survey of

31

108 women academics in the UK, a significant proportion of whom voiced their perception that the occupation was experienced differently by men. Becher and Trowler (2001) provide a critique of the small number of women in Becher's (1989) original sample (22 out of 221), and summarise the research on women academics published since 1989.

In Britain, therefore it would not be possible to 'explain' lower publication rates by heavier teaching loads. There is, however, a feature of publication in the social sciences which could tie in with fewer PhD students and lower publication rates, and that is co-authorship. The prevalence of single authored, jointly authored, or multiply authored publications varies from one discipline to another. Multiple authorship is commoner, indeed normal, in engineering and the sciences, and rarest in the arts. However, in any discipline, men are more likely to have some joint publications than women, and this partly 'explains' why men publish 'more' than women. This issue is not just a matter of the total length of an academic's CV: the presence or absence of joint publications can be interpreted by those who consider scholars for jobs, grants, promotions and distinctions. In C.P. Snow's novel about crystallography, *The Search*, two successful scientists are described advising an unsuccessful one how to build his career so that he will become eligible for promotion. The failure is told that he must 'Publish a great deal, some in collaboration, some by yourself. If it's all by yourself, the jealous men will say you're impossible to work with; and if it's all in collaboration, they'll say you're no good on your own' (1934: 324).

Men are much more likely to publish jointly than women are in all disciplines, perhaps because women have fewer higher degree students, and so have fewer potential collaborators. Underlying those issues lies a third – whether women in general, and feminists in particular, feel at ease in their jobs and in higher education. The research on chilly climates, sacred groves and so on would suggest many do not. Caplan (1993), Statham et al. (1991), Brooks (1997), Aisenberg and Harrington (1988), Morley and Walsh (1995), Morley (1999), Becher and Trowler (2001). Clark et al. (1996) report some chilling examples of harassment in higher education. Noticeably Henkel (2000) does not index gender or women. Networks of women, and/or feminists, can provide some shelter in chilly climates, opportunities for increased publication, and increase citations to women's work. Women's caucuses and learned societies can increase publication opportunities. However, it is not clear that joint publications by two women have the same status as joint publications with mixed authorship. My career advice to women is to publish with and without men.

Turning specifically to sociology, these general features of a deeply segmented occupation seem to have applied at the beginning of the feminist movement and to have persisted since. Chubin (1974) looked at a sample of men and women with PhDs in Sociology from American universities. She found that there were many silent women, and that the vast majority of those who were ever going to publish had done so for the first time within five years of their doctorate. Among those who had published she found that women were much less likely to be co-authors than men: that is women were more likely to have *only* solely authored publications. When women did co-author, they were rarely listed first. Women's publications were cited less than men's. Mackie examined the articles published in 14 sociology journals in 1967 and 1973 and found that: 'In 1967 and in 1973, women sociologists were more likely than men to publish alone' (1976: 286). In the period he studied, the proportion of articles that were jointly authored was rising steadily.

The feminist sociologists wanted more women employed in sociology, wanted the good ones promoted, and wanted some equalisation of the loads inside the occupation. By this I mean that many feminists valued the pastoral care and introductory teaching, they felt that many male colleagues disdained it, but wanted a re-balancing of the value system of higher education so the lower status work became more highly valued, and all tasks were more equally shared.

33

SOCIOLOGY TODAY

Sociology in Britain in 2001 is very different from 1968. It is much bigger: far more staff, students and departments, and far more sociologists teaching medical students, dental students, nurses, social workers, and other professions. Whole new areas of empirical research have been opened up, which I have discussed in Chapter 3. There is, however, a wonderful contrast between the gritty, smelly, practicality of research on, for example, hospital cleaners, and, to quote Rosemary Deem: 'the increasing malestream sociological obsession with the Internet, Los Angeles and various facets of the hyper-real' (1996: 16).

To emphasise the changes, let us return to Burminster.

vignette 2.2

Burminster has changed. There are now over 200 students doing various undergraduate degrees, including 'joints' with subjects, such as media studies, peace studies and gender studies, unknown and undreamed of, in 1968. The department now has 16 full-time staff, and a penumbra of eight part-time 'tutors'. The department now runs courses for the medical and dental students, and a masters' course in gay and lesbian studies. There are now seven professors, four men and three women including Tamzin Wrankester, none of whom is head of department. Mr Whaddon, a senior lecturer, now 60, is head of department.

Tom Twisdon is still on the staff, still a lecturer at 62: he has never recovered from his shock at the fall of the Berlin Wall. Miss Glynde retired in 1975, very disturbed by feminism: she sometimes comes in to departmental events: usually retirement parties and reunions. There are four women lecturers, all under 40. Professor Tamzin Wrankester teaches the level three theory, the methods course includes a compulsory essay on either feminist or queer methods, and all reading lists are required to include at least one-third of items authored by women. There is a compulsory course on gender in Year Two, and a final year option on sexuality. Miss Glynde's worst fears have come true: no course on marriage. If Professor Westwater were to return from the grave, he would find Burminster sociology unrecognisable.

three

the new forms possible to women?

the achievements of feminist sociology

A manda Cross (1981: 148) writes of 'the new forms possible to women'. This chapter focuses on the achievements of feminist sociology in making those new forms, and in colonising the old forms which were male strongholds. Achievement is in the eye of the beholder. As there are many different beholders of feminist sociology, one group's achievement is another's retrograde step. A liberal feminist may see a gain which both an anti-feminist and a radical feminist could discount or even regard as a reversal of fortune. A radical feminist may cherish a publication or insight that makes some male sociologists uncomfortable and is unknown to most men in the discipline. There are female sociologists extremely hostile to the work of all feminists, and men such as those lauded in Chapter 7 who have built the 'new men's studies' enthusiastically scaffolding their concepts from feminist work. The Feminist Scholars in Sociology (1995) claim as major achievements, feminist work which had been condemned by a series of eminent men in *Sociological Forum* in a 1994 Symposium on 'What's Wrong with Sociology?' The men felt feminism was one of the things wrong, the feminists felt it was one of the discipline's strengths.

For the purposes of this chapter I have focused on five areas of achievement:

1 feminist presence in public manifestations of sociology;
2 tenured posts in top sociology departments;
3 the opening up of new topics;
4 the creation of new intellectual spaces;
5 the creation of new definitions of 'knowledge'.

The area of research methods is the subject of Chapter 4. The chapter ends with one final indicator of impact and achievement: the backlash. There are never backlashes against ideas that are thought trivial: counter-arguments are lodged against ideas thought to be powerful.

FEMINIST PRESENCE IN PUBLIC MANIFESTATIONS OF SOCIOLOGY

To capture the achievements I have juxtaposed some of the published manifestations of sociology in the 1970s with their equivalents today. Good examples are the contents of reference books, new journals, and the editorial boards of journals. Reference books do show changes produced by feminist sociologists. In 1977 Bullock and Stallybrass edited the first edition of *The Fontana Dictionary of Modern Thought*. It had nine consultant editors, all men. The third edition came out in 1999 with 3,764 entries, by 326 contributors. There were 984 new entries. The editors recognised the change in their coverage of feminism: 'Movements like feminism have now matured into full-blown disciplines with a history that is long and complex, complete with schools, factions, revisionists and a vanguard that continues not only to explore concepts but to exert powerful influence on our social structures' (ibid.: v). In the first edition there was one entry on feminism about two-thirds of a column long. In the 1999 third edition, feminism has a three-column entry followed by separate entries on feminist criticism, geography, history, psychoanalysis, psychology, and theology. Elsewhere socialist feminism, radical feminism and liberal feminism have their own entries.

Reference works are only one public manifestation of sociology. The journals in which research is published are another. Feminist sociology has established its own journals and made inroads into the existing ones as editors, editorial advisors and authors. There are some obvious achievements. In the USA, Sociologists for Women in Society (SWS) is 34 years old (founded 1975) and its journal *Gender and Society* had reached volume 15 in 2001. Arlene Kaplan Daniels (1999) provides a brief account of the growth of Sociology for Women in Society (SWS). Two women who were presidents of SWS became presidents of the ASA itself (Alice Rossi and Joan Huber). In the UK, there has not been a generic BSA journal officially sponsored by the British Sociological Association launched on gender or women, but there is a plethora of journals on gender or women which carry sociological papers. A feminist sociologist wanting to publish a paper on work has *Gender and Work*, on education *Gender and Education*, on violence *Violence Against Women*, on ageing *Women and Ageing* and so on. There are also the feminist journals, such as *Signs* in the USA (up to volume 26), and *Feminist Review* (67 issues), *Women's Studies International Forum* (up to volume 24), and the *European Journal of Women's Studies* and *Feminist Theory*.

Feminist sociologists have also made some impact on the management and content of the generic journals. In the UK the achievements can be traced by comparing 1967 with 1992 and 2000. We can compare the three generic sociology journals in Britain, *Sociology* (the baby, but also the official journal of the BSA), *The British Journal of Sociology* and *The Sociological Review*. It is appropriate to look at the sex of the editors, the review editors, the editorial board/advisory board, and the authors of the papers. When *Sociology* began in 1967, it was embedded in a very different social context. The first set of editorial advisers is a glimpse into another world. They were listed as: Joe Banks, Basil Bernstein, P. Collison, Stephen Cotgrove, John Goldthorpe, David Lockwood, Donald MacRae, John Madge, F.M. Martin, J. Clyde Mitchell, Bryan Wilson and Mrs (*sic*) Margaret Stacey. Those advisers came from a restricted set of institutions, in terms of geographical spread and the status of their universities (and they *were* all universities): Liverpool, London (two), Newcastle, Cambridge (two), Oxford, Edinburgh, Manchester, UC Swansea, 'Bath University of Technology' (*sic*) and Political and Economic Planning, London. The editorial board in May 1992 looked quite different. The 18 members (six more than 1967) were ten females and eight men, with the chairperson a woman. Two people were based in Wales and two in Scotland, and one was from a polytechnic. Oxford and Cambridge were conspicuously absent. The February 2000 issue of *Sociology* (volume 34, number 1) showed an editorial board of 21, 12 men and nine women, seven from post-1992 universities, and still none from Oxbridge. The editors were a man and a woman, so too were the review editors.

In 1967 *The British Journal of Sociology*, which is based permanently at LSE, had an editorial board of ten; nine men and one woman. In 1992 the board had 13 members; ten men, three women. The 2000 volume of *British Journal of Sociology* (51) shows an editorial board of 14, with three women, a male editor and male review editor.

The Sociological Review for July 1967 (volume 15, number 2) had an editorial board of 14, all men. The institutions of the editorial board members were not given (they may all have been at Keele where the journal is based). The February 1992 issue (volume 40, number 1) shows an editorial board of 18, seven of them women. The three editors were all men, one of whom acted as review editor. The February 2000 issue (volume 48, number 1) shows 28 people on the editorial board, seven of them women. One of two editors is a woman, the review editor male. These changes in board membership are summarised in Table 3.1.

The pattern of authorship of the articles, and the ways in which the authors are listed has also changed, as Table 3.2 shows.

In January 1967 in the first issue of *Sociology* there were six papers, produced by 12 authors, of whom one (Jennifer Platt) was female. The authors were sometimes listed by initials (S.R. Parker) and sometimes by first names (Anthony P.M. Coxon). The contents of that issue can be contrasted with that of May 1992, when there were 11 articles; three by women. All the authors were listed by their first names and family names (e.g. Geoff Evans). What is really inconceivable today is a listing in the September 1967 issue, where a paper's authors are W.P. Robinson and Miss (*sic*) S.J. Rackstraw! There were 11 papers in that issue, three by women, the same as May 1992.

Journal	Total (women) 1967	Year Total (women) 1992	Total (women) 2000
Sociology	12 (1)	18 (10)	21 (9)
BJS	10 (1)	13 (3)	14 (3)
SR	14 (0)	18 (7)	28 (7)

Table 3.1: *Board membership of three generic journals*

Journal	Total (women) Jan. 1967	Year Total (women) May 1992	Total (women) Feb. 2000
Sociology	12 (1)	11 (3)	13 (3)
BJS	7 (1)	4 (2)	11 (2)
SR	6 (1)	7 (2)	6 (2)

Table 3.2: *Gender and authorship in three generic journals*

If we turn to the content of *BJS*, in 1967 (volume 18, number 1) all the authors were listed by initials in the table of contents (J. Rex, J. Ford), and by their full names on the actual article. There were seven articles by men and one by a woman. In 1992 (volume 43, number 1) there were four papers by men and two by women. In 2000 (volume 51, number 1) there were 11 papers by men and two by women. *The Sociological Review* for July 1967 had six articles, one by a woman (Roisin Pill). Authors were listed by both names 'Gordon Rose'. In February 1992 (volume 40, number 1) there were seven papers, two by women. Authors were listed by both names 'Helen Roberts'. Authors are still referred to by both names, in February 2001 when there were six papers, two by women.

Sociology and to some extent *Sociological Review* have changed more than *BJS*. The BSA membership elects the board of *Sociology*, and so the number of women involved is a reflection of a culture change in the association's membership and their priorities. Similar analyses of the two generic journals in the USA, *The American Journal of Sociology* and *The American Sociological Review* were conducted by Ward and Grant (1985) and have already been summarised in Chapter 2. They scrutinised the years 1974–83. In 2001 both *AJS* and *ASR* had male editors, each supported by three assistant editors of whom two were women.

TENURED POSTS IN TOP SOCIOLOGY DEPARTMENTS

Judith Glazer-Raymo (1999) reviews the progress made by women in American higher education generally. In part, this advance was due to the growth of women's studies courses and degree programmes. By 1995 The National Women's Studies Association had more than 600 women's studies programmes in higher education listed. However, women were making progress in all disciplines, particularly by gaining the entry qualification to academic life: the doctorate. Some 47 per cent of the PhDs earned by Americans in America in 1994 went to women. In 1995, 16,333 women got PhDs – nearly 10 times more than in 1965 (1,760). In Social Sciences (not including education or psychology) 487 women got PhDs in 1969–70 and 1,313 in 1993–4 going up from 12.6 per cent to 36.1 per cent. The breakdown of social science reveals that women are 61 per cent of the anthropology PhDs, 51 per cent of those in sociology, 27.8 per cent in politics and 24.3 per cent in economics. The fact that women gained 51 per cent of the PhDs awarded to Americans in America in 1995 shows a rapid rise.

39

However, it is not clear that the increased female percentage of the qualified pool of labour will turn into an equal proportion of women actually holding academic jobs. In the American system there are two types of job: casual versus tenure-track and tenured. Gaining a tenure-track position does not, in itself lead to tenure (Clark et al., 1996). The three grades of posts that matter are assistant professor, associate professor and full professor. Across all the types of higher education in the USA, in sociology, in 1991 women were 29 per cent of all tenured and tenure-tracked posts. However, 46 per cent of the assistant professors were women, 30 per cent of the associate professors and 20 per cent of the full professors. So there were few full professors (Glazer-Raymo, 1999). Even where women sociologists have achieved some parity of appointments in the discipline, they may well be employed in lower status institutions where there are no PhD students to be supervised. In the USA, departments vary widely in prestige, and the institutions themselves are in a hierarchy from community colleges which offer only two years of teaching through places that offer only a bachelor's degree and do not have graduate schools through to the elite universities with big doctoral programmes. Women were concentrated in the lower tiers, and relatively scarce in tenured posts in the top two tiers (Glazer-Raymo, 1999). The hierarchy of American higher education institutions is shown below, most prestigious first:

1 Fortune 100 research universities
2 Other doctoral and master's-granting universities
3 Comprehensive universities
4 Liberal arts colleges
5 Community colleges

In 1970, the USA had 2,525 higher education institutions (HEIs) with 450,000 academic staff, of whom 23 per cent were women. By 1993 there were 3,632 HEIs, with 933,373 staff, 38.7 per cent female. Of the 554,903 full-time staff, 33.5 per cent were female. Between 1975 and 1993 women as a percentage of full professors rose 9.6 per cent to 17.2 per cent. Women still spend more time teaching (58 per cent) than men (46 per cent) and less time on research (16 per cent to 27 per cent) – probably because more women are employed in teaching only HEIs: the lower tiers of the hierarchy. Part-time (PT) and non-tenure-track (NTT) staff do large amounts of teaching in all types of HEI, and it is in those grades that women are concentrated. Women are 33 per cent of tenure-track (TT) faculty and their tenure rate is only 48 per cent compared to men's 72 per cent. That is, women are less likely than men to get tenure.

Progress for women in the USA would ideally mean the best women getting tenure in the elite schools, such as Berkeley, Yale, Harvard, Columbia, Stanford and Chicago. In the discipline of sociology there has been only a small amount of progress since feminist sociology began, partly because the elite schools had, typically, *no* tenured women in 1968. At Chicago no woman had ever been tenured in the Sociology Department when feminist sociology became established in the late 1960s. The changes began with Rita Simon, in 1978, who was also the first woman to edit *ASR*. In 1993–4 Chicago had 20 tenured men and four tenured women. The Berkeley Sociology Department was founded in 1948. It awarded 126 PhDs between 1952 and 1972, 32 to women. These were the department's golden years, because it was rated the top sociology department in the USA in 1964 and 1969 (Orlans and Wallace, 1994). Berkeley sociology grew after Blumer came from Chicago in 1952. Then it had only nine staff, whereas by 1964 it had 36. From 1948 to 1970 no woman was hired in a tenure-track position. (A few women had temporary posts as NTT adjuncts.) In 1997 women were 12.5 per cent of the tenured faculty at Harvard, 13.3 per cent at Stanford, and 13.8 per cent at Yale (Laslett and Thorne, 1997).

The slow progress of women into tenured posts, especially tenured posts at elite schools, can be traced in the three volumes of published autobiographies. Laslett and Thorne edited a collection, *Feminist Sociology*, published in 1997, with 11 autobiographical essays. It followed two earlier collections by Goetting and Fenstermaker (1995) and Orlans and Wallace (1994) which used 'gender' and 'women', rather than the 'f' word. The Laslett and Thorne volume was thought important enough to get two reviews in the ASA's review journal *Contemporary Sociology* (Hess, 1999; Whittier, 1999). Laslett and Thorne provided essays themselves and commissioned chapters from Evelyn Nakano Glenn, Judith Stacey, Joan Acker, Susan Krieger, Sarah Fenstermaker, Marjorie De Vault, Desley Deacon, the three women who founded The Center for Research on Women at Memphis University (Weber, Higgenbottom and Dill), and one man, R.W. Connell. I have discussed Connell's contribution to feminist sociology in Chapter 7 on the malesteam. Of 46 autobiographical essays by women, it is striking that only 23 are by women who are full professors in elite American universities. Many of the others taught in lower status places, such as community colleges, and/or never achieved tenure at all.

Britain is rather different from the USA, both in the nature of the higher education system, and in the lack of published analyses of women's position in and contribution to the discipline. Whereas in the USA there has been a stream of analyses of the place of women in the discipline, Britain has not had that introspection. The status of universities and other HEIs is a matter of tacit, expert knowledge, and in theory, all universities are equal, in that all have the right to award doctorates. However, there are competitions between them for students, for staff, for grants, for prestige, and most of all for research rankings in the quinquennial Research Assessment Exercises. There is evidence that knowledge and understanding of the hierarchies in British higher education are pervasive among large employers (Brown and Scase, 1994) but very unequally spread across potential students and their parents (Pugsley, 1998). Working-class families have little understanding of status differences between HEIs, and suffer symbolic violence at every stage from application to employment after graduation. In the early days of Third Wave feminism there were detailed analyses of women's place in universities (e.g. Acker and Warren Piper, 1984; Blackstone and Fulton, 1975; Rendel, 1980), although they rarely looked down the data to the level of individual subjects such as sociology. Recently, such work has become sparse, and there is nothing of the detail of the American self-scrutiny. For the 2001 RAE all the data are being made public, and it would be possible for a study looking at the percentage of tenured women in the top ranked sociology departments, or to investigate whether women were less likely to be returned in the RAE than men. (There were rumours and press stories of this modern exclusion in the months before the 2001 submissions were made.)

It is true that across all the HEIs in Britain women are clustered in temporary posts, in research posts, in part-time work, and in the lower ranks (Lecturer A and B) of the tenured jobs. There is no reason to believe that sociology has a different pattern from other disciplines. It would be possible to count the women returned as research active in the 2001 RAE to give some measure of female involvement in the discipline, but there is no equivalent base figure for 1961, or 1971. However, this research has not been done for publication. The government statistics for higher education publish the data for groups of subjects, making it impossible to disentangle sociology from some allied social sciences. In Britain, in 2000, 11.9 per cent of the full professors in administrative, business and social studies were women. It is not possible to disaggregate this figure except by checking staff lists in every individual HEI. So the official statistical data are not being mined for feminist analysis on the position of women in the discipline. Nor has Britain produced the range and variety of published autobiographical essays by women, or men, which would enable the statistics to be fleshed out.

42

It would be illuminating to take the 'top' departments – for example, the LSE – and see when women got tenure and when they got professorships. However, whereas in the USA there are departments with century-long histories, the discipline in Britain is much younger, and few departments are more than 50 years old.

NEW TOPICS

There is no doubt that feminist sociology has opened up new topics. If, for example we take the sociology of families and households, there are at least nine 'new' topics opened up by feminist sociologists, which aim at unpicking and doing high quality research upon 'marriage', 'family', 'household', and 'the private'. They provide us with a new angle on marriage and households: the scrutiny of the private. These topics are:

1 Housework
2 Caring
3 Money
4 Domestic violence
5 Food, drink and cooking
6 Childbirth
7 Emotional 'work'

8 Leisure
9 Control of time

Much of the sociology of the past 25 years has been about the apparently mundane: who pays the rent? Who buys the children's school shoes? Who empties the kitchen bin? Who cleans up when granny soils herself? Who hits whom? Whose hobbies get time and money, whose get squeezed out? (see McKie et al., 1999).

housework

Ann Oakley's (1974) pioneering study of housework, or rather of housewives, is the best-known example of a feminist sociologist opening up a new topic. When Ann Oakley (1974) set out to study housework, as work, in 1968 her topic was seen as 'odd'. That research, on 40 London housewives with small children, became a pioneering classic. Two findings were strikingly novel in the early seventies. First, the hours spent. On average, housework took women 77 hours a week, far longer than most paid employment. Second, the class difference. The working-class woman liked the role and disliked the tasks, the middle class hated the label but did not mind the chores. They had far better working conditions (central heating, unlimited hot water on tap, fitted carpets, washing machines, freezers and vacuum cleaners) and got pleasure from interacting with their small children. The working-class woman lacked good working conditions, and faced conflicts between their childcare and the housework. For example, if washing has to be carried down several flights of stairs to the pavement before being done in a laundrette, manipulating the pram and the toddler and the washing is hard work. Reading to a toddler while the washing is in your own machine in your own kitchen is not 'the same' experience. Since Oakley's original study, research has diversified, so that both men and women are studied, as are households early in their life cycle and those of the elderly, families where there are two wage earners or none, with and without children, and so on.

After Oakley's pioneering books other feminist sociologists conducted research on the work done inside families and households, and so, too, did scholars not particularly interested in feminism. The methods of data collection have diversified, and research has been done on men, on adolescents, on children and on the elderly to see how domestic work is done. Because Oakley opened up a new topic, we now have evidence about how the domestic work is, or is not, being or not being redistributed or mechanised. Some recent studies, outlined below, show how the original achievement of Oakley has been routinised in sociology.

43

Sullivan (1997) collected time diaries from both partners in 408 couples. These data enable us to see not only which sex does which task, but which tasks are done together and which alone. These data come from the large Social Change and Economic Life Initiative (SCELI) study in six cities in Scotland and England, not just London. Men's domestic work is mainly gardening and DIY, women's is mainly cooking and cleaning. Women frequently report doing more than one task at once: 'washing-up while at the same time operating the washing machine and keeping an eye on the children' (ibid.: 231). It appears that domestic tasks are still gendered, and that women are more likely to be doing several at once. Valentine (1999) reports a survey by a major supermarket chain which got 43,000 respondents. Women did the bulk of the shopping in 62 per cent of the households, and the cooking in 75 per cent of them. In the households of these respondents the traditional division of labour was more prevalent in the working-class households than the middle-class, (or was *reported* as more traditional). Baxter and Western comment that:

> Most research still shows a clear division of labour within the house-hold with men participating mainly in outdoor work and women taking primary responsibility for childcare and indoor activities such as cooking, cleaning and laundry ... Moreover wives spend over twice as much time on domestic work as their husbands. (1998: 101)

The body of data now available on housework is a definite achievement of feminist sociology.

caring

Janet Finch opened up the field of research on caring when she conducted a study of mothers using pre-school playgroups (Finch, 1984) and when she edited the landmark volume on women as carers with Dulcie Groves (Finch and Groves, 1983). In that book nine women and one man reported studies of women's caring *work* for the chronic sick, the disabled, and the elderly. There is evidence that women continue to provide domestic care for able-bodied adult children long after they could share the work. 20 years ago I argued that when women continued to perform domestic duties for relatives (such as adult sons), it served partly as a hedge against loneliness: as an insurance policy (Delamont, 1980: 218–21). By providing domestic services women ensure that they are not lonely: the child who comes home with a load of laundry *has come home*. Research on such apparently mundane issues as housework, cooking and money is illuminating about the 'big' topics of power, gender and identity. Women's continuing performance

44

of domestic work for children, men and elderly relatives is a striking continuity in modern Britain. Underneath the talk about families and their changing place in Britain, the work goes on, women feel that shopping, cooking, cleaning, childcare, elder care and even family happiness are their responsibility. If women are not shouldering the bulk of the physical and emotional labour, they feel *guilt* so they continue to perform the bulk of the cooking, cleaning, shopping, clothes maintenance and childcare. The research on divorce, and on new families after divorce (e.g. Burgoyne and Clark, 1983) shows how divorcees, and those who establish new families after divorces, have to renegotiate the division of physical and emotional labour, with added burdens of guilt (Finch and Mason, 1990).

Crompton (2000) has developed the research on caring in studies of how employment and caring are interrelated in contemporary Europe. Her quotes from women in France, Norway and Britain show doctors and bankers planning their work lives in ways that help them deal with guilt. The same issues of responsibility and guilt predominating in women's lives show well in the research on caring. There is a clear relationship between gender and caring. While elderly and disabled married women may get care from husbands (Arber and Ginn, 1995; Taraborrelli, 1993), the vast majority of carers are female, and bear the double burden of the physical labour and the guilt. The caring that starts with motherhood extends far into the future, while the duties of being a daughter loom on the horizon. Dilemmas regarding caring are a regular feature of the problem pages of the women's magazines:

> My sister looks after our elderly father. I couldn't have him myself as I live in a small flat and work full-time. She has a big house, works part-time and is better off than me. Recently, she asked if I'd take Dad so she could have a break. Although I wanted to help, it came at a very bad time, so I suggested a few alternative dates and even offered to pay for Dad to go into respite care, but my sister's taken the huff and won't speak to me. Help! (*Woman*, 9 August 1999)

The ways in which caregiving has been explored are a second achievement of feminist sociology. So too is the third theme, money.

money

Jan Pahl (1990) pioneered research into the ways money was used by British households, based on interviews with 100 couples. Her original study found four different ways in which couples organised their money: a typology expanded to six styles in her later work. Subsequently Vogler and Pahl (1994) interviewed 1,200 couples in six different towns. In this project they distinguished between strategic control and the day-to-day management of money. The poorer households, where money management is an endless struggle, a chore, and a burden, more usually have everyday money management in the hands of women. Wealthier households, where money can be used for fun, more frequently have male money management. The six different ways of organising money management commonly found in Britain are: Female whole wage, male whole wage, housekeeping allowance, pooling with female management, pooling with male management, and pooling with joint management. Some 2 per cent of couples keep their money entirely separate, and this is an unexplored 'system'.

The female whole wage system was a feature of working-class families in areas of heavy industry such as mining or steel manufacture. A good husband, a respectable man, handed his unopened wage packet to his wife, who gave him back 'pocket money' and then ran the household finances. The male whole wage system keeps all the money in the man's hands. He pays all bills, and takes the wife to the shops where he pays for the goods. She has no money, unless she earns some or collects the child benefit. The housekeeping allowance system involves the man giving the woman a fixed amount of 'housekeeping' which she is to use for specified purposes. Women in such households may not know what the man earns, and the 'housekeeping' may not be related in any clear way to the costs of what it is meant to cover. The pooling systems involve all sources of incoming money being brought together (into one bank account, or one teapot), and then dispersed. There can be female, male or joint control over spending from the joint pool.

Pahl had become interested in money management after a study of domestic violence victims who had fled to a refuge. Her informants included women whose husbands earned large wage packets, but spent most of their earnings on drink, gambling or hobbies, leaving the children hungry and ill-clad. She then investigated in her study of 100 couples how non-violent households organised money. In the Vogler and Pahl (1994) study the more egalitarian systems – pooling systems – were associated with women in full-time work, and better educated men (with A levels or above) who held non-traditional views about gender. Men with fewer qualifications and traditional ideas about male and female roles were more likely to impose a housekeeping allowance system. However, the system men grew up with also effects the one they operate: that is, if a man's father used the housekeeping allowance, he is likely to do so too. The housekeeping system is closely associated with an ideology of a male breadwinner. Women who feel they lack control over money are likely to value earning some 'of their own' highly when they take paid employment, because they can spend it without feeling they need to ask permission. Vogler (1998) argued that the ways in which money is organised set the agenda for talk about family finance. For example, if the household works on a 'housekeeping allowance' system, discussion will be about the size of that allowance, not about the proportion of the man's wage that he keeps for himself. Burgoyne and Morison (1997) build on that work in a study of money management in second marriages. In these 20 couples, there was a much higher incidence of separate, independently managed money than in any studies of first marriages. Pahl (2000) has more recently explored how the use of credit cards is or is not changing patterns of money management inside households.

This area of research, opened up by a feminist sociologist, provides a platform from which the assumptions of the welfare state, of financial institutions, and of government about how money is spent can be subject to feminist scrutiny. The research done since 1980 on this topic is a definite achievement for feminist sociology, as is that on the fourth theme: violence.

the dark sides of the family

One of the major achievements of feminist sociology has been the recognition of, and research on, the dark sides of family life (Dobash and Dobash, 1992, 1998). The re-discovery of domestic violence in the 1970s, (it had been a feminist campaign topic in the 1870s) and the establishment of refuges for battered women by feminist activists, were followed by a body of research. Greater recognition of the other five ways in which families may be sites of abuse followed. The six types of abuse are shown in Table 3.3.

47

Against	Physical	Sexual
Children	1	2
Women	3	4
The Elderly	5	6

Table 3.3: *Six types of abuse in families*

Such a typology does not include mental cruelty, which frequently accompanies the other types. All six types produce stigmatised victims, who are ashamed to tell 'outsiders' of their injuries. The research on all six types has been advanced by feminist sociologists and criminologists. The growth of feminist criminology, with its successes in expanding the range of topics that deserve research attention, has been similar to the rise of feminist sociology. The exemplary research now available on crime and violence in private settings such as the family has frequently been conducted by feminists who identify primarily with criminology.

It is very hard to estimate how many families contain abusers, and the official statistics are notoriously unreliable. Young children and the elderly may be unable to report abuse; many other victims are too frightened to do so, or unaware of where to go or whom to tell. In the early 1970s, the police in the UK were very unwilling to record complaints of domestic violence, so the incidents reported to them frequently did not make it into any statistics. Domestic violence is the best researched of the six dark sides, and has led to the biggest efforts towards protecting victims and changing society. Here the community action of the feminist movement went hand in hand with feminist research on its causes and consequences. Dobash and Dobash (1992) trace the rise of the social movement against domestic violence. They describe the establishment of refuges for victims, the attempts to change the law, to alter the practices of the police, the sentencing decisions of the courts, and to find ways to treat violent men. These are particularly controversial, with strong claims that schemes do and do not work put forward by practitioners and evaluators. At the heart of the debates around domestic violence is an issue of power. Men who batter their wives are exercising control over them, because they believe they have a right to do so. Women report being beaten up because: 'his tea was too weak' (Pahl, 1985) or 'there was too much grease on his breakfast plate' (Dobash et al., 1977) because they asked for money to feed the children, because they asked where their men had been, because he was drunk, because he had lost at gambling, because they had smiled at the butcher, because they were asleep when he came home, because, because, because ... At the root of the violence is a man's belief that he has a right to control 'his' wife, 'his' children, 'his' household. Studies of male aggressors show that they rarely express guilt: rather, the victims feel guilty.

Police recognition of the existence of domestic violence has grown over the past 30 years, along with a reluctant recognition of the physical abuse of children. There is much less acceptance that there can be rape in marriage, that children are sexually abused, or that old people may suffer both physical and sexual abuse. Children are taught to fear 'strangers' not 'Uncle Fred', even though they are more in danger from family and friends than from any stranger. In the summer of 2000 the *Observer* (16 July 2000) claimed that there had been an explosion of domestic violence, but it is more likely that public tolerance, police tolerance, and victim tolerance have declined sharply, so that fewer women suffer in private silence. When the girlfriends and the wives of celebrities reveal that they have been beaten up (as a former girlfriend of the retired cricketer Boycott, and the ex-wife of soccer player Gascoigne have done), it is possible that the stigma may be starting to decline.

Research on the six dark sides of family life has been an achievement of feminist sociology, closely tied to political campaigns and community action. See Charles and Davies (1997) for a study of Welsh identity and domestic violence. Less obviously feminist at first glance is the fifth theme, that of research on food, drink and cooking.

food, drink and cooking

In the late 1970s and early 1980s three feminist sociologists, Anne Murcott in South Wales, and Nicky Charles and Marion Kerr in Yorkshire, opened up another previously private and unconsidered research area, that of food, drink, and cooking. Charles and Kerr studied families on benefit, to see how women managed to provide food when the family income was very low. Anne Murcott's background had included community studies. She was involved with Meg Stacey's second study of Banbury (Stacey et al., 1975) and medical sociology. In mid-career she conducted a study of women having a baby in the South Wales valleys to discover their ideologies or cosmologies of food (Murcott, 1983). From this came a whole sociology of food and drink, eating and drinking. Studies such as Charles and Kerr (1988) and *The Nation's Diet* initiative (Murcott, 1998) on food choices in contemporary Britain teach us about gender, identity and social change. *The Nation's Diet*, includes projects on newly established households, on African-Caribbean and white families in London, on rural Wales, on older people, and on Italians and South Asians in Glasgow. What people eat, whether it is prepared from scratch, bought ready to microwave, carried home from a takeaway or eaten in a pub or café, is an important element in their sense of self: their race, their religion, their respectability.

Valentine (1999) reports a study of 67 people from 12 households in Yorkshire. Valentine argues that food choices were one of the ways that families and households established and maintained their identities, whether religious, cultural or sub-cultural. Her informants include a Muslim couple who use food, along with sending their children to after school Islam classes at the Mosque, to maintain their cultural identity, and vegetarians self-consciously creating a new, meat-free identity for themselves. Valentine's study of food choices at home is complemented by research on eating out. The interrelations between food, drink, religion and identity are explored further in Delamont (1994). Here again, feminist sociologists opened up a new topic, which grew into a whole research area of interest beyond feminists (e.g. Purdue et al., 1997; Warde et al., 1999). The sixth theme, childbirth, has remained of more concern to women.

49

childbirth

Under this heading there are two related topics which have been opened up by feminists. These are the experience of childbirth, especially of maternity care in hospital, and the wider topics of motherhood, fatherhood, and of reproductive ideologies. Ann Oakley (1979) followed her pioneering study on housework with a parallel project on a small number of London women having their first baby. That project made 'becoming a mother' sociologically strange, and encouraged other subsequent studies of becoming a parent. A series of studies of women's passage to motherhood (such as Bailey, 1999; Oakley, 1979; Phoenix et al., 1991) has confirmed the persistence of what Joan Busfield (1974) called the dominant British reproductive ideology. There is a powerful set of beliefs that motherhood is fulfilling for women, and that married couples who do not become parents are 'selfish'. Bailey (1999) interviewed 30 women in Bristol about to have their first baby. They were all white and their average age was 32. These women all reported a raising of their status because of their pregnancy: they saw themselves as being 'responsible', brought up to the level of other adults, and saw themselves 'slotted in to what a woman can do' (ibid.: 341). Feminist sociologists have analysed the considerable stigma still attached to the involuntarily childless or to being child-free, even though one in five women born in 1961 will remain childless or child-free (ONS, 1998).

Sally Macintyre (1977), in an equally pioneering study to Oakley's, showed how the reproductive ideology impacted on single, pregnant women. The medical profession assumed that all illegitimate pregnancies were undesirable and all legitimate ones desired. Macintyre's rich ethnographic showed that, from the mother's viewpoint, this was not necessarily true at all. She found single women who had planned to be pregnant, and married ones desperate not to be. Here feminist sociology has accompanied a major shift in British society: the decline in the 'shame' attached to illegitimacy, both for the mother and the child. One-third of live births in 1997 were 'illegitimate', but four-fifths of these were registered by both parents, and three-quarters of them by cohabiting parents (*Social Trends*, 29: *Social Trends*, 50). For individual women illegitimacy may still be stigmatising, but in general it is an acceptable 'choice' for a woman over 20, and only frowned on in a young teenager, a 'girl' of 12 to 16. For the married woman, and those over 18 in 'secure' cohabitations, becoming a mother is a source of securing an adult identity. Removing the stigma of childlessness, and taking on the identity of mother, does, however, bring women up against the health service and for many, into a series of hardships (Graham, 1993). In 30 years of feminist sociology, the research on reproductive ideologies, on pregnancy, on abortion, on childbirth, and on the relationships between motherhood and poverty has been a major achievement. The studies of fatherhood and of grandparents grew out of this pioneering feminist sociology.

The studies of childbirth and reproduction go back to the early years of feminist sociology. The seventh theme is newer, dating from the 1980s.

'emotional' work

Feminist sociologists led the development of research on the intimacies and emotional temperature of relationships, and the idea that there is 'emotional' *work*. Mansfield and Collard (1988) reporting a study of 60 newly wed couples found the women were disappointed that marriage had not produced emotional reciprocity, a close exchange of intimacy, a common life of empathy (ibid.: 178–9). The men refused to talk about love and intimacy at all, or reduced the whole agenda to sex. Lewis and O'Brien (1987) found a parallel lack of emotional intimacy with children. Duncombe and Marsden (1995) conducted interviews with 80 heterosexual couples, and their data are our main sociological source on this aspect of married life. They report that women told the interviewer they wanted their partner to signal intimacy, by 'unprompted' intimate or romantic gestures and actions, because these would make them feel emotionally 'special'. The men in the study 'appeared' neither to understand nor accept their wife's desires. They either reduced the issue to sex, or felt that they were working so hard to provide economically for their families that they had nothing left to give. Women wanted the emotional intimacy and romantic specialness before sexual intercourse, men wanted the sexual intercourse to serve as the intimacy and romance. Duncombe and Marsden entitled their 1995 paper 'Workaholics and whingeing women' to emphasise this gulf between the sexes.

Related to the research on intimacy is the investigation of such issues as gift giving (Cheal, 1987), sharing of clothes and the maintenance of social and familial ties by remembering birthdays, anniversaries and so on (Finch and Mason, 1990). Jacqueline Scott (1997) addresses a similar range of topics using data from the British Household Panel Study on 5,000 households. The popularity of Beck and Beck-Gernsheim (1995) and the turn towards intimacy as a sociological topic by Giddens (1992) can be seen as developments from a research agenda opened up by, originally, feminists in sociology.

51

leisure and time

Feminist sociologists opened up research on control over time. Rosemary Deem's (1986) pioneering research into the leisure activities of married women in Milton Keynes showed that men expected and took time for their leisure, whereas women only had time for their leisure if their male partner supported the activity. The dynamics of the households were such that men owned their time, and controlled the time of their partners. The importance of including time in any feminist analysis of the private sphere was emphasised by Barbara Adam (1996).

Across these nine areas of domestic life, then, feminist sociologists have opened up new research topics, and pioneered new ways of studying 'the private'. This was not the result of neglecting all the traditional areas of sociological enquiry. It is possible to demonstrate the achievements of feminist sociology in other fields, such as education, health and illness, (and these are covered in Chapter 7) or work and employment. In education, for example, Amanda Coffey and I (Coffey and Delamont, 2000) have written a whole book on feminist sociological research of relevance to teachers. AltaMira Press has a whole series of books, each showcasing feminist work in an empirical area (The Gender Lens series, with eight titles already published). There is not room to explore them all here.

RE-FOCUSING ON CLASSICAL TOPICS

I have chosen one example to illustrate this heading: the interrelated topics of women's social mobility and the proper way to construct class systems in modern Britain. Other examples, could, no doubt, be chosen, but the sociology of class, stratification and social mobility is a particularly central one in the UK. The feminist sociologists (women and men) in Britain, particularly inspired by Joan Acker's (1973) critique of American research on social stratification, developed arguments against the traditional ways in which the topic had been researched (see Chapter 4) and theorised. They then moved on, in the past 20 years, to develop new coding frames, and new ways to discuss stratification (Delamont, 1989c; Brown, 1986).

After Acker's landmark paper, three issues, related but not necessarily all researched at once, were made problematic by feminists. First, was it sensible to treat the household as the unit of analysis, with its class location treated as that of the male head? Second, were the very categories of occupation, which were used to group occupations together into classes, inherently sexist? Third, what empirical and theoretical insights would result if women were treated as having their own occupationally based class identity and therefore their own social mobility? These feminist interests were an addition to a series of debates about social class itself, and the role of class analysis in sociology (Savage, 2000) which have raged in the UK between 1970 and the present. This volume is not the place to open up the wider questions, discussed elsewhere in the series (Holmwood, forthcoming). Nor would it be appropriate to rehearse the full debates about the three questions here. The furore around the first question, and the opening up of new vistas following the second and third are briefly summarised here, and also briefly discussed in Chapter 7 from a different angle.

The debates surrounding whether the household should be the unit of class analysis came to prominence in British sociology after the publication of the results of the Oxford, Nuffield, mobility study in 1980. The project had gathered data in 1972 from an all-male sample in England and Wales, but by the time it was published (Goldthorpe, 1980; Halsey et al., 1980) that sampling strategy was under attack from commentators, male and female, feminists and non-feminists. An all-male sampling strategy that had been taken for granted in 1972 seemed worthy of comment, and even old-fashioned in 1980. During the 1980s a debate took place between Goldthorpe, who aggressively defended the traditional position, and a loose coalition of sociologists who wanted to explore alternatives. (Britten and Heath, 1983; Goldthorpe, 1983, 1984; Heath and Britten, 1983; Stanworth, 1983). Goldthorpe was confident that the male was head of the household, and that his occupation determined its class location, even if women worked for longer and took their careers more seriously than their mothers had done. He was uninterested in any differences between, for example, a household where the man was a doctor and the woman a secretary compared to a household where both adults were doctors, or one where the man was a routine clerical worker and the woman a doctor. Commentators who wanted to argue that these three might differ in sociologically interesting ways were, he argued, simply mistaken.

In the aftermath of that controversy Crompton and Mann (1986) edited a collection of thoughtful and judicious pieces which explored neo-Marxist and neo-Weberian aspects of gender and stratification. The importance of the debates to the discipline as a whole was apparent from the space allocated to it in Morgan and Stanley (1993) in which Helen Roberts (1993) rehearsed 'The women and class debate'.

The second question was, in many ways, more important, but received less attention. As Coxon and Jones (1978, 1979a, 1979b) and Coxon et al. (1986) had shown from a substantial empirical research project, there were deep-seated problems buried in the classification systems of occupations used to allocate places in the class

53

hierarchy. One of these problems is that the occupational titles used to elicit prestige ratings are themselves suffused with gender stereotypes: a 'nurse' is taken to be a woman, an 'engineer' or 'miner', a man. The resulting list of occupations is itself sexist, and reproduces a range of sexual inequalities and stratifications. So gas fitter is a skilled manual trade (Class 3 M) while hairdresser is Class 4, reproducing the sexual inequalities of pay between men and women prevalent in twentieth-century Britain. If women were to have their own social class, based on their own occupation, rather than that of their father and then their husband, it was unclear whether *their* occupational ranks, and therefore class positions, were usefully captured by the classification schemes used by government or sociologists for men (Roberts, 1986; Thomas, 1986).

Finally, there was a new body of research that tried to study the social mobility of women, either using existing data sets, because there were no lavishly funded surveys of large samples as there had been on men, or collecting new data. Heath (1981) pioneered the former approach, Marshall et al. (1988) the second for England. Work on Scotland, and in both parts of Ireland, was conducted with a view of gender very different from Goldthorpe's. The collection edited by Payne and Abbott (1990) represents the achievements of that work, following Abbott and Sapsford (1987). To any open-minded sociologist, the results of studying women's mobility patterns are interesting, not only for what they show about the life chances of women and how these are affected by education, marriage and motherhood, but also for what they reveal about the whole occupational system of the nation.

Feminist sociology has certainly changed the parameters of the debates about class, stratification and social mobility. The achievement can be gauged by comparing, among the introductory texts for undergraduates, Worsley's (1970) treatment of stratification and social class with that of Worsley (1977) and then with Savage (2000). In the more advanced literature, aimed at professional sociologists, the feminist achievement can be seen in Appendix G of Marshall et al. (1997) on 'The class and gender debate'. Here they devote six pages to a thorough discussion of the debates. In their main text they treat gender seriously, and they cite the feminist arguments. It is, of course, ironic that feminist sociology changed the shape of the sociological literature on class just as there was a switch in emphasis in the discipline from work to play, from occupation to consumption, from modernity to postmodernity. That, however, is a debate for another book.

54

THE CREATION OF NEW INTELLECTUAL SPACES

sexualities

Sexualities are the final example of a research area initially opened up by feminist sociologists as an appropriate sphere for sociological enquiry. The paper by Jackson and Scott (1997) for example, would have been inconceivable in 1957 or 1967, but it contained over 20 citations to sociological research and theorising done after 1980. The HIV/AIDS panic produced another impetus propelling sexuality into the sociological mainstream, of course, but the importance of feminist sociologists in (re)claiming the topic from psychology, psychoanalysis and anthropology is incontrovertible.

NEW DEFINITIONS OF 'KNOWLEDGE'

The biggest achievement of feminist sociology has been the changes in the very definition of feminist sociological knowledge. The depth of work in, for example, Ahmed et al. (2000) and Andermahr et al. (2000), would have been beyond the wildest dreams of women in sociology in 1968.

55

The final achievement of feminist sociology to be addressed in this chapter is of a quite different kind. Rather than a positive indicator, it is a negative one. The polemical backlash against feminist sociology is, in itself, an achievement which must be explored. Counter-arguments are, by their very existence, a mark of the importance of feminist ideas in the discipline (Clark et al., 1996). During the 1990s several male sociologists accused feminism, and feminist sociology of going too far: particularly by destroying fatherhood, male authority in the family and the concept of the 'breadwinner'.

THE BACKLASH/THE DISCOURSE OF DERISION

There are commentators, mostly but not entirely men, who attribute to feminism as a social and ideological movement, and therefore partly to feminist sociologists, an enormous *negative* influence. *Contemporary Sociology*, the ASA's journal of book reviews and review essays, carried five essays on the state of the discipline in the May 1999 issue, with the specific focus of 'values, science, social movements, and sociology' (Risman and Tomaskovic-Devey, 1999: viii). The first such essay, by Jonathan Imber (1999) who teaches at Wellesley, a college founded by feminists in the nineteenth century, attacks feminist sociologists for attention seeking, bringing sociology into disrepute with other social scientists, stifling serious debate, being left-wing, providing political therapy rather than education, and being ungrateful successors to the founders and great sociologists of the past. Imber objects to the ASA tendency to 'fiddle endlessly with race and gender balance' (ibid.: 258), and complains about the ASA's commitment to 'promoting as scientific data its political conviction about the necessity of affirmative action' (ibid.: 258). This backlash diatribe was typical in several ways. First, it cited no women, and no feminist work except for one polemical group statement (Feminist Scholars in Sociology, 1995). Joyce Ladner, an African-American woman, appears in the text, but not in the references, so does not get a citation 'count' from Imber. Second, it fails to recognise and distinguish any schools of feminism: positivist liberal feminists hate what Imber hates as much as he does, yet he fails to cite and use his intellectual allies. Third, absolutely no evidence is provided to substantiate any of his claims.

In Britain, more of the hostility has been directed at feminist sociology's pernicious effects on the family than on the 'pollution' of the discipline. One such author is Dench, and I have presented his ideas as an example of a backlash argument, or a discourse of derision. The issue of marriage is central to Dench's (1994 and 1996) work on men in contemporary Britain. In a pair of polemical books, Dench argues that feminism has gone too far, and men have become detached from society and their financial responsibilities for children. In the working class men are too often turning at worst to crime and at best to welfare dependency idleness. His argument is essentially the same as that perpetrated by the conservative feminist Catherine Beecher in the mid-nineteenth century, who argued that America's economic, political and social stability depended on women sacrificing themselves for the greater good. Beecher claimed that women should run happy, healthy, religious homes and sacrifice any other ambitions, feelings or desires so that America could be a stable democracy (Sklar, 1973). In 1951 the American functionalist Talcott Parsons produced essentially the same argument (although he did not acknowledge Beecher). Dench is therefore writing in a long, if sexist, tradition within sociology.

Dench argues that there are two different types of family culture in contemporary Britain, one he calls 'traditional' or 'conventional', the other 'alternative'. The latter is similar to what Young and Willmott (1975) called the symmetrical family and to what the Rapaports (1976) termed a dual career family. Dench uses 'alternative' as a negative term. The traditional or conventional family is, for Dench, one where the man is the main breadwinner, and the woman the main homemaker, and where all members of the family should provide reciprocal support. This type of family is seen by Dench as central to a stable society. It is essentially similar to what Bernstein (1975) terms a positional family. The 'alternative' family in Dench's model is similar to Bernstein's concept of the personal family. Here each person negotiates roles, duties and workload in ways that suit them as individuals and are best for their family. They are not bound by stereotypes of sex roles, age, or position in the family. The best cook cooks, the best driver drives, the person most attached to his or her job works the longest hours and does least at home and so on. Two-thirds of Dench's interviewees (221 people in London) believed in the superiority of the positional family, one-third believed the personal was morally better. A few people lived in a 'traditional' family but believed in a 'personal' one. Dench describes them as confused.

Dench states that older people, those who were or had been married, and parents, were more enthusiastic about the positional family, while the young, the child-free and women in full-time work were keener on the 'personal'. Dench draws from this a doom-laden and conservative message: he claims that the chattering classes are destroying the traditional family even though most ordinary people can see it is essential for social stability. He also argues that the 'personal' family allows men to escape from their moral and financial duties, to the long-term detriment both of the man, and society as a whole. This view of men, as selfish, wicked skivers who will abandon their children unless shackled to them, and of women, who must behave like the wives in 1950s' sitcoms if Britain is to avoid a crime wave, is deeply depressing. It is grounded in a naïve 'biology', which assumes that men are unable to behave in co-operative or egalitarian ways. Dench's conviction that only a traditional, positional family is desirable for both sexes, children and society is over-simplistic. His attack on feminism, and feminist sociologists, for advocating the personal family, undermining the positional family, and flying in the face of biology is typical of the backlash against feminist sociology.

There are two issues here. First, there is no evidence at all that any of the social changes or attitudinal changes are the result of feminist sociology. The causes are much more likely to derive from the labour market and the globalised economy. However, if the changes were due, in any way, to the ideas and the dissemination of research done by feminist sociologists, these ideas and findings have been influential because they revealed the harsh realities of patriarchal positional family life. If the price of keeping working-class men shackled to their families (for these male sociologists rarely suggest that male intellectuals should or could be kept tied to *their* families) is the unequal division of labour, the male control of money and time, and, in the worst cases, the pretence that there is no violence or sexual abuse, rather than attempting to evolve a more egalitarian, personal family style, then feminist sociology could claim the undermining of the positional family as its proudest achievement. It seems extremely unlikely that feminist sociology has actually had any impact at all on the everyday private lives of the working classes. There are issues of class, of labour market experience, and of sex differences which need to be explored. Additionally, we need to separate the emotional aspects of family life from the practical and material, and face up to the dark side of the family too. A man who routinely rapes his wife and beats his children with a belt may be very happy with his family life: the victims of his aggression may not be as content.

Dench is not alone. Norman Dennis, once a Marxist sociologist, who was one of the authors of the most famous study of coal miners (Dennis et al., 1956) has been equally horrified by what he claims are the destructive effects of feminism. (Dennis, 1997; Dennis and Erdos, 1993, 2000). He has written attacks on the negative impact of feminist ideas in general and feminist sociology in particular parallel to Dench's. It is interesting that the author of a study criticised by Frankenberg (1976) for exploring the capitalist exploitation of men's labour in the mines while ignoring the domestic exploitation of women is so horrified by contemporary Britain, by modern women, *and* that he sees feminism as complicit in what appals him.

58

There is a far more powerful explanatory frame for explaining changes in the British family; the theories of Basil Bernstein. Bernstein (1975) argued that the upper class and most of the working class lived in 'positional' families (where roles are fixed by age and sex) because this reflected and prepared children for the labour markets they experienced. In the middle classes, Bernstein argued, a split had occurred between the old middle class, who worked with property, money and material goods, and the new middle class who handled symbolic property (psychiatrists, advertising and PR, the arts, etc.). The old middle class kept to the positional, traditional family: the new middle class had evolved the personal family (see Delamont, 1989b, 1995 for more details on this). Men with different labour market experiences in different sectors of the middle class, will value different types of family. Bernstein's argument, that some sectors of the middle class, whose business is the manipulation of symbolic property, live in different types of family from the 'old' middle class is more plausible than Dench's condemnation of the personal family as a feminist mistake, or a mirage espoused by the young, the naïve and 'career' women. To summarise, it makes sense to see different family types grounded in the class and labour market experiences of the adults, who will try to rear children to 'fit' the outside world as they have experienced it. As the world of work diversifies, so too does the family. Dench and Dennis believe that only one type of family 'works' for British society: more sensitive commentators know that different types of family can 'work' and the Dench or Dennis 'traditional' family can be a hell of violence, inequality and misery.

CONCLUSION

There have been achievements for feminist sociology. However, its influence and importance are nowhere near as great as its detractors claim, and are certainly contained inside the discipline, often at the subject's margins rather than its citadels of power.

four

organising the necessary work

the question(s) of method(s)

T he title of this chapter comes from a passage in which Kate Fansler describes how in academic life one is either 'happily unorganised', or 'One kept up with it, organising the necessary work in a provocative way, one wanted to get it done' (Cross, 1981: 119). Kate Fansler was referring to the routine tasks of writing references, doing the minutes of meetings, and refusing requests to do six impossible things before Easter. I have appropriated it to refer to social science research methods, the focus of this chapter. Specifically this chapter deals with the debates around 'feminist methods' in sociology. Before embarking on the debates, feminist methods need defining. The best of the many definitions of feminist methods is that provided by Virginia Olesen (2000: 215) 'incisive scholarship to frame, direct, and harness passion in the interests of redressing grievous problems'.

The debates surrounding feminist methods encompass the biggest impact that feminism has made in sociology. Far greater than any impact feminism has made on theory, or in any empirical areas, the controversies aroused by 'feminist methods' have been angry, far-reaching and long-lasting. None of the attempts by feminists to reinstate founding mothers, or enthrone contemporary women thinkers have captured the attention of the discipline the way the methodological debates have. James Davis (1994: 188), for example, includes 'feminist methodology' in a list of infections, 'foreign objects', 'bunk', which have damaged sociology because it has 'a weak immune system'. The list reveals Davis to be a very conservative positivist, because he also stigmatises 'grounded theory', 'ethnomethodology', 'postmodernism', 'critical theory', 'humanistic sociology' and 'ethnic studies'. However, it is still startling to find feminist methodology described like botulism.

The chapter deals with the methods issue in seven sections.

1 The early days (critiques of gaps and instruments), 1968–80
2 Two early sciolisms

3 Sandra Harding's trivium
4 Liz Stanley
5 Male hysteria
6 Queer theory and methods
7 Postmodernism

Issues of research methods, and of methodology have been central to feminist sociology for 30 years. There are debates among feminists, and between feminists and their critics/opponents about what topics to study, what methods to use to collect data, how to analyse those data and how to write them up. These are all categorised as methods questions in this chapter. Over-arching these debates are serious methodological and epistemological disputes about the very nature of research. Since the 1970s there has been a philosophical debate about the nature of 'scientific' enquiry in Western capitalist societies (see Harding, 1986) and whether its whole basis was actually contaminated by *unexamined* assumptions about masculinity versus femininity, male versus female, objectivity versus subjectivity, mind versus body and reason versus emotions. These debates are acutely relevant to studies of gender, because there is no neutral ground from which a scholar can investigate males and females (see Haste, 1994). Such concerns led to developing feminist research methods (Maynard and Purvis, 1994). Maynard (1994) presents the interrelated arguments over qualitative *versus* quantitative methods and whether feminist research must use the former to be true to the experiences of women. All sociologists need to be familiar with debates on feminist methods and epistemologies. Twenty-five years ago there was a strong claim being made for non-sexist research methods (Eichler, 1988), which has now largely dissipated, because there is much less sexism in the ordinary, non-feminist project than there was in 1980.

61

EARLY DAYS

In the early days of feminist sociology (1968 to 1980) the main focus of writing on methods was intensely *practical*. Women pointed out that researchers had posed their research questions in a sexist way; that empirical studies had sampled from the population in a sexist way; that they had used research instruments that were grounded in sexist ideologies and therefore reproduced sexist findings; or that they had analysed and written up their findings in sexist ways. There were also accusations that funding agencies were at least reluctant, if not downright unwilling to sponsor research on women, or even on mixed samples, rather than on men. This needs to be illustrated, because it is quite hard in 2002 to reconstruct how sexist much research was, in all these five ways, as recently as 1968–80. In this section, therefore, there are two examples of each type of criticism from this era: many more can be found in my book from that period (Delamont, 1980, and in Chapters 7, 8 and 9 of Delamont, 1989b).

Underlying many of the criticisms is the issue of language. English uses 'man' to mean both the male animal *and* the whole species. It is, therefore always ambiguous in ways that 'woman' is not. Sometimes the two meanings of 'man' can be distinguished by the context. So for example, a sentence such as 'man is a social animal' probably means the whole species, while 'when man plays football' probably means the male. However, such extrapolations are problematic, because many sentences of the first type do actually only mean males, and some apparently male-specific sentences are actually intended to be generic. This ambiguity in the English language has been a problem for feminists for over 300 years: when Paine wrote *The Rights of Man* did he mean humans or men? Contemporary feminists in the Anglophone world have, in both public and academic spheres, struggled to disentangle and clarify the meanings. In public life they have argued to replace Chairman with Chairperson or fireman with firefighter, because too often Chairman and fireman means a male, either to those running the committee or the fire service, or to the general public, or, especially, to children.

In the academic sphere, feminists (for example, Thorne et al., 1983 who cite 44 articles on this point) have done research to show that children, and students, do not see or hear the generic 'man' to mean the human species. Reading a text on 'caveman', or Palaeolithic Man or Medieval Man or Nineteenth-Century Man, children and students think it means *males*. A geography module called 'Man and Transport' is taken to mean men and transport, one on 'Urban Man' is taken to mean that males live in cities. Harrison (1975) even found that adolescents who had studied 'The evolution of man' had learnt that women had not evolved. Social scientists are not immune from this either: and many of the criticisms of how research questions were posed actually turn on language.

In the feminist critiques of research questions, sampling, date collection instruments, selective reporting of findings, analysis and writing up, three interrelated issues were raised.

1 Did the researchers claim universality when actually only studying males?
2 Did they study only males without justifying the omission of women?
3 Did they build sexist assumptions into their research processes?

To be fireproof, a piece of research has to state clearly whether its focus was men, women or both; either sample both sexes or explain why only males were chosen; and the study has to be designed to avoid embedding stereotypical assumptions. Then the analysis, the writing up and the publication of the research have to avoid making sexist assumptions and reporting conclusions in a sexist manner. The third of these criteria is, of course, the hardest to meet.

sexist research questions

The choice of research question sets the agenda for any research project. In the past, many sociologists set themselves research questions which, when scrutinised by feminists, turned out to have been embedded in sexist assumptions and/or actually focused on only the male sex while purporting to be universal. If we take the research question from a well-known, respected, and much cited project conducted in the 1970s, this general point becomes clear. The authors pose their research question as follows: 'Does the labour market objectively allow to the worker a significant measure of choice over his economic life? Does he subjectively perceive this as choice?' Given the pattern of using male pronouns to cover both sexes, this *could* be a research question about workers of both sexes. However, it was not. The research question comes from Blackburn and Mann (1979: 2) characterising their study of 1,000 workers (actually 1,000 men), in Peterborough. The project is a study of semi-skilled men in a local labour market with a choice of jobs. It is an interesting read. However, it is *not* about workers. It is about male workers. Feminist sociologists needed to point out that failing to specify gender in the research question *reduces* clarity; specifying gender sharpens the research question.

63

The same point can be made about research on education and social mobility. Sandra Acker (1981), for example, highlighted how much of the empirical research in the sociology of education in Britain had been done on all-male samples. For example Hope asks 'What did it feel like to be a *child* in the Scottish system in 1947?' (1984: 19), Hopper (1981: 13) asked what are 'the personal and interpersonal consequences of social mobility?'. Both men actually only studied males. Hope researched what is was like to be a *boy* in the Scottish system, and Hopper what the consequences of social mobility in England were for *men*. There is a relationship between the research question and the choice of a research setting or the way the sampling is done. Some of the most criticised sampling was done on social mobility issues.

sexist sampling procedures

The 1972 Oxford Mobility Study (Goldthorpe, 1980; Halsey et al., 1980) sampled only men in England and Wales. The Oxford Mobility Study was based on data collected in 1972, when it was entirely normal to draw an all-male sample for a study of social mobility. By the time it was published in 1980 the climate had changed, and many reviewers queried or criticised the all-male sample. The Oxford team in 1972 were operating in the same way as other British researchers on social mobility such as Richardson (1977), Coxon and Jones (1978, 1979a, 1979b) Stewart et al. (1980), Hopper (1981), Payne (1987a, 1987b). Payne was the only author to deal with women and mobility, as a topic, compensating for an all-male sample drawn by the sociologist who had originally designed the study. Feminists (including Roberts, 1986 and Delamont, 1989a) criticised the all-male sampling, and the way in which it was often not defended and sometimes not even mentioned. Hope (1984) for example, re-analysed data from the 1947 Scottish Mental Health Survey. The original survey was of 1,208 11 year olds, of whom 590 were boys. Hope focused only on the boys in his re-analyses, but never explained or justified his decision. Similarly, Hopper (1981) never explains or justifies drawing an all-male sample to test his hypothesis about the subjective effects of social mobility.

Helen Roberts (1986: 56) criticised Coxon and Jones for choosing an all-male sample. In fact, they had applied to the SSRC for a grant to study the occupational cognitions of both men *and women*, but the SSRC rejected the idea. The sum awarded was half the amount applied for, and Coxon and Jones were instructed only to study men. It is a comment on the time that they did not 'go public' and invoke the support of other sociologists to challenge this decision by the funding body – instead they did the research on men only. Most feminists did not object to all-male samples when explicitly justified by the investigators, because that allowed a debate. It was the all-male sampling left unexplained, unjustified, and undefended by the investigators that aroused criticisms.

Alongside the feminist criticisms of the sampling in quantitative, especially statistical survey research, were parallel objections to the choices of field sites in qualitative studies. Lyn Lofland's (1975) critique of urban sociology, a classic of its kind, has been described in Chapter 3. McRobbie and Garber (1975) produced a critique of the British research on adolescence which made similar points about the sites and sampling in the obscure and famous qualitative studies of teenagers. Ward and Grant summarise feminist position on single sex samples as follows:

In a few cases single-gender subjects were appropriate (e.g. analyses of women's adaptation to motherhood or men's responses to impotence) or understandable (e.g. studies of professional football players or nursery school teachers). Occasionally single-gender subjects were logically related to the researcher's institutional base: the staff of a man's prison or the faculty of a woman's college. Some authors also analyzed archival or longitudinal data collected on males only. (1985: 148)

In other words, no feminist objects to an all-male sample if the researcher has thought carefully about why it is sensible for the particular project. By 1985, therefore, single-sex samples were only acceptable in these types of research projects: otherwise, the use of a single-sex sample had to be defended if the investigators were not to be severely criticised. Alongside the criticisms of the sampling strategies were the objections to the sexist nature of the research instruments.

research instruments

I have illustrated this point from a detailed critique of a study conducted by Irene Jones. Murdock and Phelps (1973) surveyed adolescents (322 girls, 299 boys) about their lifestyles. They had designed separate questionnaires for boys and for girls, with some identical items and some which were different. When their original research instruments were scrutinised by Irene Jones (1974) it was clear that preconceptions, of a stereotyped sort, had shaped the data collection instruments. Murdock and Phelps gave Jones unrestricted access to all their unpublished data, so she could scrutinise all their instruments, analyses, and reasoning. One set of questions offered a variety of adolescent roles that the respondents could choose to identify with. Both sexes were offered 'good pupil', 'rebel', 'ritualist', 'good bloke/good friend', and 'pop fan'. Boys were also offered 'street peer', 'sports fan', 'boyfriend', and 'natural leader'. These were not offered to girls. Instead girls were offered 'homemaker', 'tomboy', 'girl friend' and 'fashion follower'. Girls could not choose to say they were leaders, or hung out on the streets, or were sports fans. Boys could not choose to be home-centred (DIY or car mechanics with Dad, building model planes, gardening, cooking, ham radio...), or to be fashion followers, or to be 'sissies'. The research instrument *itself* polarised the two sexes in stereotyped ways. The two questionnaires ensured that the results of the research revealed a gulf between the leisure patterns of teenage girls and boys, with boys out on the streets following sport and girls at home trying on each other's clothes. By restricting the choices, the opportunity to find out how many female leaders and sports fans, or male home-bodies and fashion followers, was lost. It is likely that the vast majority of the adolescents would have claimed affinity with the stereotypes Murdock and Phelps expected, but because they built them in to their instruments, it will

65

never be possible to explore how many 'home boys' and 'street girls' there were.

Inside the detailed wording of the items there was further sexism. The male sports fan is good at sport, watches TV sport and goes to matches. His clothes and cleanliness are not mentioned. The tomboy likes swimming and gym but 'does not like dressing up and would rather wear her old jeans all the time'. These are not equivalent. There is no equivalence between liking sport being closely associated with being unfashionable for girls, and a passion for sport being unmarked for fashion and sexual attractiveness *for boys*. It was equally stereotypical that the questionnaire nowhere provided for a boy to mention a passion for clothes or fashion. Irene Jones showed that the preconceptions about adolescent sex roles held by Murdock and Phelps had produced a stereotyped pair of questionnaires which were bound to produce a polarised set of results. Of course, it is possible that there were no young men who were fashion followers, or homeboys or sissies; and no young women who were in street gangs, or loved sport *and* fashion. However, because the full range of choices was not offered to both sexes, we will never know.

Exactly similar criticisms can be levelled at the research on social mobility. Hopper's (1981) study of the 'personal and interpersonal consequences of social mobility' (ibid.: 13) is permeated with similar unexamined sexist (and heterosexist) assumptions. Hopper wanted to see how men compared themselves to their reference groups, and has a series of questions about other males in his informants' lives. He took it for granted that no one was gay, and that the reference groups were all male. Thus, Hopper asked his informants, men in their 30s in 1965–6, about their 'friends' (explicitly men), who had 'wives' (ibid.: 125). In the retrospective questions about school, the men were asked about their 'group of friends' (males) and the 'girls' who they had 'gone out with' (ibid.: 255). When Hopper asked about relatives he focused on 'their brothers and brothers-in-law' (ibid.: 118).

The central point here was that if a researcher asks women about housework, or the quality of nursery provision, while questioning men about DIY and the quality of the railway network, it is not a legitimate *finding* that women hold views about nurseries and men about railways. Only if both sexes are asked about both topics, and answer differently, can the researcher legitimately report a sex difference. Many researchers in the 1950s, 1960s and 1970s would ask women if their husbands influenced how they voted, *not* ask men if their wives influenced them, and then report that women deferred to their husbands in political matters.

Most of the feminist criticism of the research methods current in sociology before 1980 focused on the research question, the sampling

66

and the instruments. There were fewer published critiques of the sexist nature of analytic processes and the ways in which writing up and publication were accomplished. This is partly because these stages were, in the 1945–80 period, usually regarded as non-problematic, and private. Very little self-conscious reflection on these topics was published by anyone, leaving less space for feminist critiques. The growth of confessional and reflexive accounts of all stages of the research process has made these topics more visible to feminist critiques.

analysis

Feminist critiques of sexism at the data analysis stages of published research are scarce. It seems unlikely that feminists were confident that analysis was done in a rigorously objective or gender-neutral way. It is more likely that feminists concentrated their criticisms on the decisions and processes which were publicly available for scrutiny. Readers cannot know how researchers analysed their findings. The research question, the sample, and the actual instruments were usually in the public domain, but processes of analysis were private, for both quantitative and qualitative research. Since the 1980s there has been a vogue for the publication of 'confessional' accounts, and a fashion to be more transparent about analysis. Today the analytic procedures used in both qualitative and quantitative research are debated, and it is possible to discover from confessional writing, and from debates about analysis, how findings were produced. However, even this increased explicitness has not produced a flurry of feminist critiques of sexism in the data analysis stages. The boom in confessional and autobiographical writing has probably been more prevalent among qualitative researchers. There is scope for feminist analyses of the confessional texts on the analysis stage, such as the papers in Bryman and Burgess (1994).

67

In practice, however, feminists have focused on the two more publicly available stages that follow analysis, what is written up and what is published. Several of the examples of criticism here draw on re-analyses/re-examinations of data sets. My main example is Irene Jones's extended critique of the Murdock and Phelps (1973) study again.

writing up and publishing findings

There are four intertwined issues here: (1) where a research team had gathered data on both sexes; (2) did they publish all these data?; (3) how authors set about describing male and female subjects in their texts; and (4) which results they highlighted in their publications, and which of their respondents they *believed* and therefore reported as 'credible' to their readers. Feminist sociologists discovered that researchers had left data on women unpublished (actually in many cases unanalysed) while reporting on males only. One famous example is the social mobility study done in Britain in 1949 by David Glass. He gathered data on men and women, but only analysed and reported on the data on men in his publication (Glass, 1954). The data, on men and women, were all destroyed, preventing further analysis. Feminists found that males and females were described very differently in their reports. One example here is Lortie's (1968) study of American school teachers. He gathered data on men and women, but described the women in stereotyped terms, blaming them for not only their lowly grades in the occupation, but also for the low status of the occupation in American society. It transpired that results pertaining to males were highlighted in publications while those on females were glossed over or downplayed. Nash (1977), for example, followed a co-educational class from primary to secondary school, but chose to write a journal article on the boys and not one on the girls.

There was another form of sexism prevalent. Re-analyses of original studies revealed that authors had *believed* male respondents' accounts of social phenomena and *disbelieved* female respondents – reporting them as 'misguided', or 'deluded'. Here Irene Jones's scrutiny of the Murdock and Phelps data revealed a blatant example. Simply put, when the adolescent boys and girls studied by Murdock and Phelps told them different things, the researchers reported the boys' version as the facts. The girls' views were dismissed as 'claims', offered to the reader as delusions. The boys overwhelmingly told Murdock and Phelps that they spent their leisure time in all-male friendship groups. Half the girls said they spent their time in mixed groups. Murdock and Phelps believed the boys' accounts and called the girls 'hangers on' who make 'claims' to belong to what are actually all-male groups. This was, as Jones pointed out, simply bad social science. Murdock and Phelps had actually discovered something interesting, and then ignored it. A finding that adolescent boys and girls see the same phenomenon differently is interesting. A stereotyped report that boys' gangs are hindered by girls hanging around is not interesting. Lesley Smith (1978) subsequently replicated, in a small qualitative study, what Murdock and Phelps had found and missed.

One response to all these types of critique was to call for a 'cleansing' of methods: to replace sexist methods with non-sexist ones. Eichler (1988) published an influential book on this topic. The other response was to develop feminist methods, and these are the subject of the rest of the chapter.

However feminist methods are defined, and as the rest of the chapter shows, they are a contested territory, there are some commonly held beliefs about what empirical work done since 1970 should look like. If it is large-scale, quantitative work, the investigator should do the following:

- either pose a non-sexist research question *or* one in which a potential sex difference is the question;
- should sample both sexes *or* explain and justify sampling only one;
- should design research instruments to test for sex differences rather than assume them in the design;
- analyse the data objectively;
- write them up so both sexes are portrayed as rational actors in their settings, and publish the data in a gender-neutral manner so stereotypes are not reinforced.

This, in short, means obeying the rules of positivist research, being objective, and not imposing one's own values.

In qualitative, especially interpretivist research, avoiding sexism involves employing a tough-minded reflexivity. A minimalist manifesto for non-sexist research would include the following: Good researchers need to do several things. First, collect and report data on gender in the field setting; second, pay equal attention to all the informants in the setting, whether they are male or female (see L.S. Smith, 1978); third, collect data on how the actors in a field setting understand and view gender; fourth, gather data on how those beliefs are enacted (e.g. in speech, or in non-verbal behaviour); fifth, examine the relation between gender and power in the field setting; and all the time the researcher needs to make his or her *own* beliefs about gender problematic (Delamont and Atkinson, 1995: Chapter 9).

In the light of all these criticisms of the existing published research in sociology, it is not surprising that in the early 1980s feminists began to develop specific feminist methods.

69

FEMINIST METHODS EVOLVE

In the rest of the chapter, feminist methods are described in five sections: on two early sciolisms, on Sandra Harding's trivium, on Liz Stanley's contribution, and on male hysteria. There were two sciolisms in the early days.

two early sciolisms

A sciolism is a superficial pretension to knowledge, a sciolist is someone who produces such pretensions. In the 1980s when articles and books on feminist methods began to appear (e.g. Bowles and Duelli Klein, 1983; Clegg, 1985; Roberts, 1981) two sciolisms were frequently offered. One recited a political slogan as if it were a guide to methods, the other reduced all research to a simplistic binary opposition.

One early definition of feminist research, which was often recited as a mantra was 'feminist research is by women, on women, for women.' That was clearly inadequate in two ways: (1) men can do feminist research, women can do non-feminist research; and (2) feminist research can be done on men, or animals, or technology or texts or anything. So, for example, a man who gathered data on men who have raped women could be, if his perspective were feminist, doing feminist research. Equally a woman who did research on homeless women need not be conducting feminist scholarship. Catherine Hakim (1995), for example, is a woman, who conducts research on women in the labour market, but is robustly anti-feminist. She has adopted a position that feminist sociologists are producing biased, inaccurate findings, which damage women. Her opponents counter-claim that Hakim's research damages women. (See Delamont, 2001: 88–91, for an account of this controversy.)

One problem with the mantra was, of course, deciding who decided what was 'for' women. Hakim believes that her defence of positivism and her insistence that women are not disadvantaged in the labour market because they do not *want* equality of working hours, and responsibility, are research 'for' women. Her opponents believe equally firmly that their work is 'for' women and Hakim's is not.

I have called this mantra a sciolism because it was so superficial. This slogan became untenable when ethnic minority, post-colonial, and lesbian women began to protest that the category of 'women' was not simple or unitary, and to argue that white, heterosexual, First World women did not necessarily do research that was *for* other categories of women. Ethnic minority women objected to white women doing research 'for' them, lesbians objected to straight women doing research for them, and so on. This was the impetus for Judith Butler's (1990) *Gender Trouble* in which she objected to straight women speaking for lesbians, for example.

These attacks came from within feminism, as it fragmented. There was also a response to the mantra from believers in the objectivity of the social sciences. The calls for research to be done *'for* women' opened up the debates about 'bias' in social research (see Hammersley, 2000, and Murphy and Dingwall, 2001) which are the subject of the section on male hysteria.

The other sciolism was that all positivist or quantitative research methods (treated as synonymous) were 'hard' and masculine, so all feminist research must be interpretivist and/or qualitative, and therefore soft and feminine. This was both insulting to the men who did qualitative research and to women who chose quantitative methods as Jayaratne (1983) argued at the time. Clegg (1985) published a paper which clearly quashed that sciolism, intellectually, but did not of course kill it. Maynard reviews this sciolism and disposes of it. 'It is likely, then, that it is not so much quantification *per se* as naive quantification which is the problem' (1994: 13). Maynard is careful to stress that quantitative studies have provided a significant contribution to feminists' knowledge base about women's lives.

Jayaratne's position, as a quantitative positivist, is echoed by other women who favour that epistemology. Ann Oakley's (1998a, 1998b) conversion to the feminist power of the randomised control trial (RCT) has moved her into this camp during the past decade. In her early work Ann Oakley relied on the unstructured interview as her main research method, supplemented in the doctoral work on housewives by the Who Am I? Twenty Statements Test used by the (now little known) Iowa School of symbolic interactionism. During the 1990s, alongside a movement from work on women's health to research on education, she became an advocate of the randomised control trial (RCT), treating it in a remarkably unsociological way. She argues that data from RCTs are powerful and can be used to inform social policy in ways that other forms of data cannot. This assumes a rationality among policy researchers that those who are not liberal feminists with a faith in the Enlightenment project do not share. Those who have studied the social realities of RCTs are less naïve about them. (See, for example, Featherstone, 2002; Latimer and Featherstone, 2002.) Moreover, the fact that policy-makers might place their faith in RCTs in reality says something about their symbolic force, but next to nothing about their adequacy for social science research.

In 1994 Lynn McDonald published a history of women who had devised and developed social science methods, simultaneously defending empiricism against its critics. McDonald was disturbed or angered by feminist attacks on 'quantification ... value neutrality ... any attempt at objectivity' (1994: 5). Men who espoused qualitative methods were equally perturbed by this sciolism. Erickson (1986) captured the absurdity in his analysis of the joke 'Real men don't do ethnography', a parody of a slogan 'Real men don't eat quiche'. Erickson reports how in 1984 a 'well-known' American process-product researcher sent round a circular containing the joke 'Real men don't do ethnography', and he found that two of his colleagues had put copies into his pigeon-hole saying how amused they were. Erickson responds with a powerful analysis of why some men active in educational research might prefer to avoid the complex nuances of ethnographic work, and might not wish to embrace its emancipatory potential (1986: 157–8).

71

The two sciolisms both confused three quite different levels of deci-sion-making about research: the first focused on the researcher, the topic and the policy outcome(s) while being silent about methods. The second confused the theoretical/philosophical underpinnings of the dis-cipline (the epistemology) with the theory of research (methodology) with the actual data gathering technique(s) (the methods). This distinc-tion, which is the subject of the next section, is usually associated with Sandra Harding's writings on feminist research.

Sandra Harding's trivium

In the USA the writings of the philosopher Sandra Harding (1986, 1991; Harding and Hintikka, 1983) have been influential. Harding (1986) distinguished between method, methodology and epistemology. Her distinction is useful. Harding limits method to specific data-gath-ering techniques and the analytic strategies that go with them. So when a researcher decides to do a postal survey and analyse the results with SPSS, or to do life history interviews and run the transcripts through NUDIST, she is making decisions about methods. Methodology is reserved for theorising about research, and epistemology for theories of knowledge. There is a methodology chapter at the beginning of Hammersley and Atkinson (1995), for example, before the rest of the book focuses on methods. Epistemology is a branch of philosophy, con-cerned with where knowledge comes from and how much confidence can be placed on it. As a philosopher, Harding is not interested in soci-ological methods, and therefore writes very little about methods or methodology, and a great deal about epistemology.

These ideas are related to her development of the trio of concepts of feminist empiricism, feminist standpoint epistemology, and postmodern feminism. Feminist empiricism is a critical practice. Male bias in research is systematically found, critiqued, and ideally removed, but the idea of scientific objectivity is unchallenged. Feminist standpoint epis-temology, in contrast, holds that objectivity is an inherently masculin-ist theory or myth. It cannot be corrected. So feminists need to make an emancipatory commitment to knowledge gathered from feminist stand-point(s). Harding argues that feminist standpoint epistemologies and methodologies were developed to oppose both positivism and interpre-tivism in social science.

Harding's work of the 1980s can be said to have been feminist stand-point epistemology, but by the late 1990s she had changed her position, to argue for a postmodern feminist epistemology. As she explains this shift, in the early 1980s 'standpoint epistemologies' developed 'in oppo-sition to the all-powerful dictates of rationalist/empiricist epistemolo-gies' (Harding, 2000: 51) *and* to the 'interpretationist' epistemologies which were the main opposition to positivism (ibid.: 51). Marxist epistemologies were, in America 'beyond the pale of reasonable discussion' (ibid.: 51). Harding states clearly than as postmodern feminist ideas developed during the 1990s she has become convinced of their explanatory power. Harding argued that the feminist potential of poststructuralist or postmodernist ideas had convinced her that feminist standpoint theory was not the best way forward for either social science or feminism, and she wished to emphasise feminist postmodernism as *the* epistemological stance.

Harding's writing has been inspirational for many feminist sociologists, but it has not provided practical guidance or exemplary sociology. For those, many feminist sociologists have looked to Liz Stanley.

Liz Stanley

Liz Stanley has been central to the debates on feminist methods and methodology for 25 years. From her paper with Sue Wise (1979) to a recent overview of the debates (2000) she has raised awkward questions. Whereas Sandra Harding is a philosopher, Liz Stanley is an active sociologist, who writes about methods, methodology and epistemology from an experience of empirical research. Consequently she is much more concerned with methods than Harding who is more interested in epistemology.

Stanley argues that feminism 'combines analytical, ethical and political dimensions' (2000: 8) and indeed, the central tenet of feminism is that these are inseparable. Indeed, she locates the uneasy relationship between feminism and malestream academia in that central tenet. Stanley borrows the phrase 'passionate scholarship' from Barbara Du Bois (1983), and links it to 'necessary research' (Stanley, 1996): that is research carried out because of the convictions of the investigators.

Stanley argues that there are two different versions of feminist methodology in the literature: one that is actually practised by feminist researchers, and another that is created and demonised by its critics. Stanley's conception of feminist methods, methodology and epistemology (and we must note she finds this analytic distinction unhelpful) has been presented consistently in her own writings. It is grounded in reflexivity, but not the reflexivity of qualitative methods texts. The reflexivity of Hammersley and Atkinson (1995) is called 'descriptive' reflexivity by Stanley (2000: 23) and is contrasted with her 'analytical' reflexivity. She is committed to 'accountable knowledge' which allows its analytic steps to be traced, re-traced, and re-analysed to produce other outcomes. Such a perspective can be taken by anyone. That person does not have to be feminist, but Stanley sees it as particularly attractive to feminists.

73

Work such as Harding's and Stanley's is not easy to read, and many 'believers' and 'critics' have failed to engage with it. Feminist methodology and epistemology have produced a violent response, and it is engagement with that response that this chapter ends. There are women, even women who claim to be feminists, who object vehemently to the very idea of feminist methods, because they are positivists who believe feminist political goals can only be achieved on the basis of objective data. Lynn McDonald (1994), for example, holds that position, and so do many liberal feminists in the UK.

male hysteria

Since 1980 there have been male responses to feminist methodology that have been hysterical. James Davis's (1994) attack using the offensive metaphor of germs and infections is entirely hysterical in tone. Of course, not all men have been opposed to feminist methods, methodology or epistemology as the work by, for example, McLennan (1985), Holmwood (1985) and Morgan (1981) demonstrates.

It is legitimate to say that men have no need to bother about feminist methods. If they do not like them, they could ignore them: no one expects, or demands that men should or could adopt feminist methods. Such methods are not taking funding from non-feminist methods, nor squeezing non-feminist research out of the journals, so they are not objectively a threat. A woman researcher might be accused of ignoring feminist methods by feminists judging her work, but no man ever has been, is, or is likely to be. Those men who attack feminist methods must find them threatening in some way. Davis's (1994) language is so extreme that Mary Douglas's (1966) ideas of purity and danger come immediately to mind. For such men, methods must be some kind of sacred enclosure in constant danger of being invaded, and therefore polluted by feelings, emotions, mess, blood, dishwater and the contents of nappies. Most men have gone on with their own research using the methods, secure in the methodology and epistemology, they prefer, and ignore feminist methods. Here Cohen and Manion, authors of a best-selling methods text, are typical of the malestream majority. In their first edition (Cohen and Manion, 1980) feminist methods are not mentioned at all. In the third edition (Cohen and Manion, 1989) they are still absent: not a section, not indexed, and none of the key references are in the bibliography. The fourth edition (Cohen and Manion, 1995) does not index feminism, has no section or sub-section on feminist methods, and does not cite key feminist methodologists. Judging these books as useful sources for students, this is a flaw. However, it is a rational response if Cohen and Manion are uninterested in feminist methods or disapprove of them, and one common in scholarship. The

74

most devastating way to deal with opponents is to freeze them out of the discourse by silence, by omission. In the fifth edition Cohen et al. (2000) added four pages of neutral description of feminist methods (ibid.: 34-8), plus two short paragraphs on other pages (ibid.: 111, 123). None of the leading exponents or advocates of feminist methods are cited, but the ideas are presented in an appropriately dispassionate, even disinterested way.

The man who has repeatedly published attacks on feminist methods, Martyn Hammersley, may not actually be the most hysterical opponent of them. Among male sociologists it is possible that there are much fiercer opponents who have not deigned to make their opposition public, and there are doubters, opponents who have not yet realised that there *are* exponents of feminist methods, methodology and epistemology, or who have not taken them seriously enough to formulate their oppositional stance. These hypothetical opponents cannot, by definition, appear in my text.

Hammersley, however, is obviously bothered by feminist methods, methodology and epistemology, as he has published attacks on them at irregular intervals for a decade (Hammersley, 1992, 2000; Hammersley and Gomm, 1997). Liz Stanley (2000) provides a detailed critique of Hammersley. There are three features of Hammersley's papers which undermine his scholarly authority. First, Hammersley does not cite (and therefore we must assume has not read) the up-to-date publications on feminist methods. In 1992 he did not cite the literature from the frontiers of the debates, in 1997 he and Gomm cited the same literature as the 1992 paper had done, in 2000 he cited nothing by Patti Lather published later than 1993, and then not her 1991 book, nothing by Sandra Harding more recent than 1992, or by Liz Stanley since 1993. Other leading feminists, such as Judith Butler, were also left uncited. Second, he over-simplified the range of positions within the 'feminist' canon; from Lynn McDonald's (1994) positivism to Patti Lather's (2001) wild postmodernism, feminist methodologists cover a large waterfront. Susan Haack (1995) and Lynn McDonald (1994) hold views on methods Hammersley probably shares, yet because he does not disaggregate 'feminist', he fails to produce a sophisticated critique.

Third, he does not address the basic premise of historical writing on science and objectivity. The history of science shows how problematic the Enlightenment idea of objectivity is; those feminists who propose that 'objectivity' is a reification of a middle-class white male historically specific view are drawing on a rich *historical* literature, which many scholars quite distant from feminism share.

Much of Hammersley's repeated attacks is focused on the two sciolisms, on Harding's position in 1986 rather than 1996 or 2000, on straw women rather than real-live articulate feminists.

Personally, I am not particularly enamoured of the idea, or the practice of 'feminist methods' (Coffey and Delamont, 2000). However, there is no doubt at all that much social science done before they, and queer theory, evolved, took objectivity, male supremacy, the male gaze, and heterosexual standpoints for granted. Ideas and standpoints were unexamined, and the ideas of dominant groups were treated as findings without any attempt to discover, explore or analyse the perspectives of muted groups. Too much research claimed an objectivity it did not and could not, in fact, have. The rise of feminist methods has coincided with, and helped to produce, a climate in which there is more explicit discussion of standpoints, of why methods were chosen, of the implications of the choices, and the interactions between researcher, methods, and findings. These are entirely desirable outcomes. I remain confident that good research will also aim to minimise sexist assumptions, whatever the paradigm or epistemology underlying it; and remain sceptical of many claims to authenticity made by feminist researchers. But I am equally sceptical of all claims to authenticity (Atkinson and Silverman, 1997).

The rise of feminist methods was swiftly followed by the growth of queer theory and methods. The following section briefly outlines the challenge to male heterosexual hegemony built into research in the name of objectivity. Noble (1992) raises some fascinating points about the exquisite irony of using an idealised view of science, and hence objectivity, grounded in the Royal Society after 1660. The men who founded the institution which canonised the approach to investigating the natural and physical world, from which we derive the idealised, mythical notions of 'objectivity', 'replication', and even peer accountability, were a distinctly odd bunch. They included Boyle, a celibate, Hooke who aimed at celibacy, and Newton, misogynist, alchemist, a virgin who suppressed his homosexuality. To take that model, problematic in the sciences as the sociologists of science have shown (Collins and Pinch, 1993, 1998), into the social sciences which are about cultures where both sexes live, is frankly absurd.

queer theory and methods

The hysteria aroused in men like Davis and Hammersley by feminist methods is paralleled by the disquiet produced by critiques of old methods and proposals for emancipatory methods coming from other 'outsiders'. The rise of the new men's studies, gay and lesbian studies, queer theory, and critical race theory has led many men to raise doubts about research epistemologies, methodology, and methods as they became engaged with investigations on men and masculinity, on gays, or on ethnic minorities. Coffey (1999) addresses many of these issues, which also featured strongly in *Qualitative Studies in Education* during the 1990s. Kong et al. (2002) discuss the relationships between the rise of feminist research practices, and the rise of queer theory and queer methodology. William Tierney, alone (1993) and with his colleague Patrick Dilley (1998, 2002), has explored how the formerly silenced, once given a narrative voice, produce challenges to traditional malestream methods which had silenced them. It is far beyond the scope of this book to explore all the ways in which feminist methods have created spaces for others to propose their challenges, but their opponents can certainly add that to the charge sheet.

postmodernism

This is the central focus of Chapter 8, and is not explored in detail here. The feminist disquiet about postmodern theorising has been largely confined to the feminist journals. The terror postmodernism has aroused in a few self-styled defenders of science has, in contrast, led to coverage in the media aimed at the general reader. The 1990s saw the outbreak of the 'science wars' (Mackenzie, 1999) in which a few scientists attacked postmodernism *and* a group of sociologists of science who were not postmodernists at all. The contributors to Koertge (1998) argued that the future of science was being undermined by 'postmodernism', as a fashionable intellectual movement and by the sociology of science.

79

Most scientists are totally untroubled by such claims – if they are even aware of them being advanced – and continue to 'do' science in the traditional way (Pearson, 2000). In practice, scientists remain content with the 'Truth Will Out Device' (TWOD) (Gilbert and Mulkay, 1984). The real 'two cultures' debate is not the phoney war fought in the 1960s between C.P. Snow and F.R. Leavis, but that between scientists and the postmodernists in humanities and social sciences today.

While the caveats of critics of postmodernism are important, and will be an element in the scepticism deployed in Chapter 8, it is also important to recognise how enjoyable postmodern analyses can be. In the unlikely best-seller of 1997, *Courtesans and Fishcakes* James Davidson writes: 'What is interesting about Foucault's work is the realisation that misrepresentations are just as interesting as representations and even more useful, when you can identify them, are outrageous lies' (1997: xxii). Studying 'outrageous lies' is enormous fun: fun I have enjoyed (Delamont, 1998).

CONCLUSION

Feminist methods are the most influential and, simultaneously, contentious development and achievement of feminist sociology.

five

unconventional but seething

were there any founding mothers?

In Amanda Cross's (1981: 33) novel, there is a scene in Cambridge where Kate Fansler is with her niece, Leighton, a student at Harvard and an aspiring actress. Leighton describes Hedda Gabler as: 'scared sh—, scared to death of being unconventional but seething underneath'. The ways in which First Wave feminists dealt with being 'scared to death' of appearing 'unconventional', while 'seething underneath' are a fascinating study. First Wave feminists developed strategies to challenge orthodoxies while appearing conformist (Delamont, 1989b). The lives and work of the pioneers of feminist sociology and anthropology show how they were revolutionaries in their careers, ideas and research projects. Most of them have been 'written out' of the histories of their disciplines in contemporary accounts, which overwhelmingly valorise men.

To take a simple example, there is Jessica Kuper's (1987) *Key Thinkers*. This is a student 'aid', which has brief entries on the life and works of 111 social scientists, or ancient figures like Plato, who pre-figure social science. Four of the 111 entries are women: Hannah Arendt, Anna Freud, Melanie Klein and Margaret Mead (Arendt for politics, Freud and Klein for psychoanalysis, Mead for anthropology). Apparently there are no female key thinkers at all in economics or sociology. All the leading male sociologists are included except, by the standards of today, Bourdieu; and among the philosophers, the omission of Derrida seems strange. But, in general, the 107 men are the people one would expect: it is the absence of women (Benedict, Kollontai, Martineau, de Beauvoir, Gilman, Webb, Wollstonecraft) that startles. Apparently, sociology students do not need to know anything about any women. The entries on the men are also stripped of any women or feminism. Althusser's entry does not warn us that he murdered his wife. Gunnar Myrdal's entry ignores Alva Myrdal's work. Sartre's entry is silent on de Beauvoir. Talcott Parsons's entry fails to discuss his sexism. It is against books such as this that feminist sociologists are driven to search for, and promote, founding mothers.

My aim in this chapter is not so much to answer the question 'were there any founding mothers?' as to explore *why* feminist sociology has addressed that question, *how* they have attempted to answer it, *what* results they have had, whether they have managed to explain the exclusion or forgetting of the founding mothers from the canon as it is taught in the contemporary era and whether they have succeeded at all in changing the canon.

The chapter is in two main sections. First, it explores the general issues around the search for, and discussion of, founding mothers. Then it gives a detailed case study of the founding mothers of one theoretical and empirical school of sociology, and their fate since 1920.

THE SEARCH FOR OUR ROOTS

Finding, or reinstating, founding mothers, has been a central task of women's studies and/or feminist perspectives, in many disciplines. Dale Spender (1983) for example, published a book of founding mothers. Lynn McDonald (1994) wrote on women who developed social research methods. Yeo (1997) includes papers on several possible founding mothers who deserve to be alongside Wollstonecraft. Lengermann and Niebrugge-Brantley (1998) produced a book on women founders of sociology. These four reference works were all produced by women of my generation, and focus primarily on scholars who lived and wrote in the eighteenth and nineteenth centuries. They wrote either before First Wave feminism, or were important First Wave figures. For people reading this book who were born during Third Wave feminism, however, there are women from the twentieth century who have to be classified as 'founding mothers', because their work has slid away into the past.

There is considerable agreement about who were the founding mothers of sociology and anthropology among feminists, but any list produced also reveals how different the histories of the disciplines are in the USA and in the UK. In anthropology, there are quite distinct 'lists' of founding mothers, reflecting the very different ways in which anthropology has developed in the two cultures. Among the feminist thinkers claimed as founding mothers of feminist sociology, the ideas of Mary Wollstonecraft (1759–97) (see Yeo, 1997), Harriet Martineau (1802–76), and Beatrice Webb (1858–1943) are usually highlighted. Sklar's (1973) biography and exegesis of Catherine Beecher's (1813–73) work make a powerful case for Beecher as a vital intellectual link between de Tocqueville and Parsons. Beecher does not figure in revisionist pantheons of historic women sociologists,

79

but her ideas on gender, the family and democracy fit perfectly into the evolution of American sociology. In anthropology, feminists in the USA see foundational motherhood in Elsie Clews Parsons, Ruth Benedict, Nora Zeale Huston, Ella Deloria, Ruth Landes and Margaret Mead. The collection by Behar and Gordon (1995) focuses on reinstating such key figures in the history of American anthropology. The view of the discipline in Britain contains quite different women, who worked all over the commonwealth, including Brenda Seligman, Camilla Wedgewood in the first generation, and subsequently Hilda Beemer Kuper, Audrey Richards, Monica Hunter Wilson and Hortense Powdermaker. There could even be a case made for treating Jane Harrison as a founding mother of social science (Beard, 2000). None of these women is revered by American feminists. Margaret Mead, in particular, is seen very differently in the USA and the UK. Rossiter (1982, 1995) and Rosenberg (1982) explore the lives of American pioneers in these social sciences.

Different types of feminist sociologist also revere and promote different women from the past. Marxist feminists are more enthusiastic about Alexandra Kollantai and Rosa Luxemburg, or even Eleanor Marks. Radical feminists are more enthusiastic about lesbians in the First Wave. Sheila Jeffreys (1985, 1987), for example, has reinstated Elizabeth Wolstenholme Elmy as a founding mother. Simone de Beauvoir is recognised as a founding mother by many feminists, although she was a philosopher not a sociologist (Moi, 1994).

Of course, *which* women we choose to reinstate and promote depends on our current conception of what sociology is. A writer on sexuality will be looking for different pioneers from one writing on trade unionism or medicine. This volume focuses not so much on unearthing lost women sociologists but rather explaining their erasure, and re-inserting them into the conventional histories. In the rest of the chapter, the focus is on one department of sociology in the USA. The story of the women of the Chicago School and of the ways in which that story is told and retold provides insight into the fate of founding mothers and of those who try to reinstate them. There is no British research on any set of women who have been systematically excluded from sociology. Whether this is because no such women exist, or because no researchers have (re)discovered any is not clear. The lessons we can draw from the (re)discovery of the Chicago women are as valid for British sociology as for American.

What is absolutely clear is that each generation of women sociologists has to rediscover the founding mothers, because they are not being (re)placed, i.e. reinstated in the malestream history of the discipline. Histories of the discipline written in 1960 ignored women, so too do histories written in 2000.

CHICAGO SOCIOLOGY: THE ARCHETYPICAL CASE?

In 1990 the University of Helsinki celebrated its 35th anniversary. The sociology department decided to have a conference on Society, Intellectuals and the University. Elina Haavio-Mannila (1992) was chair of the department and invited me to speak. The conference took place in English, although I was the only British speaker, among Finns, French, German, Italian and one American Swede. Elina Haavio-Mannila asked me because she had read *Knowledgeable Women* (Delamont, 1989b), and gave me the brief of speaking on women. I presented a title 'Can a woman be an intellectual? Can an intellectual be a woman?' and wrote a paper on the women of the first Chicago School (Delamont, 1992a, 1994). Four things about the trip, the conference and the paper have stayed with me. I fell in love with Helsinki, which has wonderful *Jugendstil* architecture that is much less publicised than Vienna's, breathtaking modern architecture and design, and a magnificent ethnographic collection on all the peoples who speak languages related to Finnish and Hungarian. At the time, the sociology department was not in the city centre near the main nineteenth-century buildings, but in a working-class neighbourhood 'across the long bridge': one of the speakers, Matti Klinge, an historian from the old elite who spoke Swedish rather than Finnish, had never been to the sociology department: he had never crossed the long bridge before.

81

As far as scholarly issues go, however, there were two related events. I was interviewed for the Finnish equivalent of *The Times* and appeared on the front page: something that would never happen to a conference speaker in the UK. Inside the conference my paper was greeted politely, but with bafflement. No Americans, nor British people either, could be intellectuals, I was told. To treat anyone in Chicago between 1892 and 1922 as an intellectual was simply absurd. Intellectuals were French, German, Scandinavian, Finnish, Italian and possibly Central European. No such people could, or ever had, existed in English-speaking countries. My paper, which queried whether women can be intellectuals because men prefer all-male cerebral communities, or whether intellectual women were denied their femininity and were 'unsexed' by their brains, was not seen as problematic because it was about women. (Or at least no one was rude enough or brave enough to raise that objection.) The doubts, and frank disbelief, came from the focus on America. Most of the papers focused on Dreyfus, or the *Tel Quel* group, or Sartre. My assumption: that the social scientists at Chicago before 1914 were intellectuals in the same sense as the *Dreyfusards* was seen as preposterous. In these lasting impressions, the marginality of sociology, of the Anglophone world, and of women in academia are all compounded. A book on feminist sociology is a multiply marginalising exercise.

These thoughts came back to me when reading Toril Moi (1994) on Simone de Beauvoir. She points out that in Norway, Britain and the USA de Beauvoir is an acceptable topic: in France 'most people take Simone de Beauvoir's lack of intellectual and literary distinction as a basic article of faith' (ibid.: 11), and writes of 'cultural terrorism' (ibid.: 12). Bearing these reflections in mind, the material on Chicago is rehearsed here, because it is the best-documented history of women in sociology. Mary Jo Deegan (1988, 1996) has produced a feminist history of the Chicago School of Sociology between 1890 and 1942. Subsequently she has analysed the Chicago women from 1942 to 1970 (Deegan, 1995). This analysis is discussed in some detail because it is emblematic. For Americans, and for many non-Americans, Chicago holds a mythical place in the history of American sociology. As Gary Alan Fine (2000) commented in his review of Tomasi (1998), the Chicago Department of Sociology is 'prominent' in the 'image' of the discipline: 'One could not imagine the publication of a volume like this describing any other school' (ibid.: 674–5). The Tomasi volume has 13 chapters all written by non-Americans, from Poland, the UK, France, Italy, Germany and Canada: an example of how important Chicago is as the location of the origin myth.

There are three feminist accounts of the intellectual climate of the era: Rosenberg (1982), Rossiter (1982) and Gordon (1990) in which Chicago social science can be located. Lengermann and Niebrugge-Brantley (1998) reinstate Jane Addams, Charlotte Perkins Gilman and eight other women into the history of American sociology. They draw on biographies of these ten women, and intellectual histories of the era. Deegan's work can be set against that other scholarship.

The rescue archaeology of Chicago sociology in the period before 1935 done by feminists has been of four kinds:

1 Re-discovering the research on gender issues.
2 Re-discovering women sociologists.
3 Re-discovering the gender politics of the department: finding the sacred grove (Aisenberg and Harrington, 1988) and chilly climate (Smith, 1999) for the women.
4 Exploring how the male powerbrokers wrote about women.

The women who were at Chicago in the period have left published and unpublished papers. Marion Talbot (1936), for example, published an autobiography which can be examined for evidence about the history of Chicago sociology. Her papers are archived in Chicago and have been used by researchers such as Deegan (1996). In the account which follows I have sketched the context: Chicago and its new university: and then moved into the history of sociology in the USA in general and in Chicago in particular. Against that background, the argument moves on to gender at Chicago.

Chicago University was founded in 1892 with an endowment of money from local entrepreneurs, especially Rockefeller oil money. The city was notorious for its stockyards, where millions of cattle were butchered to feed the industrial centres of the north east and the coastal cities of New York and Boston. It was booming in the 1890s, with thousands of immigrants arriving: especially Irish, Italian and Eastern Europeans, predominantly Catholic, but with some Jews escaping pogroms in Europe. The new university was part of a move to turn the wild west frontier town into the civilised city. The first President, William Rainey Harper was only 34. He set out to make Chicago a university different from the elite, Ivy League, men's colleges of the East Coast (Brown, Dartmouth, Yale, Harvard, and so on). He chose the universities of Prussia as his model rather than Oxbridge. In an important way Chicago was not like either because it was co-educational: partly because there were a lot of women teachers keen to upgrade themselves by part-time and summer school courses and the new university needed the fee income they provided. In its first 50 years there were proposals to make Chicago all-male to raise its status, but these were never implemented, and Chicago always had male and female students. Partly because Harper wanted Chicago to be different from Yale, and partly because he could not persuade the leading scholars in the ancient subjects (Latin, Greek, Hebrew, Theology and Philology) to leave the Ivy League to take up chairs in a cowtown, Chicago specialised in new subjects. It pioneered sociology, social administration, psychology, anthropology and sciences.

Harper looked for keen young men to lead his new subjects. For sociology he found Albion Small who became chair of sociology at 28 in 1892 and continued to do so until 1934 when he was 70. Small also founded the *American Journal of Sociology* (*AJS*) and edited it from 1895 until 1935. Abbott (1999) provides the official history of *AJS* and the Chicago Department. The men Harper drew to Chicago – John Dewey and G.H. Mead, great philosophers, leading psychologists, economists and anthropologists, and in sociology: Small, W.I. Thomas, R.E. Park and E.W. Burgess – made Chicago a world leader in social science scholarship. In Chicago, sociology became established as a discipline, symbolic interactionism as it was retrospectively labelled by Blumer crystallised as a theoretical perspective, and empirical research (collecting both quantitative and qualitative data) rather than just speculating and theorising about social phenomena, became *de rigueur*. There are many studies of the golden age such as Faris (1967), Carey (1975), Rock (1979), *Urban Life* (1983), Bulmer (1984), Kurtz (1984), Harvey (1987), Smith (1988), Deegan (1988), Tomasi (1998) and

Abbott (1999). Abbott himself recommends Fisher and Strauss (1978a, 1978b, 1979a, 1979b) for a thoughtful view.

Chicago University sociologists dominated the whole discipline in America through the ASA and the *AJS* and by their sheer numbers and prestige until 1935–6 when sociologists elsewhere in the nation rebelled. The rebels took over the American Sociological Association (ASA), and founded a new journal, the *American Sociological Review* (*ASR*) to challenge the *AJS*. Small's department dominated the new discipline until his retirement, but by 1928 there were sociology departments in 99 of the 236 colleges and universities in the USA (Abbott, 1999). By the 1930s there were about 40 new PhDs in the discipline each year. However, as late as 1950, half the practising sociologists in the USA had been through Chicago. The period of rebellion saw the cosy relationship of the ASA, the Chicago Department and Chicago University Press end: the *ASR* began with the best papers from the ASA's annual conference which Chicago University Press no longer wanted to publish as an annual volume (Abbott, 1999). In this era, American sociology was also purifying itself. Abbott (ibid.: 105) points out that in the 1930s: 'the last of the do-gooders drifted out of the ASA'.

In the period from 1942 to 1962 there was a second flowering of sociology at Chicago (Abbott, 1999; Fine, 1995). After 1945 this was partly fuelled by the GI Bill which funded veterans to attend college. There were 200 graduate students in sociology at Chicago in the 1950s: a number far beyond the experience of any British sociologist where ten graduate students constitutes a critical mass (Delamont et al., 1997). The people who taught at Chicago, and even more those who were trained there in this era, spread out across the USA taking the gospel with them in their diaspora. Chicago sociologists had been the leaders of the Society for the Study of Social Problems (SSSP) and were the founders in 1973 of the Society for the Study of Symbolic Interaction (SSSI) (Lofland, 1997). The papers published in *Social Problems*, and then later in *Urban Life* founded in California by the self-styled 'Chicago Irregulars' (Lofland, 1983) originally as *Urban Life and Culture* and now published as the *Journal of Contemporary Ethnography*; and the 'official' SSSI journal, *Symbolic Interaction*, embody the work of the scholars who were taught by the people trained in the second Golden Age.

GENDER AND CHICAGO SOCIOLOGY

Abbott (1999: 24) contrasts the 'profound' impact that the literatures on urban issues and on 'race-ethnicity' have had on the history of Chicago sociology with the lack of impact made by encounters with feminism. In the main part of this chapter it is that lack of impact that I am going to address. Noticeably, Abbott himself ignores the feminist work on Chicago in its first golden age by Rosenberg (1982), Rossiter (1982), Gordon (1990) and me (Delamont, 1992a), dealing only with Deegan (1988, 1995).

Before plunging into the argument offered by Deegan, it is important to understand the *Zeitgeist* of Hull-House. The idea of settlement houses, in which white intellectuals from the upper middle classes chose to live in slums, conducting adult education classes, providing community leadership, being the role models of a Christian, celibate, literature, orderly lifestyle including temperance, is now a very alien one. In the nineteenth century it was popular in Britain and the USA. Feminists were keen on the idea of leaving their stifling Victorian families to live communally with other like-minded ladies and build celibate career-centred lives (Walkowitz, 1992). Vicinus (1985) has an excellent account of their desirability for British First Wave feminists. In Chicago, Jane Addams founded and championed Hull-House for 40 years, and it was America's most famous settlement. It was modelled on Toynbee Hall in London, and provided a home for many of the women staff of Chicago University and some men. There was a communal dining hall, and women could live there cheaply, respectably, and provide social and educational services to the neighbourhood. For many years Hull-House was an annexe of the university, especially of the sociology department, because it was the centre from which empirical research on its neighbourhood was conducted. In 1895 the earliest empirical research on Chicago, modelled on Booth's *Life and Labour of the London Poor* was produced as *Hull-House Maps and Papers*.

Deegan's (1988) *Jane Addams and the Men of the Chicago School* was an attempt to rewrite the orthodox histories of Chicago Sociology to re-centre Hull-House in the departmental chronicle, and the sociological identities of at least 15 women scholars and feminist activists of the period 1892–1920. As well as (re-)claiming these women for sociology, she also stressed that their research *topics* are recognisably sociological today, even if they were deemed to be *not* sociological between 1920 and 1980. Lengermann and Niebrugge-Brantley (1998) draw essentially similar conclusions, and, for an essentially similar argument, see also Bernard, (1987). The story of Chicago is told, contested, retold, recontested. Like any origin legend, any powerful myth, it is endlessly fascinating. There is no consensus, only controversy. Scholars dispute membership, influence, love and hate, power and impotence, and the relative importance of different research methods, theories and epistemologies. For the purpose of this chapter, only two issues are important: women as researchers and gender as a topic. There is no attempt to deal with any other aspects of the myths of Chicago sociology.

85

There are 14 women who were active in Chicago sociology in the 1892–1920 era, whose publications, research, teaching and even existence are not acknowledged in the malestream histories before Abbott (1999). I have selected these 14 from the accounts of Abbott (1999), Deegan (1988), Lengermann and Niebrugge-Brantley (1998) and Rosenberg (1982). They are:

- Edith Abbott
- Grace Abbott
- Jane Addams
- Sophonisba Breckinridge
- Alice Chapman Dewey
- Charlotte Perkins Gilman
- Florence Kelley
- Frances Kellor
- Julia Lathrop
- Annie Marion McLean
- Helen Castle Mead
- Marion Talbot
- Dorothy Swaine Thomas
- Helen Bradford Thompson Woolley

It is not appropriate to describe all these women's lives and work in any detail, even if the research on them had been done and was available. Rosenberg (1982) discusses Helen Woolley at some length; Fish (1981) has written on Annie Marion McLean, and Marion Talbot (1936) published a readable autobiography; Lengermann and Niebrugge-Brantley (1998: 229) draw on a biography of Florence Kelley by Blumberg (1966), of the Abbott sisters by Costin (1983), of Florence Kelley by Sklar (1995) and of Julia Lathrop by Wade (1977), as well as two histories of women and reform in that era by Muncy (1991) and Gordon (1994). I have discussed some of the 14 in more detail to draw out the lessons about the fate of founding mothers.

Edith Abbott had a PhD in political economy from Chicago, studied with the Webbs at LSE, taught sociology at Wellesley, and was then a Chicago staff member in sociology from 1908 to 1920. She published books on *Women in Industry* and on truancy from school in 1916. Her specialism was statistics: her post was 'Lecturer in Methods of Social Investigation'.

Jane Addams is the most famous woman on the list, although she is much less known outwith the USA. She is remembered in the USA as a pacifist, a settlement worker, a feminist, and a social worker, not a sociologist. However, she taught sociology, was a member of the ASA, published in the *AJS*, and identified herself as a sociologist. She edited one of the pioneering empirical studies of urban Chicago, *Hull-House Maps and Papers* (1895).

Sophonisba Breckinridge was the first woman to qualify as a lawyer in the state of Kentucky in 1894. She moved to Chicago to become Assistant Dean of Women: a pioneering feminist post combining administration and pastoral care. Once in Chicago she completed two PhD degrees, in law and in political economy. Her law doctorate was the first Chicago awarded to a woman. Breckinridge taught sociology in the sub-department of home economics, which was a sub-division of sociology. She published *The Delinquent Child in the Home* in 1912, and with Edith Abbott, in 1916, a book on truancy. After 1904 Breckinridge and Julia Lathrop concentrated on establishing the School of Social Service Administration (SSA) which was a professional training centre for social workers.

Marion Talbot was the first Dean of Women at Chicago. If she is remembered at all today, it is as the founder of the American Association of University Women, not as a sociologist. However, she taught in the sociology department before she created her sub-department of home economics. Her intellectual interests were in the area of overlap between urban studies, town planning and home economics. However, many of the topics considered to be part of the sociology of everyday/everynight life today; such as housework, food and drink, and use of space in homes, were within Talbot's scope. Deegan (1996) has explored her passionate friendship with Breckinridge.

Charlotte Perkins Gilman came to Chicago from California in 1895, and wrote the feminist book *Women and Economics* (1898). She is remembered as a feminist, but not as a sociologist. However, she published in the *AJS*, spoke at the ASA, and worked with Lester Ward, who is seen as a founder of American sociology.

Florence Kelley was born in 1853, and moved to Chicago in 1891 as a divorcee with three children. She had done a PhD in Zurich, had known Engels, and had translated his works into English. She was the leading force in compiling the *Hull-House Maps and Papers*. This was an American attempt to emulate Booth's *Life and Labour of the London Poor*.

Frances Kellor was born in 1873, lived in Hull-House intermittently between 1898 and 1905, studied crime, and became head of the New York Bureau of Industries and Immigration in 1910.

Helen Mead, Alice Dewey and Dorothy Thomas were the wives of three of Chicago's most famous pioneer scholars. Deegan (1988) argues that they have been eclipsed because they were wives (as, in a later generation Helen McGill Hughes was eclipsed by her husband). Deegan highlights Helen Mead and Alice Dewey's active campaigning for female suffrage: a social reform goal intertwined with social science in the nineteenth century (Delamont, 1989b). Dorothy Thomas (W.I. Thomas's second wife) wrote *The Child in America* with him in 1928. Alice Dewey was an enthusiast for the fiction of Zola. Zola's fiction was influential on the style of Chicago urban sociology, and Deegan suggests Alice Dewey may have brought Zola's novels to the attention of the male sociologists.

Helen Woolley grew up in Chicago, and entered the university in 1893. She completed her PhD there in 1900. Her research was on the psychology of sex differences, and challenged the dominant ideology that men and women had very different mental abilities. Rosenberg (1982) documents how convincing her findings were. W.I. Thomas had believed that men and women had biologically determined mental abilities that differed sharply. After Woolley's research he changed his position in print, citing her experiments as evidence that socialisation and environment separated males and females and that produced differential mental abilities.

Deegan (1988) claimed that these women had been expunged from the history of Chicago sociology, unjustly and because of the active misogyny of Park. The process she describes is explored by Rossiter (1982), in her history of the professionalisation of American science, a process which involved clearing out all amateurs, all school teachers, and all women. Lengermann and Niebrugge-Brantley (1998) plot the links, both academic and emotional, between eight of these women (the Abbott sisters, Breckinridge, Kelley, Kellor, Lathrop, McLean and Talbot) in detail, as well as confirming their sociological credentials. They devote whole chapters to Jane Addams and Charlotte Perkins Gilman. They also describe the different research methods the women deployed, and list some reasons why they should be considered as founding mothers of contemporary sociology.

THE EXPULSION AND THE EXCLUSION

There are two versions of the events in Chicago after 1920. In the dominant, male, version of the story, three men of great perspicacity – Faris, Park, and Burgess – inherited the department, purified it, and created a recognisably modern sociology there. In other words, they separated academic sociology as an objective, scientific discipline from social administration, social policy, social work, home economics, and from political activism of all kinds. Scholars were to focus on research, not on helping tenants campaign against slum landlords or helping workers organise unions. Disciplines which trained people to work among the poor were to be separated from their scientific discipline of sociology. This version, which is a 'Whig' account of the history, can be found in Faris (1967), Matthews (1977), Rock (1979), Kurtz (1984), Bulmer (1984) and Harvey (1987).

This purification of discipline and department involved clearing out all the women lecturers, and removing their publications from the canon. Rossiter (1982) chronicles similar processes in the learned societies of many American sciences and social sciences. In Chicago there were no women tenured or even tenure-tracked in sociology from 1940 to 1960. For example, Evelyn Kitagawa joined the staff in 1951, did not get a professorship till 1975, and eventually became its first woman chair (Deegan, 1995). In the years between 1945 and 1975 one badge of excellence for a sociology department in the USA was to be all male: top departments in top universities did not give tenure to women. Rossiter argues that purging women from universities and learned societies was one of the ways that disciplines professionalised themselves in the nineteenth century.

Deegan (1988) has offered a feminist minority account of the period after 1920. She argued that Park was unable to work with women, and therefore drove them out of sociology. Subsequently he wrote up the history of the era, expunging all the women's names, and their publications, from its history. Organisationally, new departments were created, such as the Institute for Juvenile Research, Home Economics, School of Social Service Administration, and so on. At the time, the women thought these were signs of progress, because they gained autonomy and self-determination. Talbot (1936), for example, saw the separation of Home Economics in this light. The women lecturers felt they could train women for good careers in these new fields, and that their graduates would go out and improve the world.

This is an ideological division between men in sociology who wanted their discipline to be university-based, male, detached from political campaigns, from social and community action, and theoretical; and women who wanted to collect data in the city to apply their results to the solution of pressing social problems. Deegan argues that in the 1892–1920 era Mead, Dewey, Thomas and Small shared the social and political goals of the women, especially suffrage, and were happy with a broader, messier sociology that combined university theory with reform campaigns in the city. When these men were gone, their successors were determined to break the link.

There was no real difference of opinion between Addams, Talbot and the other women and the men about the proper roles of males and females in social science. Both thought women were 'better' at gathering data and analysing them, while men were 'better' at abstract thought in the ivory tower. Where the two sexes differed, Deegan argues, was in the value they placed on the two activities. Each sex thought that what they did was the more valuable.

89

As the history of social science developed in the USA after 1920, the male view won. Sociology developed as an abstract, ivory tower subject, quite separate from the messy real-world realities of political campaigns, unions, rent strikes, social administration, domestic hygiene and charitable activity. The work of Addams, the Abbott sisters and Talbot was redefined as social work or home economics, and excised from the malestream histories of sociology at Chicago.

As long as Albion Small was Chair of the Sociology Department there seem to have been friendly relationships between sociology and the women in the new sub-departments. Later in the 1920s and 1930s the relationships became extremely hostile. The male historians do not offer any explanation for the hostility, if indeed they even *mention* the women or the hostility. Deegan blames Park for the rift, arguing that he was obsessively, fanatically hostile to Addams, Breckinridge and Talbot. He had come to Chicago from elsewhere, was kept in a junior role for many years, but eventually became Chair and the custodian of the official history of the Chicago School. Park was involved with the black activist Booker T. Washington, and the Chicago Commission of Race Relations after a race riot in 1919, but he seems to have loathed feminism and feminists. He was also opposed to trade unions and welfare rights work, and committed to purging American sociology of 'political' taints. His written accounts of Mead and Thomas focused entirely on their academic work, and ignored their political activism. Harvey (1987: 31) quotes Park saying that Chicago had suffered more from 'lady reformers' than it had from organised crime and gangsters; and that 'reformers and do-gooders' were 'lower than dirt'. As reformers and do-gooders were centred in Hull-House, and were mostly women, this was de facto an anti-woman statement. Park's memory is treasured by many graduates and historians of Chicago sociology who do not mention his sexist attitudes and hostility to Jane Addams and the other women. Abbott (1999: 28–9) calls Park 'the enigma and talisman of the department's history'. He published relatively little, and his family life was problematic. Abbott states firmly that 'there have been suppressions about Park'.

Of course, a history of sexism and even misogynist behaviour does not usually prevent men from being eulogised, whereas racism, especially anti-Semitism, does. Deegan (1988: 154–5) reports that American historians of sociology avoid Park's quarrels with Abbott and Breckinridge strenuously. Park's biographer was, Deegan says, told to omit it from her biography by senior figures in the discipline. Winifred Raushenbush's biography of Park, published in 1979, is a positive one, and she did not respond publicly to this claim by Deegan. Deegan also states that she herself was threatened that if she discussed Park's treatment of women *she* would be blackballed from American sociology. The informants who told her about the feud asked to remain anonymous.

There is no reason for British chroniclers of Chicago sociology to fear being blackballed, but the four male historians, Rock (1979), Bulmer (1984), Harvey (1987) and Smith (1988), all seem to have accepted the male orthodoxy. Smith, Harvey and Rock do not mention *Hull-House Maps and Papers* at all, and Bulmer gives it one mention but no bibliographic details are provided. In general, male historians of Chicago treat the war between Addams and Park as normal, only to be expected when old, feminist virgins have to be dealt with, especially if they work in low-status areas like home economics or social work.

Here, then, are two competing origin myths. In the dominant malestream story, after 1920, brave men purify the discipline by separating sociology from social reform, political activism and feminism. In the minority feminist version coined by Deegan, a group of male chauvinists strip out all the policy-related sociology and its exponents, and then excise them from the history of the department.

Elsewhere (Delamont, 1992a, 1996a) I have used the theories of Mary Douglas (1966, 1970, 1982) to explore the competing belief systems of the men in the department and the women focused on Hull-House. Deegan has no explanation for the post-1920 male revulsion against women in Chicago except for Park's dislike of women, especially older, academic spinster feminists, and of social reformers. Rossiter's model (1982) is more powerful as an explanation. After 1920 there was a revulsion against the celibate, separatist feminism of the First Wave, among intellectuals fed by the enthusiasm for Freudianism (Delamont, 1992a; Vicinus, 1985). The next generation of women did not, even if they were feminists, want to live celibate lives in settlement houses with other spinsters.

91

1920–65: A DARK AGE

Deegan labels the years 1920 to 1965 the 'dark era of patriarchal ascendancy' (1995: 333). It is in this period that the pioneering women died or retired and were not replaced. She argues that the only two senior men who were remembered positively by women graduate students were W. Lloyd Warner and David Riesman. Riesman, however, had been parachuted into Chicago, and was marginalised by the powerful men. Championing women and holding feminist ideas merely confirmed his marginality. The women trained from 1939 onwards tended to marry (Helen McGill Hughes, Carolyn Rose, Alice Rossi, Rose Laub Coser, and Rosalie Wax were all married to distinguished sociologists). Anti-nepotism rules prevented them from being given posts at the elite universities where their husbands worked.

Much of the history of the period from 1945 to 1965 is regarded as a second golden age, and that is discussed in Chapter 7. In the remainder of this chapter I have drawn out three general issues, none apparently 'about' gender, which actually became points of struggle about women and/or feminists in sociology, which can be seen to underlie long-standing problems over what sociology is, and whether women's concerns have any place there. There are three issues here: (1) qualitative versus quantitative methods; (2) research topics; and (3) the distinction between pure and applied social science.

qualitative versus quantitative methods

Deegan (1995: 338) points out that in the pre-1920 era mathematical sociology was women's work, because it was technical rather than innovative, repetitive and uninteresting. After 1930, statistics became redefined as masculine. She criticises Bulmer (1984), who emphasised the importance of the quantitative tradition at Chicago, for searching for men across several disciplines to create one, yet ignoring the women, like Edith Abbott. In the first golden age, and under Park, the elite power group in the department valued qualitative research, and women were despised for their demographic and survey work.

Then, when quantitative methods rose in the discipline, they became associated with the elite work done by men. Once computing became available, of course, the drudgery of statistical work vanished, and the painstaking methodical 'clerical' work of doing statistics vanished altogether in favour of mere sophisticated mathematics. By the 1950s, although there were doctoral students and staff doing qualitative research, the image the department projected to MA students was overwhelmingly quantitative.

Jennifer Platt (1995: 94–5), an MA student in 1959–60, found that the programme was dominated by statistics courses: at that period the staff of the graduate school was all male. LeCompte recalls her period there late in the 1960s:

> I was trained as a sociologist, but from the Chicago School of fieldwork, rather than from the highly quantitative and statistically rigorous sociology of the times. I am often thought of as an *ethnographer* ... the term ... used ... for sociologists trained, as I am, in the Chicago School of sociological fieldwork. (1998: 201)

Suttles who supervised her master's thesis, was 'the last practitioner of field sociology, resident at the University of Chicago's sociology department' (ibid.: 202).

92

research topics

One of the reasons for the exclusion of women from the history of the Chicago School may be related to focus of their research. Topics which are currently part of sociology, and were legitimate topics in the 1890–1920 period, were not regarded as sociological between 1920 and 1980. For example, Annie Marion McLean (1899/1998) studied, by participant observation, women's work in the new department stores. Florence Kelley (1899/1998) studied the Consumers' League. Both these topics fit perfectly into contemporary sociology, which sees consumption as an important focus of attention (Lury, 1997). Frances Kellor (1900/1998) studied women criminals, again, a topic acceptable today. Yet neither consumption nor women criminals were sociologically fashionable topics between 1920 and 1980. Marion Talbot's (1910/1998) analysis of the educational system for women in the USA deals with issues in education that would fit any contemporary analysis of gender and education.

pure versus applied

Alongside the exclusion of women for being women, there was an issue about where the boundaries of *sociology*, as opposed to social policy, social work, home economics, charity work, socialism, and political campaigning, were to be drawn. The women of the Chicago School were a polluting, contaminating factor *both* because they studied topics which were defined as social policy, social work, and home economics *and* because they were campaigning activists, who wanted to work *with* labour organisations, anti-poverty campaigners, and socialists to change America. Florence Kelley corresponded with Engels until his death, Edith Abbott and Sophonisba Breckinridge were active in the National Association for the Advancement of Colored People, Frances Kellor studied the 'justice' system in the American South. In the years when such 'political' and 'radical' causes were seen by the silverbacks as dangerous pollutions of a science, or would-be science, those who wanted to harness sociology to activisms had to be driven out.

There have also been fashions in what empirical topics are seen as legitimate for sociological enquiry. Some topics have been legitimate for sociological enquiry, then re-defined as *not* sociology, then re-defined into the disciplinary frame again. For example, no one reading this book would be surprised, or disconcerted, to see a publisher's advertisement for a book called *Food as a Factor in Student Life*. It might be listed as a sociology book, or as one on higher education, but if it were listed as sociology we would not be startled. In 1960 or 1970 it might have raised eyebrows, because there was little or no sociological work

93

on food, or other aspects of consumption. In 2000 it would be seen as a perfectly plausible contribution to the discipline. In fact, that book was published in 1894 by two of the Chicago women Ellen Richards and Marion Talbot. It was sociology *then*, it could be sociology now: but between 1920 and 1970 it could not have been. In the purified 'scientific' discipline it was a research topic for home economics or social policy or education: not for sociology. Student *anomie*, yes: student diet, no.

However, there is a wider meaning to the term purity, which has deeper and greater explanatory power. Rossiter (1982, 1995) made a historical study of how American scientists and social scientists professionalised their disciplines during the nineteenth and early twentieth centuries. To create the disciplines as we recognise them today, the men purified them. They excluded amateurs, those without formal qualifications, women, ethnic minorities, and polymaths. By creating the learned societies, and the departments in the top universities as mutual citadels, they excluded those who were not paid lecturers and researchers, those without doctorates, and other undesirables. A chemist became a paid expert with a PhD in Chemistry from one of the few doctoral-granting universities who was a member of the self-perpetuating American Chemical Society. Rossiter shows in detail how this was done by physical and biological scientists, and by social scientists such as anthropologists and sociologists. A pure academic discipline, like a profession, had to police its boundaries; control its entrance, and be free of women, ethnic minorities and amateurs. The purification strategies are a classic example of Mary Douglas's (1966, 1970, 1982) ideas about purity and danger, and, in her later work, group and grid. The exclusion of W.I. Thomas for his political (and possibly sexual) activities, and of the Chicago women, can be seen as classic exclusionary tactics undertaken as part of the professionalisation of American sociology. In that light, the histories of American sociology, without any awkward women, are the heroic origin myths of a discipline. Cluttering the heroic myths by adding women into the legend, especially if those women disputed the boundaries of the sacred kingdom or promised land, merely damages the deviant bard. Rewards come from repeating the known story which gains prizes for the teller of tales, while complicating the legend merely marginalises the teller. Deegan's work has only been written into the origin myth by Abbott (1999) and he is self-consciously arguing an unpopular and uncanonical line.

Britain has not yet produced an equivalent to Deegan about the women at LSE or Leicester, but when one is done, the author will be ridiculed, the scholarship ignored, and the heroic origin legends will continue unabated. Discovering, rediscovering or trying to reinstate founding mothers is like washing the kitchen floor. It has to be done, but no one important ever notices, and if the result is loudly proclaimed, the author or floor washer is despised as a neurotic obsessive.

CONCLUSION

The work of Deegan, and the others who have challenged the malestream histories of Chicago, is a thought-provoking example of the search for founding mothers. It is a vital part of building feminist sociology, but those who do it are not thanked or revered for the labour. Britain needs its Deegan, and it needs a McDonald (1994) and a Lengermann and Niebrugge-Brantley (1998) to search out and champion its founding mothers.

six
the brotherhood of professors, males all
the founding fathers of sociology

A full-fledged member of the brotherhood of professors, males all. (Cross, 1981: 79)

T he previous chapter focused upon the search for founding mothers. This one deals with the uneasy relationships between feminist sociologies and the intellectual patriarchy: the founding fathers and the brotherhood of professors who write about them in the modern world. There are six feminist responses to the grand narrative of the history of sociology as it is usually told:

1　Identification and reiteration of the ways in which the grand narrative omits women as creators or subjects in the past and present.
2　Identification and reiteration of the omission of feminism as a theory, and of its key concepts, from the grand narrative of sociology.
3　Scrutiny of the works of the founding fathers to see the sins of omission and commission practised on women.
4　Searches for alternative founding fathers whose treatment of women or feminism is more enlightened.
5　Critiques of the current accounts of the history of sociology (usually the history of sociological theory) for their failure to undertake the tasks listed in 1–4 above, or include the founding mothers.
6　Use of the theories developed by the founding fathers and their successors to create feminist analytic approaches to sociological phenomena.

Two of these responses (4 and 6) can be seen as wholly positive: the other four are essentially critical or even negative.

In this chapter there is a very brief summary of the orthodox grand narrative as told by British and American sociologists, and then some explanation of the six feminist responses to it.

THE GRAND NARRATIVE

The orthodox histories of sociology tell how the discipline was founded, and has been developed since the 1850s, by the brotherhood of professors, who were all men. The discipline of sociology began in the turmoil after the French Revolution, while Europe and then America were changing from rural, agricultural societies into urban, industrial societies. The founding fathers were thinkers (empirical research came later) who debated what, if anything, made the new urban industrial societies function. They argued about the possibilities for social order in the new cities, unsure whether such societies could avoid breaking down into revolution, crime and immoral disorder. The origins of feminism lie in the same era, and the different schools of feminism have roots in exactly the same ideological debates among the same social classes in the nineteenth century. Insofar as there is an historical feminist sociology and/or a feminist challenge to the malestream sociology these, too, have roots as far back as the Enlightenment.

All the malestream histories of sociology recapitulate that account, *all* without drawing the parallels with the history of feminism. Giddens (1971), Hawthorn (1976), Rhea (1981), Collins (1994a), Bottomore and Nisbet (1978a), Lee and Newby (1983), Craib (1997), Barnes (1995) and Scott (1995) all offer the same history, as indeed did Aron (1965, 1967) in France. A detailed criticism of the ways in which women as topic, as scholars, and feminism as a theory or as a social movement are excluded is presented in Appendix 1.

In the histories of sociology in the period from 1790 to 1920 the leading figures are French and German, only a few thinkers from the UK, Italy, and the USA appear in the accounts. After 1920 the American historians began to stress the importance of the American giants of the discipline, and in all Anglophone narratives, after 1940 Talcott Parsons and Robert Merton are lauded. In the period after 1970 the histories list dominant figures from Europe once again: Lévi-Strauss, Bourdieu, Foucault, Althusser, Lacan and Lyotard from France; the Frankfurt School, Habermas, and Beck from Germany, plus Gramsci from Italy, and Freud, the Austrian. These latter, 40 years dead, appeared in histories of sociology after the paradigm shifts of 1968–70. While the precise list of who is, and who is not, held up as a seminal theorist varies slightly between Hawthorn (1976) and Craib (1997), the total omission of all women scholars, and feminist ideas, and all feminist critiques of the grand narrative has not changed at all. As Jo Eadie wrote: 'There seems something oddly old-fashioned about assessing the contemporary of a critical text by the number of women writers that it recognises – but then there are times when only the bluntest of tools will do' (2001: 575).

Having searched for a 'core text' to use on a social theory module, Eadie concluded that: 'reading the most recent surveys of the field, one could be forgiven for thinking that gender played a negligible role in the functioning of contemporary society' (ibid.).

Eadie reviewed six texts, and concluded that most of them 'construct feminism in ways that effectively exclude it from what purports to be a coherent and comprehensive overview of social theory (ibid.: 576). It is perhaps surprising to find Eadie simultaneously labelling the approach that scrutinises histories and overviews of sociological theory for their omission of women and feminism as 'oddly old-fashioned' and yet still being forced to do that task. It was one of the first things feminist sociologists did: see, for example Delamont (1980: 7–10). However, as Appendix 1 demonstrates, Eadie is entirely correct in her summary: histories and overviews of the grand narrative of sociology ignored women and feminism 30 years ago, *and still do*. So, although feminists were undertaking the first two tasks 30 years ago, the malestream has taken *no notice at all*, and the fifth task is still necessary. A recent history such as Craib (1997) does not bother to acknowledge the feminist argument that Harriet Martineau should be seen as an important sociologist alongside J.S. Mill. Hammersley (2001) writes as if Deegan (1988) had never existed. These male chroniclers may disagree with the feminist work, but if so, they do not do it the courtesy of citation and disagreement: it seems more likely they have not read it, because they 'know' it is irrelevant, or have never heard of its existence.

Rather than dwell on the negative work at length, important though it is, this chapter focuses on the feminists' third, fourth and sixth strategies.

FEMINIST FOCUS ON THE FOUNDING FATHERS

There are three feminist strategies to be explored: how feminist sociologists have revisited and criticised the founding fathers central to the malestream grand narrative; how feminists have searched out alternative founding fathers; and how feminists have used ideas from the founding fathers to build feminist sociology.

At one level, the way the history of sociology is presented is a reasonable way to chronicle the history of the subject. Women in the European countries where sociology began after 1770 were denied access to formal education, could not attend universities, and had no scholarly occupations available to them. Women contemporaries of Comte, Marx, Weber and Durkheim *were* less likely to be able to invent and develop sociology. It is unreasonable, and unscholarly, to expect a twenty-first-century sensitivity to gender issues in eighteenth-century and nineteenth-century people. No feminist sociologist would expect a twenty-first-century position on gender by nineteenth-century theorists. However, what feminists can reasonably expect, do expect, but do not find, is texts about founding fathers which alert students, novices, and even their peers, to the nature of sex roles in their heroes' era, and sets their views on women into that context. Exegeses of founding fathers should, feminists argue, address what they thought about First Wave feminism (if that is known), what they wrote about women, and why they did not have female colleagues. These basic standards are simply not met.

Second, there has been a pattern of re-reading the canonical work, and the more minor, less well-known publications by the founding fathers, to see if they dealt with gender, at all, and if they did, to see what they actually said. Frequently, such re-readings discover that the founding fathers thought, wrote and theorised about gender issues, even though those ideas have been screened out of the malestream modern accounts of their central ideas. Such re-readings can discover that the founding fathers held positions on gender which were context-bound, stereotyped and unscholarly, but sometimes innovative and challenging material is found. Lorna Duffin (1978) re-evaluated Spencer's sociological work. J.R. Martin (1984, 1985), not only re-read Rousseau's *Emile*, but excavated *Sophie*, his much less well-known treatise on the appropriate education for girls. Taking the two texts together reveals Rousseau as a much more reactionary social theorist than he appears to be if one only studies *Emile*. B.D. Johnson (1972) scrutinised Durkheim's *Suicide* in this way. Bologh (1990) presents a feminist reappraisal of Weber. Where founding fathers did write on gender, their work has been subject to feminist critique.

In this chapter I have taken Marx, Weber, Durkheim, the American Pioneers of 1890–1930, Freud, Parsons, Merton, Bourdieu and Foucault as founding fathers and Grand Old Men whose work has been scrutinised and used by feminists, and Engels as a theorist outside the normal grand narrative whose claims to be added to the canon are advanced by feminists.

Marx, Weber and Durkheim, three men, are the founding fathers, and feminist sociologists have to relate their epistemologies to those three. There is a clear difference between them. Marx (and his collaborator Engels) is still revered by Marxist feminists (Sayers et al., 1987), and sociological insight is still found in his writing. Contemporary feminism has a more uneasy relationship with Weber and Durkheim, partly because they did not have a collaborator who produced ideas adaptable by feminists. The American pioneers are not discussed in the UK, but

99

have received feminist scrutiny in the USA. Freud is massively problematic for feminism. Parsons and Merton make an interesting contrast: contemporaries, one of whom has become a feminist bogey, the other ignored.

Marx

There is a relatively large literature in feminist sociology which starts from Marx. Hamilton (1978), for example, used Marx as the fundamental theorist for understanding how women experienced the passage from feudalism to capitalism in Europe. Feminist writers in Third Wave feminism were critical of Marx's failure to address sex differences among workers, explore exploitation inside the family, make the labour of reproduction as significant as that of production, and theorise sexuality. Marx's own life, especially his treatment of women in his family and household, also causes problems for feminists. However, key concepts, such as ideology and false consciousness with Marxist origins are widely used in feminism. The empirical studies of women in employment (e.g. Cavendish, 1982; Cockburn, 1983) used Marxist ideas to address issues that both Marx himself and contemporary feminists could recognise. From 1968 until the fall of the Berlin Wall in 1989 many Marxist feminists worked with a dual system approach, in which Marxist theories were used to analyses the means of production, but other sources were used to theorise sexuality. Michèle Barrett (1988) is a leading exponent of such an approach. Heidi Hartmann (1979, 1981) wrestled with what she called 'the unhappy marriage' of feminism and Marxism. Several feminist sociologists researched and challenged the ways in which Marxist ideas had been implemented in state socialist countries such as the USSR, and Czechoslovakia (e.g. Heitlinger, 1979; Scott, 1974), in the process critiquing Marx himself.

Weber

Feminist sociology owes a debt to Weber, but one which is rarely acknowledged. Weber brought into sociology the concept of patriarchy, or to be more precise, patriarchal authority. He differentiated three types of authority (charismatic, bureaucratic and patriarchal), as part of his attempt to theorise nineteenth-century European societies. Feminists after 1968, especially separatist radical feminists have not always located the Weberian roots of the term, but have found it a powerful label for male domination. The most sociologically sophisticated deployment of the term is Sylvia Walby's (1997) six structures of patriarchy. Walby conceptualises 'a system of patriarchy' (ibid.: 5) as 'a system of social structures and practices in which men dominate,

100

oppress and exploit women'. She separates six structures which are, in effect six spheres of social life, or six dimensions of the social world. These are: (1) household production; (2) paid work; (3) the state; (4) violence; (5) sexuality; and (6) cultural institutions. Walby finds male domination in all of these spheres or dimensions. Her model allows for a variety of gender regimes, because the six spheres or dimensions can be articulated in different ways. The six spheres articulate in different ways for women of different ages, social classes, sexualities, ethnicities, religions and regions of the country. This model of patriarchy also allows the sociologist to engage with spatial issues, and those of time (Adam, 1996). Walby is clearly arguing against an orthodox Marxist view when she states that 'In the UK gender shapes class as much as class shapes gender' (1997: 13). Walby does not explicitly locate here ideas of patriarchy *vis-à-vis* Weber: indeed, in Walby (1997) she does not cite or index him at all, but her nuanced development of the concept of patriarchy is, in fact, a sophisticated use of the Weberian tradition.

Durkheim

The majority of feminist sociologists, unlike feminist anthropologists, have been unable to draw analytic concepts from Durkheim as they have from Marx and Weber. Liberal sociologists have de facto used the approach to official statistics that Durkheim pioneered, but there are no feminists harnessing *anomie* or *conscious collective* as there are feminists using ideology or patriarchy. This is because Anglophone sociology has inherited the wrong Durkheim, as I demonstrate later in the chapter.

Freud

Freud is not generally regarded as a founding father of sociology, although he does appear in some texts. Freud, whose ideas became widely known in intellectual circles after the First World War, was not a sociologist, but his ideas have been regarded as seminal by many male sociologists since 1920. Freud's theories are particularly problematic for feminist sociologists. The relationship between Freud's own ideas, the popularisation of those ideas in the Anglophone world after 1918, their effects on First Wave feminism, the rise and fall of Freudian ideas among sociologists, and the response from feminists, all need some unpicking here. The best explanation of the devastating impact that Freudian ideas had on the First Wave feminists can be found in Vicinus (1985). The impact was recognised at the time by Second Wave feminists such as Winifred Holtby (1936) and Josephine Tey (1946).

Although Freud was never a sociologist, his ideas, because they decentred God and centred the socialisation of the individual, were as revolutionary for the intelligentsia as Darwin's and Einstein's. When the work done in nineteenth-century Vienna reached the Anglophone world, it had two powerful thrusts forcing it into acceptability. The First World War had left many men mentally damaged, and Freud's therapeutic ideas offered some way to help them. This is vividly portrayed in Pat Barker's trilogy (1993, 1994, 1995). The need for some help for mentally ill officers is clear in contemporary anti-intellectual novels such as John Buchan's *Mr Standfast* (1919) which opens with Richard Hannay visiting an invalid colleague, Blaikie, who is paralysed by shell shock, and stresses that he is not getting any effective treatment. Second, Freudian ideas were opaque, foreign, mysterious, glamorous, and because of their sexual content, 'modern'. For young intellectuals, they were splendid because they were shocking. For men, they had a wonderful bonus: they destroyed the 'old' morality, the ideology that women were morally superior beings whose mission was to raise men to their level. In Freudian theory, as it was understood, women were sexual beings too, and repressing that, through celibacy, or expressing it in Boston marriages, was a form of illness or deviancy. This view of the doyens of First Wave feminism is clear in Clemence Dane's (1917) novel *Regiment of Women* and in the sexist writings of Meyrick Booth (1919, 1927). By advocating Freudianism, men could force women back into a heterosexual world or damn them as 'inverts' or 'repressed' and be thoroughly modern and scientific. The majority of the population never adopted a Freudian viewpoint, of course, but it was among the intelligentsia that First Wave feminism lost its intellectual support (see Delamont, 2003, for an elaboration of this argument).

Freudian ideas were part of the backdrop of American universities in the 1950s, and were blended with Parsonian sociology of gender. This was why Friedan (1963) devoted so much space to an attack on Freud. The sociology of the Frankfurt School (Jay, 1973) was imbued with Freudian ideas, and this gave Freud a new place in sociology after 1968 when that humanistic neo-Marxism became fashionable. Thus in the 1970s most Third Wave feminists were expressing scepticism about Freud, while he was re-appearing in sociology. A minority of feminists set out to reinterpret the Freudian legacy, noticeably Juliet Mitchell (1975) who retrained as an analyst, Sayers (1991) who revitalised the work of four of Freud's female disciples, (Anna Freud, Melanie Klein, Karen Horney and Helene Deutsch) and Nancy Chodorow (1978, 1987) whose work is routinely cited by feminists. The relationship between psycho-analytic ideas and feminism also produced controversy when Lacan and Irigaray came to Anglophone notice: Lacan's Freud was radically different from Parsons's Freud or the Frankfurt School's

102

Freud, but because Lacan had been Althusser's analyst and because the most energetically self-publicising school of French feminists were the Psych-Po group (Psychoanalysis and Politics), a Gallic Freud was forced onto the feminist agenda. In general, feminist sociologists have remained unenthusiastic about Freud as a sociological founding father. As Joan Acker puts it: 'intense encounters with Freud left me highly suspicious of the value of a psychoanalytic perspective' (1997: 30).

American fathers

Schwendinger and Schwendinger (1971, 1974) examined the thinking of early professors of sociology in the USA, and criticised them for their supine attitude to capitalism and for their sexism. Bernard and Bernard (1943) and Coser (1978) provide accounts of the pioneers of sociology in America. Many of the men who established the discipline: Albion Small, George Vincent, William Sumner, Lester Ward, and Edward Ross, for example, are unknown in Britain and do not figure in current American sociology. Thorstein Veblen (1857–1919) is still read, as are Charles Horton Cooley, and the Chicago giants, Mead, Thomas and Park. However, apart from the Schwendinger and Schwendinger revisionist critique, the former group here not been subjected to contemporary feminist re-appraisals. Veblen has not become redefined by feminism as a legendary sexist or misogynist: perhaps he is due for a feminist analysis. The only historically significant American founding fathers still taught, analysed and reanalysed are those associated with symbolic interactionism and Chicago, whose work has already figured at some length in this book.

103

In the USA, a specifically American sociology grew up in Chicago from 1892 onwards, which was discussed in detail in Chapter 5. This American sociology was the first to include women as lecturers, researchers, members of learned societies, and referees of journal articles. Symbolic interactionism, with its intellectual roots in G.H. Mead and W.I. Thomas, is the theoretical school which developed in Chicago, as one strand of Chicago sociology. The women of the Chicago School were not symbolic interactionists, and had little interest in theory at all. So although American sociology produced the first women sociologists, and the first feminist sociologists, there was no feminist symbolic interactionism. Deegan (1988) contrasts W.I. Thomas, a supporter of women's suffrage, with male contemporaries who opposed the goals of First Wave feminists, and has edited a collection on women and interactionism (Deegan and Hill, 1987). This collection has one historic paper, by Jessie Taft (1987) extracted from her 1913 thesis. She was a student of Mead and Thomas. Even Deegan has not claimed that interactionism had women theorists in the pre-1918 years.

Parsons and Merton

In the period from 1930 onwards two Americans are regularly pre-sented as founding fathers to today's students: Robert Merton and Talcott Parsons. These two American men dominated sociology in the era of Second Wave feminism (1930–68). One of them, Talcott Parsons, became a symbol to feminists of all that was pernicious about malestream sociology, while Robert Merton has been left unattacked. Talcott Parsons (1902–79) wrote extensively on theoretical issues, offering American sociology his version of the ideas of Weber and Durkheim. He wrote about age and sex in the social structure of the USA, and it is his vision of the proper roles of men and women in the economy and the family which has been the symbol for feminists of everything that was wrong with sociology between 1930 and 1970. Parsonian ideas were reproduced in textbooks, and taught widely beyond sociology. The argument was that the stability of American democracy depended on men striving in the world of work, while women ran homes in which men could discharge their pent-up emo-tions. These ideas can be traced through Catherine Beecher back to de Tocqueville (Sklar, 1973) although Parsons does not cite Beecher.

104

This sociology was under attack from Gouldner (1971) as theoreti-cally and empirically sterile when the Third Wave feminism blossomed. For feminists, the stultifying sexism of Parsonian theory was laid bare by Friedan (1963). Clearly, neither Marxist feminist sociologists, nor radical feminist sociologists could look to Parsons for inspiration. Miriam Johnson (1989) a liberal feminist, is the only feminist sociolo-gist who identifies as a Parsonian. Parsons's ideas are simply not flexi-ble enough to allow most feminists to see them as stimulating. It is also striking that not one of the 42 women sociologists whose autobio-graphical essays have been published (see Chapter 7 for details) remem-bers him with warmth either as a theorist or as a person. Indeed, Mary Haywood Metz recalled how when she was a student in the 1960s: 'my male peers at Harvard and Berkeley expected a "real" woman to be on her way to becoming a good Parsonian wife-mother' (1994: 221). Holmstrom was rejected for graduate study at Harvard by Parsons: 'I arrived at Emerson Hall in ivy-covered Harvard Yard for my interview with Talcott Parsons. He made it clear that *married* women were not welcome – not a surprise for anyone who knew his position' (1995: 263).

The theories of Parsons were taught to many of the feminists whose autobiographies have been analysed. The reminiscences of 42 women only mention meeting him or being taught by him three times, but five of them describe being taught his theories. Cavan (1994: 62) for example describes how Garfinkel taught her 'the prodigious writings of Talcott

Parsons'. However, the baleful influence of the work is part of what these women are delighted to have challenged.

In contrast to Parsons, with whom he is sometimes associated, Robert Merton (born 1910) used the ideas of Weber to explore American history, and then developed a sociology of science. He has not been pilloried by feminists at all. He is absent from the reminiscences of the 42 women sociologists analysed perhaps because there is no volume focused on women who did PhDs at Columbia where he was based. Four women recall being taught his ideas, and one (Laslett) that he attended her oral. There are distinguished women sociologists who were trained by Merton, especially Harriet Zuckerman (Zuckerman et al., 1991) and Cynthia Epstein (1970), and they have drawn feminist inspirations from his ideas.

BRINGING IN OTHER FATHERS

There has been a trend since 1968 to re-engage with founding fathers who did address gender issues, but had been marginalised in the 'official' histories of the discipline compared to their contemporaries. The rediscovery of writings about gender by the big names, and the calls to put other founding fathers forward as important because they did address gender, are best exemplified by the attention paid to Engels (e.g. Delamont, 1972, 1996b). Engels has been the focus of far more scholarship since the rise of feminist sociology than he received between 1950 and 1970. Marxist feminists have been particularly active in their re-examinations of Engels's writings. Feminist attention to Engels began in the late 1960s, because he wrote *The Origins of the Family, Private Property and the State*. This book, though absolutely suffused with nineteenth-century ideas about the evolutionary development of human societies including family forms, did address sex, gender and the reproduction of labour power. Quotes from *Origins* were an obligatory part of the manifestos of all the Marxist women's liberation groups, and in the early academic feminism (e.g. Juliet Mitchell, 1966). Because Engels recognised that the Victorian bourgeois family was not the acme of an evolutionary process, but merely a transitory form, his ideas were useful for feminists arguing for social change. Sayers et al. (1987) is a collection of contemporary feminist essays on Engels.

So far, the chapter has presented a relatively non-contentious history of sociology, complicated only by interweaving some discussion of feminism. In Appendix 1 the focus turns to how that history is presented in the texts used to teach it to current students. Here the feminist voice becomes more intrusive into the grand narrative. So far, this

105

chapter has been a calm deep sea. In the next section the Gorgona rises.

The Gorgona is a giant mermaid, a sister of Alexander the Great. She appears beside a boat, grabs the gunwale, and asks if her brother, King Alexander, lives. Woe betide the sailor who tells her Alexander is dead. Wise mariners answer 'He lives and reigns: *zei kai vasileri!*' or 'He lives, he reigns, he rules the world'. If she hears this, the Gorgona takes you swiftly to your next port of call. If the Gorgona is told Alexander is dead, she either hits the ship with her fist and sends it to the seabed, or she starts to chant *mirologhia* (the mourning laments, the songs of fate). The *mirologhia* of mermaids become powerful typhoons, she tears out her hair which becomes bolts of lightning, and her sobs cause great waves to batter the ship (Stewart, 1990; Storace, 1996). In modern Greek folklore, the Gorgona is condemned to swim the seas for all eternity because she spilt the water that would have given Alexander eternal life. She was cursed to live for ever as half a fish and half a woman. Fancifully, in the next part of the chapter, the Gorgona of feminist sociology has risen and grasped the gunwale of the theory boat. She is asking whether theory is a calm sea: that is an area of male consensus about dead white men: or is it a contested arena where feminist critics have to produce a typhoon?

HARNESSING THE FATHERS

In the earlier section on feminist responses to the major figures in the classic grand narrative of sociology I used women whose work is recognisable to all but the most blinkered malestream sociologists. In this part of the chapter the focus is on feminist developments from the founding fathers which deviate further from malestream sociology, and might provoke disquiet among the malestream disciples. Weiler (2001) is a collection of papers in which women, most of them self-identified as feminists, reflect upon how they have used various theorists but none is a foundational sociologist. In this section, feminist use of Marx, Weber and Durkheim is explored. Dorothy Smith's advanced work on Marx, Witz's (1992) development from Weber and feminist work by Ardener, Douglas and myself drawing on Durkheim, are all explained.

Marx

There are several feminists whose work could be discussed here, but the most interesting is Dorothy Smith. In her early work she combined a Marxist analysis of macro-structures with an ethnomethodological take on micro-processes to create an innovative feminist sociology

(Smith, 1972, 1973). Her later work is much less influenced by any male theorists, as she points out (Smith, 2000). I have focused on Smith's early work here, not to categorise her as a Marxist now, but to show how one feminist sociologist was developing a novel and thought-provoking sociology grounded in or on Marx but not recognisable to most 'Marxists' at the time.

Dorothy Smith was publishing in the early 1970s, but her work did not become widely known outwith Canada until later in the decade. Her paper 'Women, the family and corporate capitalism' was delivered to the Canadian Anthropological and Sociological Association in 1972, published in 1973 (Smith, 1973; Stephenson, 1973) but not picked up in the USA or Europe until 1977 (Nelson and Olesen, 1977) when it was republished (Smith, 1977). Her 'An analysis of ideological structures and how women are excluded' (Smith, 1975) was published in a Canadian journal and therefore many of us missed it through ethnocentric reading habits. 'A sociology for women' (Smith, 1979) was in an edited collection (Sherman and Beck, 1979) that went out of print before its merits were widely recognised. Only with her first book (Smith, 1987) and her paper in an American collection (Smith, 1989; Wallace, 1989) did Smith's work become accessible outwith Canada, and by 1989 she had moved beyond the innovative uses of Marxism in the work of 17 years before into a more autonomous and free-standing feminist sociology without the deference to founding fathers. Her anger with Hekman (Smith, 2000) is partly due to Hekman's (2000) failure to provide an accurate chronology of Smith's work, or recognise its paradigm shift from Marxism and ethnomethodology to a distinctive feminist position.

107

While she has moved on theoretically, the early work illustrates the shape-shifting use of Marx in the feminist sociology of the 1970s. As Stephenson wrote at the time: 'Smith has extended Marx's historically constrained explanation of the nature of oppression. She incorporates the enduring facets of his analysis, brings them up to date, and expands them by dealing with ... oppression as it is experienced by women' (1977a: 16).

Smith starts her paper by arguing that whereas Marx and Engels had predicted that the 'public' or social sphere would expand, submerging the Victorian 'private' sphere, in late-twentieth-century corporate capitalism, the public/private divide was stronger than ever (although it took rather different forms). Marx and Engels had expected that as the 'public' sphere extended itself, the domestic arena, and with that the private arena, the personal servitude of women within it, would vanish. The individualised domestic labour and care of children would become public matters. Smith argued that this had not happened, and that the American and Canadian sociology of the family had failed to recognise the ways in which the economic base (corporate capitalism) determined the familial superstructure. The *bourgeois* family was, Smith noted, grounded upon a corporate capitalist economic system.

Smith then explored how the rise of corporate capitalism had created the alienation of the bourgeoisie. In the nineteenth century the workers were alienated, while the bourgeoisie were not; in the late twentieth century, the bourgeoisie were also alienated labour. She wrote: 'Both worker and manager are expropriated by the corporate enterprise ... But in the case of the manager ... his ethical being, his motives, his strategies of thought and communication – it is those that are appropriated. It is an alienation of the person, not of the product' (1977: 25–6).

This alienation of the managerial cadre, who are overwhelmingly men, transforms the working conditions of women. Smith contrasted the ways in which family life had developed under corporate capitalism in working-class and middle-class families. Much of the paper focuses on the ways in which the middle-class wife and mother has been alienated, by changes in the economic base, which make her work a service to the system of corporate capitalism, rather than to an individual man. She summarises this: 'In appropriating the home by legislating its merit and concrete order, the corporate enterprise establishes women as its 'executives', analogous to their husbands' positions as managers. Nothing is left to women but the execution of an order whose definition is not hers' (ibid.: 37).

There are, of course, parallels here with the popular attack on suburban bourgeois households as damaging to women and to America in Friedan (1963). At the time of its success, Friedan's left-wing and activist credentials were not known, and her best-seller does not use the analytic tools of Marxism explicitly. Smith's early work was a reworking of Marxist concepts to draw conclusions about women (or rather *married mothers*) which went far beyond any other feminist theory.

Smith herself did not pursue the creation of a feminist neo-Marxism. Rather, she was simultaneously exploring ethnomethodology especially in her paper 'K is mentally ill' (Smith, 1978) and her work on the social construction of psychiatry (Smith and David, 1975). Melding the Marxist concepts of alienation, and ideology, with the insights from the ethnomethodology and the critical, feminist engagement with psychiatry, Smith produced the manifesto of 'A sociology for women' (1979), with the central tenet that such a sociology needs to treat 'the everyday world as problematic'. This phrase became the title of her first book (1987), and opens up an agenda not relevant here.

108

Weber

The example chosen to illustrate the feminist use of Weber is Anne Witz (1992). Witz took the idea of patriarchy onwards from Walby (1990) and developed the neo-Weberian concept of closure to explore the history of gender in medicine, midwifery, nursing and radiography between the 1850s and 1930s. Witz does also draw on Marxist ideas, but her use of neo-Weberian concepts is particularly innovative. Crompton (1987) had previously worked with neo-Weberian ideas, in her studies of pharmacy in France and Britain (Crompton and Sanderson, 1989), and she subsequently focused on neo-Weberian and neo-Marxist ideas about professions and the class structure (Crompton, 2000).

Witz's work is part of a large literature on the history and sociology of the professions, going back to the 1920s. There were two quite distinct traditions, one functionalist (its experiments are sometimes called trait theorists) and the other symbolic interactionist. In the early 1970s Terence Johnson (1972) changed the paradigm, followed by the work of Atkinson (Atkinson, 1983; Atkinson et al., 1977). None of the work up to 1980 had treated sex segregation, or sex stratification in the professions seriously, rather, it was a topic in which stereotypes were repeated with intellectual laziness (see Atkinson and Delamont, 1990). Witz does not discuss Atkinson, or any of the work done in the interactionist tradition before or after Atkinson. She focuses instead upon the growth of neo-Weberian approaches to professions after the work of Johnson.

Witz (1992) drew on the neo-Weberian, Parkin (1979) who had defined professionalism as a strategy of exclusionary closure, in which an occupation aims to limit the number of entrants, and control the entry standards, so that the existing members can earn more, increase their social status, and gain power. However, as Witz (1992) points out, neither Johnson nor Parkin paid serious attention to the way gender figured inside, or at the boundaries of professions. Crompton (1987) had argued that neo-Weberian approaches to closure were more useful when studying gender issues than neo-Marxist ones. Witz (1992: 43) builds on this, focusing on closure, rather than following Crompton's interest in class formation.

Witz (1992: 44) follows Parkin in separating four distinct strategies of closure that an occupation or profession can use. A dominant social or occupational group engages in demarcationary and/or exclusionary strategies. Subordinate social or occupational groups engage in inclusionary and dual closure strategies. So surgeons engage in demarcationary and/or exclusionary strategies and occupational therapists in dual closure and inclusionary ones. Exclusionary strategies close occupations

109

to outsiders, creating a monopoly of skills and knowledge for the insiders. In Britain before 1920 many 'traditional' professions such as law and accountancy kept women out until a new law forced them to stop that exclusionary strategy. Demarcationary strategies involve a superior group monitoring and regulating the work and knowledge of other subordinate occupations in the division of labour. Witz (1992: 48) shows how the relations between the largely male medical profession and the mainly female occupations of nursing, midwifery, radiography, physiotherapy and occupational therapy, in the period from 1900 to 1950 demonstrate demarcationary and exclusionary strategies.

Inclusionary strategies are used by subordinate groups who seek to move upwards into the sphere of a superior group, for example, women in the nineteenth century campaigning to get into medicine, or in the late twentieth century to get ordained as ministers in the Anglican Church. Dual closure strategies are used by subordinate groups who simultaneously resist being excluded by those above and fiercely exclude those below. Witz was especially interested in gendered strategies of dual closure, which are complex and varied. In her discussion of how dual closure strategies are gendered, Witz develops a specifically feminist use of Weber, which goes beyond the Weber used by many male sociologists.

110

Witz and Crompton are feminist neo-Weberians. They have moved a considerable distance away from the gospel of Weberian sociology as it is usually presented in malestream sociology. That orthodox Weber is not seen as a sound basis for feminism. There are no feminists proudly (re)claiming the same Weber as their inspiration as Rex, Albrow and Collins do (though Bologh, 1990 makes a brave attempt). Some feminist revisionists have argued that Weber's mother, Helene, and wife Marianne were sociologists of importance (Lengermann and Niebrugge-Brantley, 1998) but male Weber scholars have ignored them. Witz and Crompton are feminists who have developed Weber's ideas, not slavish adherents of the original.

Durkheim

There are two distinct Durkheimian traditions in contemporary social science, and so it is important to clarify which Durkheim is under discussion before exploring modern feminist responses to his work. There is the mainstream sociological Durkheim, promulgated by Parsons, who is an empiricist, a positivist and a conservative. Then there is the Gallic Durkheim of anthropology, whose legacy through Mauss and Van Gennep and Lévi-Strauss gives us structuralism. That is a powerful tool for contemporary feminist thinking. There is little or nothing for feminists in the classic sociological Durkheim, fed into Anglophone

sociology via Parsons. That Durkheim appears to be a biological deter-
minist, an evolutionary thinker who sees the division of labour by sex
to be a mark of civilisation. The *other* Durkheim, however, is a rich
source of feminist analyses.

In France the legacy of Durkheim was carried forward by Mauss
and Van Gennep, in a version of structuralism that led through Lévi-
Strauss to Bourdieu today. This French tradition is much more influential in Britain in anthropology than in sociology, with the exception of
Basil Bernstein's work (Atkinson, 1985, 1995). Only those sociological
feminists who have adopted Bernstein (Arnot, 2001) could be seen as
heiresses of Durkheim in British sociology.

It may seem odd, even perverse, to offer a structuralist perspective,
rather than a poststructuralist or postmodern one. I make no apology
for it here. Traditional structuralism offers enormous insight, is a powerful analytic tool for feminist sociology, and should be much more
widely taught to, understood by and used by feminist sociologists than
it has been.

One of the leading exponents of the Gallic Durkheim in structuralist anthropology is Mary Douglas, a woman theorist. She has not written explicitly as a feminist, nor commented on feminism, nor focused
her research on gender or women. Douglas may or may not be a feminist: she has not published explicitly feminist work. She is, indubitably,
a Durkeimian, who has taken the Gallic Durkheim and built an elaborate theoretical framework (group and grid) that provides ways of
exploring feminist themes.

In her first general theoretical work, *Purity and Danger* (1966)
Douglas showed how dirt is 'matter out of place', 'disorder'. As we
organise our environment we try to eliminate dirt and disorder, both
physical and symbolic. We classify as dirt or disorder, as pollution, as
outrages against moral or religious order, everything which is out of
place. So, for example, shoes are not inherently polluting, but in Britain
we do not place them on a table unless we have redefined it as a work
space to clean them. We call the placing of shoes on the table unlucky
or unhygienic. Cigarette ash is tolerated in an ash tray, but revolting
and repulsive suspended in the jellied consommé we serve for dinner.
Nail varnish is pretty or striking on our nails, but a stain, needing stain
removal, on our best skirt. As with physical pollutions, so too with
moral ones. A relatively harmless fornication becomes a serious sin,
and an illegal act, if the sexual partners are siblings. A fight becomes a
potential parricide if the combatants are actually father and son. It is
not the act itself which has absolute value, but the social classification
of it. Much of Douglas's (1966) book was concerned with exploring
why ambiguous and anomalous things are so disturbing for many cultures, many individuals, many systems. The solutions to the problems

111

posed by 'anomalous beasts' and 'fearsome monsters' occupy much of the monograph. She outlined five solutions to the problems posed by anomalies (firm categorisation, physical control, avoidance, pollution beliefs, celebration in art). Douglas was herself interested in pollution beliefs: (1) about bodily emissions and invasions; (2) reinforcing social boundaries; and (3) arising from conflicting aims in a culture.

When Douglas moved on she developed two dimensions, called group and grid, to help us understand different types of cultures, societies or organisation (Douglas, 1970). Group is about membership. Strong groupings are hard to enter, are exclusive, and demand high commitment and loyalty. In the UK the Royal College of Surgeons is located at the strong end of the group continuum, whereas the AA is at the weak end of the group continuum. Grid refers to the degree of social control or regulation exercised over members or participants: so prisoners are subjected to strong grid, while new age travellers are *attempting* to live in a weak grid. In her later work on group and grid she developed a typology of organisations or cultures, where each could be high or low, giving four types (a. strong group weak grid; b. strong group strong grid; c. weak group weak grid; and d. weak group and strong grid). In each of these the pollution beliefs are different, and their strength/importance also varies. In cultures where grid and group are both weak, there is little concern with pollution, where both are strong, there are fiercely held and enforced pollution beliefs, both at the boundaries and protecting the hierarchies. The explanatory power of the group/grid mapping for feminist analyses is explored at length in Delamont (1989b), and applied to the myths about the Chicago School in Delamont (1992a).

In the same tradition is Shirley Ardener, an anthropologist who has published feminist work (1985) and edited the work of others on feminist themes (1975, 1978, 1981; Callan and Ardener; 1984; Dube et al., 1986; Macdonald et al., 1987). Unlike Douglas, Ardener is little known in sociology but her work has enormous analytic power.

Shirley Ardener (1975) is also a Durkheimian, and developed a theory about the ways in which societies, cultures or organisations will have dominant and muted groups. The models of the society, culture or organisation held by the dominant group will have more coercive power than the models held by subordinate, or muted groups. Muted groups have to use the dominant group's model to survive, because it has the power of the dominant group. In Delamont (1989b) I used this idea to explore male and female models of adolescent sexual behaviour. Later work by Holland et al. (1988), *The Male in the Head*, uses the same idea, though without citing Shirley Ardener at all.

Alongside Douglas and Ardener the structuralist Durkheimian tradition is found in Bernstein and in Bourdieu, both of whom wrote thought provokingly on women. Through 25 years of feminist scholarship I have used this Durkheimian tradition to analyse a range of phenomena, from wedding meals (Delamont, 1983, 1994), through life on a gynaecology ward (1987b), the gender stereotypes in pupils' urban legends about secondary school (1991), the myths of the Chicago School (1992a), the role of sociology of education in British sociology (2000a) and most consistently, the ways in which the feminist pioneers of women's education constructed their 'forgotten safeguards' against the dangers both they and their critics saw threatening the health, reputations and marriage prospects of the pupils and teachers (Delamont, 1978a, 1978b, 1989b, 1993).

FUTURE FOUNDING FATHERS?

In this last section I have focused on three male theorists who will, I hope, be added to the grand narrative, whose work and views on women are very different from their predecessors. Of course, such predictions are hazardous, and some feminists have responded with very negative comments to the work of distinguished sociologists. Deegan and Hill, for example, criticise Goffman for writing in an entertaining way: 'Goffman plays with words. The temptation to be humorous and clever weakens the writings of Goffman' (1987: 15). Deegan and Hill thus explain why they have not included anything by Goffman in an edited volume on women and symbolic interactionism. Such failure to recognise genius weakens feminist sociology.

I have dealt in this section with three future founding fathers, Bernstein, Bourdieu and Beck. Bernstein's contribution to building a feminist sociology is relatively undeveloped but is explored in Arnot (2001) and Delamont (1995). The central way in which Bernstein's sociology has feminist potential is his emphasis on the different roles of women in the old and new middle class, and on how the labour market experiences of women impact upon the educational careers of their children. As the sociological reputation of Bernstein rises in the years after his death, its feminist potential will be increasingly recognised.

France and Germany produced two of the leading contemporary sociologists. Pierre Bourdieu (1930–2002) and Ulrich Beck. Leading figures from two different schools of thought – Bourdieu as a structuralist and Beck as a sociologist of reflexive modernity – they epitomise change and continuity in the orthodox history. They can be seen as a continuation of the classic theories of Marx, Weber and Durkheim and, in their refusal to perpetuate lazy stereotypes of women, as a radical break from that 175-year history. They are representative of a change in both malestream sociology and in feminist sociology's relationship to it. These two, are, of course, related: if malestream sociology is changing, then feminist sociologists will find they can use it. Both Bourdieu and Beck have written books in which the role, status and feelings of women are considered with some serious thought given to feminist perspectives.

Bourdieu is both an anthropologist and a sociologist. His ideas are currently fashionable in cultural studies and sociology of culture, having been important in the sociology of education since 1970. In *Masculine Domination* (published in French in 1998 and in English in 2001) he applies the structuralist framework to the gender regime of contemporary France, starting by challenging its familiarity by revisiting his anthropological work on the Berber (Kabyle) of Algeria.

Beck became well known in the Anglophone world after his works were published by Polity – and his theories of risk society and reflexive modernity were publicised by his collaborations with Giddens, Lash, Urry and Adam. In *The Normal Chaos of Love* (Beck and Beck-Gernsheim, 1995) published in German in 1990. Beck and Beck-Gernsheim seriously address the gender regime of (West) Germany, raising questions that are only 'askable' because of the rise of feminist sociology.

114

CONCLUSION

The relations between feminist sociology and the malestream has frequently been stormy like the giant mermaid rocking the boat and calling up the tempest. At best, there is an ambivalence about grounding feminist sociology in ideas originally produced by men whose theoretical and personal views on women are, by contemporary standards, unsound.

seven

simply invisible

feminist sociology and the malestream

T his chapter takes its title from Amanda Cross (1981: 47) and is drawn out of a comment made by her heroine Kate Fransler about her lack of impact on and in Harvard: 'Because as a woman ... she was simply invisible.' This chapter faces, Janus-like, in two directions. There are two possible responses feminist sociologists might wish for from the malestream. Feminist sociology could aim to become mainstreamed, so that sociology changed fundamentally and became non-sexist. Alternatively, feminist sociology could aim to be a separate, distinct territory within sociology. The latter aim would demand nothing from malestream sociology except benign neglect or tolerance. Just as a sociologist of medicine is neutral about political sociology or demography, so too non-feminists should be neutral about feminism. This is an improbably utopian vision, because different subfields are in fierce competition for funds, posts, prestige, students, and publications, and there are elaborate hierarchies of prejudice and esteem. Just as theory ranks above all empirical areas except stratification (perhaps), and within the empirical areas science ranks much higher than sport, education or rural life, so too feminist perspectives would have to fit somewhere in an hierarchical system.

As well as these two models for feminist sociology inside the discipline, there is a third future, outwith the discipline. The third model would be for feminist sociology to migrate from sociology to women's studies, where it would be one of the many disciplines. This last vision is probably the easiest to imagine. Just as there are researchers from a variety of social sciences in business schools, or education departments, so too in departments of women's studies or gender studies, sociology would be one discipline among others. Malestream sociology would be largely irrelevant, and making an impact on malestream sociology would be a low priority. Feminist sociology would be indifferent to malestream sociology as ethnomethodologists are indifferent to mainstream sociology.

For the purposes of this chapter that last model is irrelevant. Here the focus is on how far feminist perspectives have been mainstreamed or have become a distinct territory within sociology. If feminist perspectives were to be mainstreamed, then men would have to have read about them, taken them seriously, and treated them as rational contributions to rational debates. This is an unlikely scenario because: 'Men ... are for the most part not competent readers, if readers at all, of feminist discourse' (Smith, 1999: 205). Mostly, men are not 'readers at all'. There is a long history of men not reading feminist discourse.

When Clifford and Marcus (1986) produced an edited collection (*Writing Culture*) which opened up to widespread debate the problematic nature of textural representation in anthropology, there was only one woman contributor, Mary Pratt (1986), a literary critic and none of the scholars whose texts were analysed was a woman either. Justifying this, Clifford stated that women were excluded because their writing was not both feminist and textually innovative. As Behar summarised his argument: 'To be a woman writing culture became a contradiction in terms: women who write experimentally are not feminist enough, while women who write as feminists write in ignorance of the textual theory that underpins their own texts' (1995: 5).

Clifford could only have believed what he said if he had not read Zora Neale Hurston (1935, 1938) from an earlier era: he had certainly not been a competent reader of her experimental texts (see Hernandez, 1995). Such non-reading has been a very frequent occurrence throughout the 30 years of feminist sociology. Getting work published is the first hurdle, getting it read is harder. For example in 1989 Ruth Wallace could get the proceedings of a conference on Feminism and Sociological Theory, sponsored by the Theory Section of the ASA published in a series *Key Issues in Sociological Theory*, edited by Jeffrey Alexander and Jonathan Turner. This is about as high status a publication as any ASA theorist could have, but it was not cited by Collins (1994a, 1994b) five years later, or by Maines (2000).

It is because of such non-readings, and incompetent readings that the fully integrated model is, as far as I am concerned, hard to imagine. However, that imagining treats the discipline as one unitary whole, which, of course it is not. An exploration of the impact feminist perspectives have had since 1968 on sociology reveals that there is not one answer but many. As Chapter 3 showed, the high status area of stratification, class and social mobility has been transformed since 1980 by feminist perspectives. A whole new topic, women's mobility, opened up. Fierce debates raged about how stratification and class were to be studied in late modernity (Savage, 2000). However, the new ideas are largely developing in parallel to the traditional debates between the established male figures, who continue their eternal struggle, like King

Kong versus Godzilla, without any serious intellectual engagement in the feminist work (Crompton and Scott, 2000). Feminist perspectives are much more mainstream in the sociologies of health and illness, and education, than they are in sociology of science, in theory, or in discussions of globalisation. The chapter opens with an analysis of one sphere in which feminist perspectives have made no impact at all, and then contrasts it with two spheres where they have been mainstreamed. The sphere which shows no impact is that of autobiographical reminiscences by the discipline's American silverbacks. A silverback is a powerful, old, male gorilla, whose back fur has gone silver: it is a term used by academic feminists to describe the powerful senior figures in their disciplines. After an analysis of the 'silverback narratives' and a brief discussion of some men who are not silverbacks, the chapter turns to the sociologies of education and medicine, where feminist ideas are much more integrated.

THE SILVERBACK NARRATIVES

This section shows how little impact all the work of all the feminist sociologists has had. It is to be contrasted with the following section, in which work by some very different men, who have treated feminist sociology with respect, is explored. The silverback narrative section begins with my personal response to the publication of an interview conducted by a Belgian sociologist, with Erving Goffman. My responses to that interview produced the motivation for the analysis.

the Goffman interview

In 1980 Jef Verhoeven conducted a long interview with Goffman in his house, as part of a series of such interviews with leading symbolic interactionists in the USA. Goffman died in 1982, during his term as President of the ASA. In 1992 Verhoeven published the text of their conversation edited to remove some 'infelicities'. The transcript runs to 29 pages, most of which are Goffman talking about his mentors, the ideas that influenced him, his contemporaries, and his approach to sociology. Many scholars are mentioned during the interview. Goffman claimed as positive intellectual influences (in alphabetical order): Gregory Bateson, Herbert Blumer, Ernest Burgess, Kenneth Burke, C.H. Cooley, John Dewey, Emile Durkheim, Everett Hughes, G.H. Mead, W. Ogburn, Robert Park, A.R. Radcliffe-Brown, A. Schutz, G. Simmel, Lloyd Warner, Max Weber and Louis Wirth. He also mentioned the importance of Parsons as a translator of Durkheim and Weber, and the negative value he placed on W.I. Thomas and Florian

Znaniecki. It is not surprising that these are all men, for reasons discussed in Chapter 6, although a reading of Deegan (1988) or McDonald (1994) produces women who *could* have been in Goffman's list.

Goffman also provided a list of his contemporaries, sociologists and social psychologists, who could be seen as symbolic interactionists. This group included, again in alphabetical order: Howard Becker, Aaron Cicourel, Fred Davis, Nelson Foote, Elliot Freidson, Harold Garfinkel, Joseph Gusfield, Orin Klapp, Ed Lemert, Alfred Lindesmith, Bernard Meltzer, Tom Shibutani, Gregory Prentice Stone, Anselm Strauss and as an after-thought, Arlene Daniels. The latter is one of only two women mentioned in the 29 published pages. The other, referred to by Goffman only as 'The woman I lived with', was actually the anthropologist Elizabeth Bott. Within this list it is not entirely clear which men Goffman regarded as his friends, although at one point he says: 'They are all my best friends: I know them all very well and I've known them all very well for thirty years. They are the only persons I eat with at meetings' (Verhoeven, 1992: 335). What is abundantly clear is that Goffman is describing an *all-male world*. His friends and his intellectual colleagues from 1950 to 1980 are all men.

118

my response

When I read the published interview, I was immediately struck by Goffman's account of the Chicago Sociology Department as if it had been an all-male environment, and his all-male friendship circle. At the time of publication I made some notes for a commentary on the interview, but merely filed them. Then Gary Alan Fine (1995) published an edited collection, *A Second Chicago School?* focusing on Chicago Sociology in the years from 1946 to the early 1960s. This collection, covering the period when Goffman was in Chicago, and using him as an example of one of its stars, forced me to return to my notes on the Goffman interview. Fine himself, explaining his decision to write of a Second Chicago School, lists the stars produced there after 1946: 'Howard Becker, Fred Davis, Eliot Freidson, Erving Goffman, Joseph Gusfield, Robert Habenstein, Lewis Killian, Helena Lopata, Hans Mauksch, Gregory Stone, Ralph Turner' (1995: 1). The Fine volume revealed that Chicago's Sociology Department in Goffman's era was not an all-male place. There were women graduate students there, even though the faculty was all male. Fine's collection includes Mary Jo Deegan's (1995) thorough analysis of the graduate students at Chicago between 1945 and 1960, the era when Goffman and his generation were trained. Fine's book also included an Appendix listing all the PhD degrees awarded at Chicago between 1945 and 1965. Many of the men

Goffman listed appear; Klapp, Meltzer and Shibutani in 1948, Becker in 1951, Freidson in 1952, Goffman himself in 1953, Gusfield in 1945, Davis in 1958, Stone in 1959. Goffman's contemporaries included Virginia Olesen, Helen Hughes McGill, Helena Znaniecka Lopata, and Rue Bucher, but he does not mention any of them in the Verhoeven interview. Nor is he the only man for that period to have 'overlooked' his women contemporaries. The Preface to Fine by Gusfield (1995) is a memoir, which is very similar to Goffman's. Gusfield lists Strauss, Becker, Blumer, Hughes, Wirth, Burgess, Goffman, Shibutani, Lloyd Warner and Freidson. The only women he mentions are his wife, and Helena Lopata, but neither is discussed as if they were part of the academic cohort. Like Goffman, Gusfield ignores Helen McGill, Virginia Olesen and Rue Bucher. Goffman and Gusfield are not alone. Fine collected over 30 self-reports from men who were contemporaries of Goffman's. Deegan analysed them, and concludes that: 'in these male accounts, there are almost no references to the 15% of their cohort who were women' (1995: 325). Goffman's account to Verhoeven fits this pattern exactly. Helena Lopata (1995b: 382), while rejecting much of Deegan's argument, does accept that the women were retrospectively invisible to men: 'While on campus, the women felt integrated ... yet the men's memory of the cohort is predominantly male.'

Inspired by the sharp contrast between Goffman's interview, the 'facts' collected in the Appendix to Fine (1995), and by the emotions aroused by Deegan's contribution to the volume, I set out on the analysis presented below.

119

an excursion into autobiography

This excursion into the histories of American sociology, as recalled by male scholars in autobiographical narratives, reveals the absence of women. The data are published autobiographical accounts of American sociology in the 1930s, 1940s, 1950s and 1960s, by men, aimed at fellow sociologists. There are some parallel volumes of autobiography and oral history about American women sociologists, which are discussed in the next chapter. The 22 narratives have been taken from the following sources:

1 The autobiographical essays by male authors published in the *Annual Review of Sociology* from 1986 to 1996.
2 The autobiographies by men in Riley's (1988) edited collection *Sociological Lives*.
3 The autobiographies by men in Berger's (1990a) edited collection *Authors of Their Own Lives*.

Between 1986 and 1998 the *Annual Review of Sociology* (*ARS*) carried a brief personal statement by a distinguished elder statesperson dealing with some aspect of his or her career and sub-specialism. The Riley (1988) volume contains autobiographical essays by eight leading sociologists, of whom four are men: Lewis Coser, William Julius Wilson, Hubert Blalock, and William Sewell. The Berger (1990a) volume contains intellectual autobiographies by 20 sociologists. Five of the authors are women (Barbara Rosenblum, Alice Rossi, Jessie Bernard, Cynthia Fuchs Epstein, Pepper Schwartz). The chapters by 14 of the 15 male authors were analysed. These men are Wrong, Coleman, Gusfield, MacCannell, Greeley, Gans, Gary T. Marx, Cressey, Gagnon, Glazer, Bendix, Guenther Roth, Pierre van den Berghe and Berger himself. The Riesman chapter was not analysed because it duplicated that in the *ARS*. The Coser paper in Riley (1988) was not included because it duplicated his piece in the *Annual Review*, already analysed, while the Sewell chapter was included because it was autobiographical, unlike his 1989 piece in the *Annual Review*. The final list of autobiographical pieces analysed is shown in Table 1 of Appendix 2.

Of course these autobiographical essays cannot be read as simple, factual accounts. Social science readers of such texts must be as sceptical about them as we should be wary of the enthusiasm for the 'narrative' gathered as data from laypeople, however fashionable that collection currently is. As Atkinson and Silverman point out:

> The collection and celebration of personal narratives have become a major preoccupation for many contemporary sociologists and others in the social and cultural disciplines. While it is by no means universal, there is a widespread assumption that such data provide uniquely privileged means of access to the biographically grounded experiences and meaning of social actors. Contemporary sociologists and anthropologists who espouse qualitative research methods often put special faith in the interview as the prime means of data collection. For survey researchers, the interview can be a reliable research instrument giving valid data on facts and attitudes. For the qualitatively-minded researcher, the *open-ended* interview offers the opportunity for an authentic gaze into the soul of another, or even for a politically-correct dialogue where researcher and researched offer mutual understanding and support. The rhetoric of interviewing 'in-depth' repeatedly hints at such a collection of assumptions. Here we see a stubbornly persistent Romantic impulse in contemporary sociology: the elevation of the experiential as the authentic. In promoting a particular view of narratives of personal experience, researchers too often recapitulate, in an uncritical fashion, features of contemporary *interview society*. In this society, the interview becomes a personal confessional and the biographical work of the interviewer is concealed. (1997)

A similar point was made by Gubrium and Holstein (1995), and is endorsed by Bauman (2000).

The autobiographical narratives published in official books are produced by senior figures in the discipline, it is an honour to be asked for one, and they are carefully crafted social products. Nothing in such autobiographical pieces can be taken as 'fact'. One might expect the leading men of American sociology to be self-conscious about the rhetorical work of autobiography and to make explicit the nature of the genre. They do not. Of the 22 narratives analysed, Berger's is the only one which warns the reader that it *is* a crafted story. All the others read as if they had been written in the 1930s or 1950s, not in the 1980s or 1990s. Berger points out that: 'The dominant norms of sociological practice discourage autobiographical thinking. In sociology, autobiography is usually regarded as risky, embarrassing and tasteless' (1990b: 152). He reminds his readers that they must 'take nothing of what I have said at face value' (ibid.: 163) and points out that while he has used the data of his life 'to do self-congratulatory ideological work' those same data can be used by others, who hold other sociological views 'to cut me up' (ibid.: 164). Berger (1990a: xv) mentions the academic debates on different 'views about the autonomy of the text'. He then emphasises that sociology exercises its hegemony by 'the rhetoric of impersonality' which is violated by the autobiographical narrative/voice.

121

To analyse the silverback narratives, I took the following steps. The chapters were scrutinised looking for four dimensions of gender consciousness.

1 I counted the numbers of men and women mentioned as friends, mentors, colleagues, fellow students, intellectual influences, and scholarly opponents. For example, in the Goffman interview, he says 'My teachers were Park, Burgess and Lewis Wirth', 'Howie Becker is very important', 'I can remember arguing with Harold Garfinkel', 'He's an interesting guy, Tom Shibutani'. These four sentences would produce six codings for men.
2 I looked to see whether or not the men made any comment on the gender of their significant others.
3 I checked to see whether or not the men analysed the gendered nature of their intellectual and theoretical environment.
4 I coded whether men comment on the rise of feminism as a theory, gender as a topic, or women's visibility in the discipline today compared to their absence during their apprenticeship eras.

The point here is not the 'accuracy' of the memory, but the ways in which male sociologists have chosen to represent their lives as lived in an all-male, or predominantly male, world. They are the authors of these accounts, and, as experienced sociological writers, have chosen the memories they present to the reader. Recognising that autobiographies are subjective and crafted, the aim of analysing the autobiographical essays was to discover how far leading male sociologists have chosen to present their discipline and their social world as a male-only one, when writing for an audience in the 1980s and 1990s. Berger (1990a: xxviii) points out that the essays in his volume have 'class and ethnicity' as 'salient themes'. He does *not* mention gender as a theme, salient or otherwise.

The first measure was the gross totals of mentions of men and women, simply counted as in the Goffman interview. The first of the codings is the most extensive because the autobiographical reflections tend to include lists of friends, mentors, and influential authors. The gross totals of mentions of men and women are shown in Table 7.1 with the Goffman interview added for comparison. The table lists together a mention of Weber and of a man friend in graduate school as 'two males', while 'I met my wife' is coded as a mention of women. William H. Sewell (1988: 122), for example, describes his move to Oklahoma Agricultural and Mechanical College as 'very favourable to my professional development', not least because Otis Dudley Duncan 'had also brought other young men, who were bright and able' there. That produces one count of a male mentioned.

Table 7.1 shows wide variations in the total numbers of people discussed from Bendix's eight and Hawley's 12 names to MacCannell's 89. However, not one man mentions more women than men, indeed, four men (Wilson, Blalock, Gagnon and Berger) list no women at all. There are a further three men (Hawley, Wrong and Bendix) who only mention one woman. Only Riesman and MacCannell list ten or more women. In most accounts 'remembered men' outnumber 'remembered women' by at least four to one. These 23 men remember having lived, or chose to present themselves as having lived, in largely male worlds.

The autobiographical narratives were also coded for the presence or absence of comments on the maleness of their intellectual environments then, or the growth of women's participation in the discipline in the past 25 years. Again, both themes were conspicuous by their absence. Not one single man mentioned that his formative environment was a male one, or that he experienced it as all male, or that he remembered it as all male. Not one single man mentioned that male undergraduates, or graduates, or young faculties in the 1990s would have a different experience because they have women teachers, and might even experience their discipline as a co-educational or feminised one.

Scholar	Men	Women
Bendix	7	1
Berger	18	0
Blalock	13	0
Blau	27	3
Coleman	50	5
Coser	33	7
Cressey	16	6
Gagnon	35	0
Gans	20	5
Glazer	43	4
Goffman (interview)	31	2
Greeley	29	2
Gusfield	38	5
Hawley	11	1
Homans	53	2
Lipset	35	4
MacCannell	70	19
Marx	24	6
Merton	45	2
Riesman	47	10
Roth	29	3
Sewell	65	7
Van den Berghe	49	8
Wilson	19	0
Wrong	14	1

Table 7.1: *Mentions of men and women by men sociologists*

A simple count of the names mentioned is an extremely crude way to discover the place of gender in the development of American sociology. The autobiographies were therefore scrutinised for mentions of the rise of feminist perspectives in sociology, and, for contrast, the intellectual importance of Marxism in sociology. The results of this comparison are shown in Table 7.2. Just as comments on the male-only nature of significant figures and on their social, intellectual or theoretical worlds were absent when names were mentioned, comments on the rise of feminism in sociology, are conspicuous by their absence as Table 7.2 shows.

For the generation who lived through the Second World War, the Korean War, the McCarthy witch-hunts, the Vietnam War, the fall of Stalin and the rise of neo-Marxist theorists like Althusser, it is perhaps surprising that only 12 of the 23 men mentioned Marxism. However, Marxism is much more commonly mentioned than feminism. The same men lived through the anti-feminist era after the Second World War, and the dramatic rise of contemporary feminism since the late 1960s, yet to a man they have chosen not to mention it. Gusfield (1990) describes his research on First Wave, nineteenth-century feminism; the only man to mention the concept at all. These men have chosen not to discuss a seismic change in their intellectual landscape.

Scholar	Marxism	Feminism
Bendix	No	No
Berger	Yes	No
Berghe	Yes	No
Blalock	No	No
Blau	No	No
Coleman	No	No
Coser	Yes	No
Cressey	No	No
Gagnon	No	No
Gans	No	No
Glazer	Yes	No
Goffman	No	No
Greeley	No	No
Gusfield	Yes	19th century, not current
Hawley	No	No
Homans	Yes	No
Lipset	Yes	No
MacCannell	Yes	No
Marx	No	No
Merton	Yes	No
Riesman	Yes	No
Roth	Yes	No
Sewell	No	No
Wilson	No	No
Wrong	Yes	No

Table 7.2: *Intellectual themes: Marxism and feminism*

These distinguished sociologists were offered editorial freedom to reflect on their careers and discipline, and the opportunity to confess to past sins of omission and commission, yet they have *chosen* to ignore women, gender and feminism. They have published unreflexive, unreconstructed accounts of experiencing an all-male, or overwhelmingly male socialisation and early career, of training in an all-male intellectual climate. They make no comments on feminism or the rise of women as a force in American sociology. Dean MacCannell (1990: 177) is the only man who specifically describes deriving any intellectual benefits from a woman's scholarship. He praises his second wife's 'evident mental abilities' and explicitly recounts intellectual work done with her over a 20-year period. He also mentions admiring his first wife's scholarship and his second mother-in-law's intellectual companionship. He is the youngest man in the three collections. Maybe the times are changing, either in the experiences, the recollections of them, or the reflections that go into producing an autobiographical text.

There are four aspects of these accounts that I want to stress: (1) the men very rarely mention any women who studied alongside them at undergraduate, postgraduate levels, or worked with them as colleagues on projects or taught with them; (2) the men make no comment on their own biographical memories being about all-male worlds: that is, they do not seize the opportunity to reflect that they remembered 'men-only' worlds; (3) the men do not analyse the extent to which either their discipline or their social worlds were *actually* male-dominated in the past as opposed to being remembered as all-male: they do not seize the opportunity to display themselves in the present as conscious of the gender balance in the various departments where they trained and later taught; and (4) the men do not comment on the rise of feminism as a theory, gender as a topic, and women's visibility in the discipline, as changes since their early years. That is, they do not seize the opportunity to display themselves as conscious of the changes in sociology. It is perhaps particularly notewothy that they do not even bemoan the pollution of their precious discipline by feminism, the invasion of women into the locker room, the coming of girls into the treehouse, or the complications of dual careers. The world of these silverbacks seems not to have changed since the 1950s, when a study of American scholars was conducted which included questions about the leading figures in various disciplines. When men were asked to name significant scholars in their field they only named men. Jessie Bernard (1964: 157) called this the 'stag' effect.

Dorothy Smith (1999: 199–203) presents an analysis of the current consequences of 'the residue sedimented by an exclusively masculine history' (ibid.: 200). Because universities were all-male for centuries, women are still 'the other'. This is, of course, most noticeable in the sciences and engineering where women are still numerically rare. Noble (1992) emphasises how the celibate, all-male, monastic origins of western science still determine much of the occupational culture, or *habitus*, of science in Britain and the USA today. Smith widens this to all disciplines when she argues: 'Men took the maleness of their university and discursive colleagues for granted' (1999: 200). As Smith (ibid.: 200) commented 'their everyday working lives were lived in a world where women were never colleagues', and 'In the past of the university, women, if present at all in an academic role ... were not members of the university on the same footing with men: their work did not count' (ibid.: 201).

To recapitulate my argument. I am not surprised or shocked that these silverbacks *say* they lived in an all-male world in the 1930s, 1940s, 1950s and 1960s. I am angry that they do not choose to comment on this, or (*pretend* to) regret the exclusion of able women then or (*pretend* to) rejoice in the more 'natural' or 'egalitarian' intellectual climate in which their successors live. A parallel analysis of a different body of silverback narratives was conducted by Yair (2001) and his students. They focus upon the published texts of the ASA Presidential Addresses from 1906 to 1998. Five women were presidents in that stretch (Hallinan, Huber, Komarovsky, Riley, Rossi). Yair's analysis found that race and ethnicity are a recurrent theme, while religion, politics and social class are relatively rarely mentioned. Only two presidential addresses dealt with gender: and they were given by Alice Rossi in 1984 and Joan Huber in 1990.

Taken together, these analyses show a total lack of impact on the malestream by feminist sociology whether liberal, Marxist or radical. That these silverbacks are silent on their all-male worlds is clear evidence that American sociological feminism has had little or no effect on the malestream of American sociology.

silverbacks across cultures

American male sociologists were chosen for this exercise only because they had made their published autobiographical narratives available. American silverbacks are no different from their peers in other cultures. There are parallel findings from other advanced societies. The autobiographical essays by two major male figures in British sociology, Halsey (1985) and Willmott (1985) are similar, and the phenomenon is equally prevalent in continental Europe. In 1989 two Finnish social scientists Rahkonen and Roos and a leading Helsinki newspaper sent out a questionnaire to 317 people who were from: 'science and scholarship and the university, literature and the other areas of the arts, the mass media and administration' (Eskola, 1992: 149).

The respondents were asked to name 'the three most prominent Finnish intellectuals living today' (Rahkonen and Roos, 1992: 114); 216 replies were received; 20 per cent of the people surveyed and 19 per cent of the respondents were women. The men voted only for men. Women voted for men and women. The results showed that: 'A typical Finnish intellectual is a scholar in the humanities, a philosopher or a writer. He is a 50–70 years old man' (ibid.: 115). That Finnish survey was modelled on an earlier French one undertaken by the review *Lire* in 1981 (Bourdieu, 1988; Rahkonen and Roos, 1992). Rahkonen and Roos comment on the structural similarities of the Finnish and French lists, including the absence of women. The French exercise of 1981 was repeated in

1987 by *L'Evénement du jeudi* but asking for five names (Rahkonen and Roos, 1992). That, too, showed that very few men consider their intellectual world to be co-educational.

Eskola (1992), dissatisfied with the newspaper survey method of Rahkonen and Roos, analysed 152 autobiographical pieces commissioned by two leading quality newspapers in Finland, which ran in seven series called 'My School', 'My University', 'Science and Scholarship', 'Science and Scholarship 350', 'My Library' and 'Listening to a Book'/'This is a Book I will read again'. Eskola's analysis of the autobiographical pieces by men showed that men wrote of their fathers but not of their mothers, referred to males in their schooldays, to men at their universities, to male scholars and authors. 'Only six per cent of references made by men concerned a woman' (Eskola, 1992: 159). Eskola concludes: 'For men it is interaction with other men that constitutes social capital, while women's social capital is based on relations between the two genders' (1992: 158). Britain, France and Finland clearly have silverbacks who do not, in general, feel any need to pretend to confess or repent of their sexism or even to comment upon it.

Scholar	Men	Women
Acker	12	9
Bernard	8	9
Daniels	25	20
Epstein	5	7
Fenstermaker	12	14
Glenn	4	13
Hacker	18	6
Hochschild	2	14
Holmstrom	16	34
Keller	11	-
Laslett	11	8
Long	4	8
Lopata	11	11
Mann	1	3
Reinharz	5	6
Roby	2	10
Rossi	6	2
Schwartz	10	6
Stacey	1	6
Thorne	25	18
Wallace	16	15
Wiseman	20	13

Table 7.3: *Mentions of men and women by women sociologists*

The American silverback narratives can be contrasted with a parallel corpus of women's narratives. Taking the collections edited by Laslett and Thorne (1997), Orlans and Wallace (1994) and Goetting and Fenstermaker (1995) alongside the Berger (1990a), I took the essays by 23 women who were full professors in elite universities in the USA from the 46 in those four volumes. The women are shown in Table 2 in Appendix 2. The analysis of significant others is shown in Table 7.3, and of significant themes in Table 7.4.

Comparing Table 7.1 with Table 7.3, it is clear that women's autobiographical style is quite different from the men's. Eleven women mention more females than males, only one woman mentions no females and most of them show the pattern outlined by Eskola. Table 7.4, when compared with Table 7.2, shows that fewer women than men mention Marxism (9 compared to 12), while many more (16 compared to 1) mention feminism.

Scholar	Marxism	Feminism
Acker	Yes	Yes
Bernard	Yes	Yes
Daniels	No	Yes
Epstein	No	Yes
Fenstermaker	Yes	Yes
Glenn	Yes	Yes
Hacker	Yes	Yes
Hochschuld	No	Yes
Holmstrom	No	Yes
Keller	No	No
Laslett	Yes	Yes
Long	No	Yes
Lopata	No	No
Mann	No	No
Reinharz	No	Yes
Roby	No	Yes
Rossi	No	Yes
Schwartz	No	No
Stacey	Yes	Yes
Thorne	Yes	Yes
Wallace	No	No
Wiseman	No	No

Table 7.4: *Intellectual themes: Marxism and feminism by women sociologists*

the exceptions

It would be very easy to assume that all male sociologists were as oblivious as the silverbacks whose autobiographies I have just discussed. This is certainly not the case. The impact of feminism has been noticeable on some men since the early 1970s. As examples, Ronnie Frankenberg, David H.J. Morgan, Robert W. Connell and Maírtín Mac an Ghaill all demonstrate in their writing, their citation patterns, their acknowledgements, and their reception in the company of feminists, how they have avoided being or becoming silverbacks.

These four men, three British and one Australian, have been chosen to exemplify the way in which men who have embraced feminist sociology have enriched their own research, and come to occupy a new type of social niche in sociology where women and men are comfortably colleagues reading each other's work profitably. There are other men who could be chosen as examples: the four I have chosen are men well known to me personally, have observed among feminists, have read, have had professional contacts with, and have spoken about with feminists over at least a decade. Because they range in age from 40 to 80, they span several 'generations' of sociologists.

These four men, listed in descending order of their ages, have all written sociological analyses which incorporate feminist ideas and self-consciously reflect on how feminist sociology has changed their ideas. Frankenberg (1976) showed an exemplary response to feminist sociology. In a review of how community studies had conceptualised women, he criticised earlier work, including his own, and attempted a thorough revision of the genre. Morgan (1981) made a very early male contribution to feminist methods. Connell, after earlier research on political socialisation and educational inequalities, began to publish path-breaking work with his *Gender and Power* (1987). He followed this with *Masculinities* (1995) and *The Men and the Boys* (2000a). His 1987 book was a vigorous rejection of functional and reductionist theories of gender. Both Morgan and Connell were founders of the 'new men's studies', but both set up the 'new' sub-specialism while making contributions to feminist ideas in sociology. Frankenberg, Morgan and Connell are all heterosexual men, who write warmly about the women in their personal lives. My fourth example of a male sociologist who relates positively to feminist ideas is Mac an Ghaill, a gay man. His first published monograph, *Young, Gifted and Black* (1988) and his subsequent study of Parnell School, *The Making of Men* (1994) both show how seriously feminist ideas can be taken by male scholars if they are so motivated.

Ronnie Frankenberg (1976) established himself as a scholar who had reflected on feminist ideas early in the 1970s in his critique of community studies. Highlighting the unconscious sexism of his own overview of the genre (1966) and of his monograph (1957), on his journey through the classic studies, he produced the best feminist comment ever. He points out that in the classic coalfield ethnography (Dennis et al., 1956); 'The relations of production at work are lovingly and loathingly described; the relations of production in the home and community are ignored with equal determination' (1976: 37).

In the concluding remarks, Frankenberg noted that 'Women ... have begun to answer the sociologists back, to claim the right not to be the inferior objects of study, but equal subjects of dialogue' (ibid.: 48). Frankenberg saw 'the future of sociology' in such dialogue. In his Introduction to Frankenberg (1982), a *Festschrift* for Max Gluckman the anthropologist, he highlighted the sexist nature of the academic profession (ibid.: 2) and drew out the gender dimensions of Gluckman's work (ibid.: 3). Frankenberg spent the latter part of his academic career at Keele, where he published work on health and illness, childbirth, childhood, and a variety of other topics. His positive view of the scholarly potential of feminist sociology is clear from his gatekeeping. As an active editor of *The Sociological Review* he ensured that the editorial board included women, that articles by feminist sociologists appeared, and that feminist sociology was present in a mainstream general journal. Classic papers such as Acker (1981), Dominelli (1986), Charles and Kerr (1986), Finch and Mason (1990) and Kay (1990) in feminist sociology were published in this era, making a vital space for the perspective in the discipline.

David Morgan spent his career at Manchester, retiring in 2001 after more than 30 years. He worked in industrial sociology and the sociology of the family: his book *The Family and Social Theory* in 1975 was the first British book to take feminist ideas seriously and rethink the conventional sociology of marriage and the family. He appeared in the Roberts (1981) collection *Doing Feminist Research*, the only male contributor alongside eight women, and produced a landmark paper taking the ideas emerging from feminist sociology about methods into a new realm. His own research moved into autobiography, into establishing the new men's studies in the UK, and then on to the body, again a newly emerging sociological topic. Here Scott and Morgan (1993) was one of the pioneering collections. His retirement event in Manchester was marked by its heavily female, feminist audience/participation. David Morgan's position in feminist sociology is demonstrated by his willingness to act as external examiner for a PhD thesis on menstruation (George, 1990; George and Murcott, 1992). Only a man comfortable with women, feminism and feminist sociology could be appointable and accept the appointment to examine a thesis on the most polluting 'sticky' topic (Douglas, 1966).

R.W. Connell's feminist credentials are more public: he is included in the Laslett and Thorne (1997) collection *Feminist Sociology*, and is one of only two men in the Allen and Howard (2000) collection *Provoking Feminisms*. Connell's (1997) autobiographical essay in Laslett and Thorne is quite unlike the men's essays analysed earlier in the chapter, both stylistically and in its referential frame. He has produced a 'messy' text, with vignettes of events from his life set in italics that dramatise them as turning points. His text is both sociological and reflexive at the same time as he says: 'I was fighting against hegemonic masculinity at the same time as I deployed its techniques' (1997: 154). He reveals mistakes he has made, and the mixture of accidents, decisions and personal events that have shaped his life. Connell writes of his daughter, and his partner, Pam, as well as many women whose work he admires. He publishes *Gender and Power* (1987) and finds that he has become a founder of men's studies:

> What is most striking is the difficulty many journals and reviewers have in categorising the book. Can't be social theory because it's not about Marx and Weber. Can't be women's studies because it's written by a man ... Seven journals work out a solution that completely throws me ... Because it's about gender, and because it's by a man, it must be men's studies. ... I have not felt so firmly positioned since the days when reviewers decided that because I wrote about class, I must be a Marxist. (1997: 159)

131

One way in which feminist-friendly men reveal their altered academic worlds is their citation patterns. The references in Connell (2000b) include Judith Butler, Nancy Chodorow, Cynthia Cockburn, Bronwen Davies, Rebecca Dobash, Cynthia Epstein, Sandra Harding, Arlie Hochschild, Margaret Eisenhart, Sue Lees, Adrienne Rich, Barrie Thorne, Sylvia Walby, and Lyn Yates. Because these feminist publications are woven into his book it is a thoroughly contemporary read.

Mac an Ghaill is the youngest of my four. He has worked in the sociology of education since the 1980s, with a pair of ethnographies of English secondary schools. In the books the interrelationships of gender, class, race, sexualities and educational success are thoughtfully plotted. He has also written books and articles on masculinities and the new men's studies, and on race and ethnicities (Mac an Ghaill, 1988, 1994, 1996, 1999). His contribution to feminist sociology is developed further in the next section.

The next section focuses on current empirical areas, where feminist perspectives are more fully integrated. Education and medicine are both sociological areas which are strong in the UK, and areas which look very different in 2002 from the way they did in 1968. Feminist sociology has had far more impact in the empirical areas of health and education than it has on the self-conscious reflections of silverbacks.

CURRENT EMPIRICAL AREAS

In these two empirical areas, each of which has a specialist journal based in the UK but with an international reputation (*British Journal of Sociology of Education*, *Sociology of Health and Illness*), which has existed for over 20 years, it is possible to demonstrate changes in the gender regime. Education will be considered first.

Sociology of education was almost devoid of research on gender, and of feminist perspectives, before 1980. Acker (1981) demonstrated the absence of gender as a topic and an analytic device by coding all the 184 articles published on education in the three generic sociology journals (*Sociological Review*, *British Journal of Sociology*, *Sociology*) between 1960 and 1979. She concluded that a Martian arriving in Britain

> would conclude that numerous boys but few girls go to secondary modern schools; that there are no girls' public schools; that there are almost no adult women influentials of any sort; that most students in higher education study science and engineering; that women rarely make a ritual transition called 'from school to work' and never go into further education colleges. Although some women go to university, most probably enter directly into motherhood ... and except for a small number of teachers, social workers and nurses, there are almost no adult women workers in the labour market. (1994: 30–1)

Lightfoot (1975) drew similar conclusions in a review of the American literature. In both countries feminist sociologists of education changed the sub-specialism, and mainstreamed their new ideas after 1980.

The changes can be seen in the specialist journals, and in the monographs and edited collections. In the UK *BJSE* was founded in 1980 with anti-sexism as one of its basic tenets, and had eight women and 17 men on its initial editorial board. Throughout its 22-year history it has showcased feminist work. In 2001 there were 17 women and 23 men on the board. British sociology of education also provided most of the editors and much of the content of a specialist journal, *Gender and Education*, founded in 1989. The explosion of research can be seen in the differences between the material available for Delamont (1980) compared to that around for Delamont (1990) and then for Coffey and Delamont (2000). A collection such as Francis and Skelton (2001) would have been unimaginable in 1981, as would the review of the qualitative research in the field by Gordon et al. (2001).

Of course, feminists cannot be complacent about their contribution to the sociology of education, or the changes they have produced in the field, or even about their scholarship being cited, recognised or remembered. There may also be a gendered, sexist, pattern of forgetting. Work by women may be forgotten when work by men from the same era survives. In Delamont (1989b: Appendix 1) there is a detailed analysis of sociology of education which includes some analysis of forgotten women researchers. Today such sexist forgetting continues. Peter Woods (1996), for example, provides a list of exemplary ethnographies in the sociology of education discussing 55 authors. He cites 33 men and only 15 women. Worse, four of the men are cited and quoted repeatedly throughout the chapter, while only one woman is cited more than once (Delamont, 2001). The women's, and the feminist, contributions to ethnographic work on sociology of education are already being 'forgotten'. A parallel analysis of contemporary quantitative work needs to be done, but it seems likely that Jean Floud, Olive Banks, Hilda Himmelweit and other women who did quantitative sociology may also be being forgotten.

The feminist contribution to the sociology of education opened up new areas for research, such as sexual harassment, sex education, and the gender stereotypes in pupils' folklore (Delamont, 1991). Mac an Ghaill's (1988, 1994) two landmark ethnographies of secondary schools in England are emblematic of the dimensions feminism has added to sociology of education, thus transforming the sub-specialism. In his study of Parnell School, Mac an Ghaill focuses on a paradox: that although masculine values and standpoints dominate English education, there had been relatively few projects making those masculine standpoints problematic (1994: 1). He opens the book with two incidents from his teaching career: a fight over homophobic insults and a boy pupil giving him a bunch of flowers. The head found the *latter* incident more threatening to the discipline and reputation of the school. In the exemplary, fine-grained ethnography of the staff room, the classroom and the playground, Mac an Ghaill explores subtleties of sexist behaviour and attitudes among teachers and pupils. Among the staff, for example, he explores how the 'liberal' male teachers:

133

> were unable to see the limits of personal consciousness-raising in relation to their own position in the institutional sexual structuring of the school. As with many politically progressive activists, in trying to understand their own contradictory position in a system of oppression, they tended to take for granted the privileges of white straight middle-class masculinity that were ascribed to them. (1994: 29)

In his exploration of this area, Mac an Ghaill's work parallels analyses by feminists such as Datnow (1998). The analyses of sex, gender, sexuality and sexual orientation among the pupils, both female and male, are built on feminist classics such as Stanworth (1983) and Skeggs (1988). By integrating and building upon work such as Holly (1989) Mac an Ghaill displays both his own engagement with feminism and how feminist perspectives have changed sociology of education for the better.

Moving on from the sociology of education to that of health and illness, a parallel enrichment can be traced. There was no equivalent British paper to Acker's (1981) devastating exposé in the sociology of health and illness. However, in the USA Lorber (1975) reviewed the field, and the subsequent explosion can be seen from Lorber (2000). When the journal *Sociology of Health and Illness* was launched in 1978, it did not have an explicit feminist agenda. However, there were eight men and only four women on the editorial board. The editor and the review editor were men. The international panel of editorial advisers contained 20 men and eight women. Feminist perspectives were not particularly apparent in the first volume. In 2002, three of the four editors, both review editors, four of the ten editorial board and five of the 13 advisers were women. Its pages provided an intellectual space for displaying the strengths of feminist analyses. Women's health had been a feminist cause throughout all three waves of feminism, so it is not surprising that women sociologists were active in changing the research on health and illness.

Central to this explosion in the feminist sociology of health and illness was Meg Stacey, and the papers published to celebrate her life and work display the ways in which the feminist ideas stimulated men and women (see Bendelow et al., 2002). Stacey's (2002) reflections on her career and on the volume dedicated to her explore several themes, but the impact of feminism on the sub-specialism of health and illness is shown to have been powerful. Bloor's (2001) review of the qualitative research in the sociology of health and illness does not explicitly celebrate feminist angles, but the topics, methods and reflexivity *de facto* reveal an empirical area transformed by feminism.

Opening up gender differences in morbidity, mortality and illness behaviour was itself a major task, especially with a feminist emphasis on studying illness behaviours, not behaviour. Challenging the medicalisation of pregnancy and childbirth, especially in the USA, and making problematic the hysterectomy, HRT and the widespread prescription of anti-depressants to women were among the topics added by feminists to the research agenda of medical sociology. Interactionist studies of doctor–patient and doctor–nurse encounters, and analyses of gender and professionalisation were also advanced by feminists (Annandale and Hunt, 2000). Feminists were instrumental in studying health workers other than doctors, especially the low-paid and the unpaid. The state of sociology of health and illness in 2002 has changed unrecognisably from the 1960s (Olesen, 2002), in large part because of a feminist engagement.

134

CONCLUSION

Sociologists of science have shown that when a new paradigm arrives in a research area, its acceptance is largely due to an older cohort of 'disbelievers' and 'rejecters' retiring, moving out of what Collins (1985) called the 'core set' and eventually dying. That is, few scientists change their own paradigm, rather, they are replaced in the core sets by younger colleagues who treat the new paradigm as the correct one for that sub-specialism. The silverback narratives can be seen as an example of an older, retired, dying generation who will take their pre-feminist, sexist, impoverished sociology to their graves, leaving the discipline in the hands of a new generation including Dean MacCannell. Reading Mac an Ghaill in education, this seems plausible. However, there are some reasons to be wary. Many of the topics and approaches which feminist sociology addressed in the 1970s and 1980s went out of favour in the discipline during the 1990s when, after the fall of the Berlin Wall in 1989 and under the influence of postmodernism, the whole discipline abandoned those topics and appropriated others. The next chapter addresses the problems this has posed for feminist sociologists.

eight

making fictions of female destiny

postmodernism and postfeminism

Feminists do not have to choose between feminism and exper-
imentalism or postmodernism as if they were unified players in
a contest, but rather must face harder questions. (Gordon,
1993: 111)

This chapter deals with two challenges to feminist sociology which
have characterised the past ten to 15 years. One, postfeminism, is
a challenge which can be found in the mass media, especially the quality or broadsheet, newspapers. Essentially, it is a claim that the feminist
movement of the 1970s has achieved its attainable goals, and has therefore vanished. The next generation of women, it is claimed, take those
advances for granted, and have no interest in campaigning for the unat-
tainable. Thus, it is claimed, the 1970s' women's movement got the
right to contraception, made advances towards equal pay and equal
access to mortgages and pensions, put domestic violence and rape onto
the political agenda, and opened up many occupations and organisations to women (the Stock Exchange, horse racing as jockeys and as
members of the Jockey Club, the Anglican clergy). Women in the 1990s
expect these phenomena, and have no interest in campaigning for other
goals, such as 24-hour state day care, or wages for housework.

Such arguments appeared regularly in the broadsheets in the 1990s,
and produced a feminist response (e.g. Coppock et al., 1995). However,
there has not been a parallel sociological debate. There have not been
sociologists claiming to establish a postfeminist sociology, there are no
books called 'Postfeminist Sociology', and no journals of postfeminist
sociology. The journals where feminist sociology appears are not carrying articles saying that feminist sociology is over, and they are not losing readers. For the purpose of this book therefore I have not dealt with
postfeminism as a sociological perspective. This chapter focuses instead
on the intellectual debate that is central to feminist sociology: postmodernism.

Some writers use the term poststructuralism to refer to the French theories now more usually called postmodernism. Butler (1990) and Weedon (1987), for example, invoked poststructuralism. Michèle Barrett used the term poststructuralism in her concluding essay in Barrett and Phillips (1992). For the purposes of this book I have subsumed poststructuralism within postmodernism. Dorothy Smith (1999: 97) makes the same elision, writing of poststructuralism/postmodernism.

POSTMODERNISM

At its simplest, postmodernism is a challenge to the consensus held among the educated classes in the Western capitalist nations, since the Enlightenment at the end of the eighteenth century, that universal, objective scientific truths can be reached by scientific methods. In this section I establish what modernity and postmodernity are, what postmodernism as a social theory is, and briefly explore two sources of resistance to its current intellectual pre-eminence. The two sources of resistance, from sections of feminism and self-appointed defenders of science, are discussed because their positions are relevant to debates on feminist sociology. Empirical research on gender and on science will also be used to illustrate some of the controversies. Postmodernism in sociology has two distinct meanings (there are other meanings in architecture and literary criticism which are not dealt with at all here). Postmodernism is both a term used to describe the era in which we live, and a theoretical perspective. The latter is the main focus of the chapter, but many sociologists are busy writing about the former. The argument that Britain, the USA, and the rich nations of western Europe have moved on from being modern nations to being late modern or postmodern runs as follows. Expressed simply, those who believe in postmodernism argue that with the agrarian and industrial revolutions, and the shift from societies of peasant farmers to societies of urban factory workers, western Europe entered an era of modernism. People's identities (or men's identities at least) were grounded in their social class, which meant identities were rooted in their role as producers. The rise of science, and the belief in objective scholarship, were inextricably linked to that modernism.

For these theorists, the past 50 years have seen the globalisation of production and the de-industrialisation of Western Europe, and thus an era of post-industrialisation. When people (or men) no longer draw their deepest sense of identity from jobs in production and thus their social class, an era of postmodernism dawns. In this era, identities are multiple and fragmented, and people (or men) structure their lives

137

around their tastes as consumers. Lyon summarises this set of propositions: 'is modernity itself ... disintegrating, including the whole grand edifice of Enlightenment world-views? And, is a new type of society appearing, perhaps structured around consumers and consumption rather than workers and production?' (1999: ix). This chapter is not an appropriate place to explore whether this is a true account of the changing social structures of North America and Western Europe. Lash and Urry (1994) address those issues, and they are not directly relevant to my topic. Here I focus on the impact of the vogue for postmodern theory in social science.

For scholars embracing postmodern theories in social sciences and humanities, the argument of the Enlightenment project that universal, objective, scientific truths can be found by applying correct methods, was a naïve, mistaken faith that could only be cherished in an era of modernism. As the developed world has become postmodern, so the Enlightenment Project has to be abandoned. Before exploring further what a postmodern position means for social science analysis, it is important to remind ourselves that this is a debate confined to a small elite in a few disciplines in a few countries in a small part of the world. The Enlightenment project and its faith in scientific objectivity, were not, and never have been universal.

138

Beliefs in the possibility of scientific objectivity have never been held by the majority in western societies, or by anyone in many other cultures. For most of the world, poverty, lack of any education, beliefs about gender, and strong religious faith, have stood between the working classes, the uneducated, all-women, and whole populations holding to other belief systems, and the scientific revolution of the Enlightenment. In Western Europe and North America the Enlightenment project was never a mass phenomenon: it was always an elite project. The masses were never part of the Enlightenment project because the elite never wanted, or never managed, to educate the masses sufficiently to make them accept rationality, objectivity or the scientific method. We can remind ourselves that only those classes or fragments of classes which had access to elaborated code speech (Bernstein, 1971) could buy into the Enlightenment project: and that the Enlightenment project has been, for 200 years, the *habitus* of the intelligentsia (Bourdieu, 1996). This point was made forcibly in a letter to the *London Review of Books*, from K.W.C. Sinclair-Loutit, recounting a conversation with a proud Orthodox Serb in 1994: 'My friend, a good Serbian Orthodox Christian, was of a culture continuous with that of the Byzantine Empire. The Renaissance, the Reformation, the Enlightenment and the Industrial Revolution had not touched him' (*LRB*, 16 April 1998: 4). Postmodernism is not a problem if the Enlightenment never occurred in your culture.

Even in advanced industrial societies many of those with access to the education which promotes the Enlightenment project reject it: most noticeably the large number of Americans who choose a literal, creationist, reading of the Bible over Enlightenment science (Numbers, 1992; Peshkin, 1986; Rose, 1986). Bearing in mind the caveat about the elite minority among whom the Enlightenment project had become the *habitus*, it is possible to explore what a postmodernist social theory is.

There is one complication which will arise throughout this chapter: many writers defending objectivity and/or positivism against what they see as its enemies now use 'postmodernism' as a portmanteau term of abuse, lumping together all their enemies under that label. Callon (1999), for example, shows how Sokal and Bricmont (1997) conflate a galaxy of French postmodernist theorists with *all* the philosophers, historians, and sociologists of science. They thus conflate the arguments of Kuhn and Popper (who held totally opposed positions on the philosophy of science) and apply the label 'postmodern' to both. The same authors and texts are being attacked as 'positivist' and as 'postmodern': Paul Atkinson was attacked in 2000–1 by Bochner (2001) for being a positivist, and by John Brewer (2000) as a postmodernist, while his whole academic career has been anti-positivist and he is deeply sceptical about claims we are 'all' postmodern now (Atkinson et al., 1999; Delamont et al., 2000a).

Post-modernists argue that we have reached the end of the Enlightenment project: the faith that we can find a neutral standpoint from which to gather objective facts and scientific truth about the world. Postmodernists argue that, in 2002, it is no longer possible for a thinking person to believe in objectivity, truth or 'science' because the epistemological basis for a belief in objectivity has been destroyed. For 200 years elite white men have believed that objective research was possible in science, social science and the humanities. Today a subset of such men, the postmodernists, are arguing that this belief was misguided: objectivity was actually the biased perspective of those same elite white men who were lulling themselves into a false sense of security by claiming objectivity. They thought that what they were doing and calling science was really objective. They did not realise that it was only their elite male view which they were extrapolating and elevating to the new status of universalism. The postmodernists who have argued for the past 30 years that there is no universalism, no objectivity, are themselves a subset of the white male intellectual elite who have broken ranks. The postmodernist subset of white men are having their biggest impact in arts and social sciences. In these disciplines a fierce debate has been raging about the need for a postmodern analysis: a debate which has mystified many onlookers. An amusing exemplification of what

139

postmodernism 'means' was printed in the correspondence page of the *Times Literary Supplement*. There had been an angry debate about the beneficial or malevolent influence postmodernism was having in various intellectual areas, which was followed by some letters printed asking plaintively what the term meant. The following letter effectively closed the correspondence.

> Sir, – Paul Boghossian mentions Stanley Fish's article, in which Fish refers to the meaning of 'ball' and 'strike'. I have not read Fish and so do not know if he mentions a well-known piece of baseball philosophy. Three umpires are discussing how they do their job. The first, who is also the least experienced, says, 'I call 'em as they are.' The second, who has been in the game a little longer, says, 'I call 'em as I see 'em.' The third says, 'They're nothing till I call 'em.' These three could be characterised as objectivism, relativism and postmodernism respectively. (Andrew Rawlinson, *TLS*, 3 January 1997: 17)

The third umpire was pointing out that there is nothing objective about whether a pitch is legal or not, only a human decision and label. A legal pitch is a ball so labelled by the umpire.

Postmodernism in this chapter refers only to social and cultural theories. There is no discussion of architecture, of literature or other media such as film. Nor does this chapter discuss whether the formerly industrialised capitalist nations have passed on into a post-industrial and/or even postmodern state. The debates in Lash and Urry (1994) or Beck et al. (1994) are not addressed here. Readers totally unfamiliar with the concept should start with Lyon's (1999) introduction. The term's notoriety is usually dated from the publication of Lyotard's *The Postmodern Condition* in 1979 in France, and in 1984 in English. Outside France, the ideas of Lyotard, Derrida, Lacan and Foucault have been treated closer than they probably were when their authors were all alive, and as the core exponents of a unitary theoretical position. Parisian sociology is rarely that coherent (Lemert, 1981). Tony Judt, for example, is scathing about the vogue for the French postmodernists in America and Britain: 'For the foreigner, occasional forays into the rich treasure chest of French cultural discourse are a cost-free exercise' (1992: 300). As Judt summarises this fashion: 'Foreign universities are full of professors who not only study the work of Lacan, Foucault, Derrida, Barthes, Lyotard, Bourdieu, Baudrillard and others, but apply their "methods" assiduously to their own research, in a bewildering array of disciplines' (1992: 299).

Charles Lemert (1981) was careful to stress the diversity and variety of the different figures important in French sociology in his collection. As several authors from continental Europe have pointed out, many of the authors lauded in the USA have been academically marginal, even unemployable, in France. Bourdieu (1988: xviii) points out that many

French scholars who are intellectual heroes in the USA held 'marginal positions' in the French university system. The women lionised abroad are even more marginal than the men. Noticeably while Lemert's collection contained papers by 22 different French sociologists, they were all men. Judt's list of the key figures is an all-male one. So while many feminists see inspiration in men and women from French circles, male commentators see only French men. As Callon says, 'It is always amusing for a French national to discover which French authors are all the rage in the Anglo-Saxon world, and to learn that they are all exalters of postmodernism' (1999: 284). Braidotti comments that postmodernism 'far from being the prestigious site of high theory – as it seems to be in the United States – has remained a marginal and radical "wing" with barely any institutional pull' (2000: 94). She explains this with named examples. Derrida was refused chairs at three universities, Irigaray has not held a teaching post since Lacan sacked her in 1974, Deleuze, Lyotard and Cixous worked at Vincennes/Saint Dennis, a marginal institution. Kelly Oliver (2000a), editor of an American collection of papers by French feminists, is careful to warn her readers that: (1) she has selected theoretical papers that have been influential in the Anglophone world, rather than papers representing all spheres of French feminism; and (2) the papers come from scholars who write on either social theory or psychoanalytic theory. Each of the French women is contextualised in an essay introducing her life and work. Thus the reader is warned that Kristeva 'has an ambivalent, sometimes hostile, relationship to feminism' (Oliver, 2000b: 155). In Hansen's (2000) introduction to Irigaray the reader is directed to thoughtful secondary sources, such as Whitford (1991). Postmodernism is an American social construction, as much as a 'real' coherent intellectual movement. However, for the purposes of this chapter, the furious reaction to postmodernism among some feminist sociologists and among some scientists is more important than arcane differences between Lyotard and Foucault.

141

RESPONSES TO POSTMODERNISM

Among scholars, there have been particularly angry responses to postmodernism among two groups: feminists and scientists. These two groups have different problems with postmodernism, which need attention here. There are feminists, including feminist sociologists, who have embraced postmodernism with alacrity and even abandonment. These postmodernist feminists are the focus of the third section of the chapter, after a discussion of the two hostile groups.

scientists against pomo

The scientific opponents of postmodernism are considered first. This campaign, called 'The science wars' was based on a conflation of, or a serious confusion between: (1) non-positivist social science perspectives such as constructivism and ethnomethodology; (2) postmodernism; (3) feminism (used as an undifferentiated term of abuse); and (4) anti-racism. The self-styled defenders of science know so little about human-ities and social science that they do not, and indeed, cannot, distinguish between them. For feminists hostile to postmodernism, the ways in which 'defenders' of science treat the two perspectives as coterminous is maddening in its inaccuracy. The 'defenders' of science including Gross and Levitt (1994), Sokal and Bricmont (1997) and Koertge (1998) are all naïve believers in a pre-Kuhnian view of science. Collins (1999), Callon (1999) and Mackenzie (1999) are well-balanced accounts of the campaign by a few scientists against social scientists' accounts of science and against postmodernism as an ideology. The sci-ence warriors, as Collins (1999) calls them, are usually just as angry about the feminist literature on science, which they also label 'post-modern'. As well as pouring abuse over Collins, Pinch and Latour, they attack Keller (1983, 1985), Harding (1986, 1987, 2000), Schiebinger (1989, 1993, 1999) and other feminists. Many of these women have queried the 'objectivity' of much science and scientific practice, but *none* of them is a postmodernist. The men from Science Technology and Innovation Studies (STIS) have defended *their* practice and episte-mology (see special issues of *Social Studies of Science*, 1996 and 1999) but they have *not* argued with the science warriors to defend the valid-ity of the feminist critiques of science.

Sullivan (1999) is a physicist who contributed to Koertge (1998), and who is prepared to engage in careful, scholarly, reasoned debate with an historian of science, Mackenzie (1999). Sullivan summarises the belief system of the science warriors as follows:

> Imbued with a congeries of ideas known as *postmodernism*, certain scholars in the humanities and social sciences question the epistemolog-ical assumptions of physical and biological scientists. In particular, the main thrust of postmodernist criticism seems to be the denial of the pos-sibility of objective knowledge, so that social factors do not just influ-ence scientific progress: it is claimed that they enter the content of scientific knowledge. (1999: 215)

This matters because these ideas are influencing public opinion about science and even worse, they have got into schools: 'Implementing a postmodernist doctrine known as constructivism' (ibid.: 215) 'special-ists' have destroyed high school science. Gross and Levitt (1994) linked postmodernism to left-wing political views, to feminism, to African studies and to gay and lesbian studies, arguing that American higher education had been taken over by dangerous subversive groups. The contributors to Koertge (1998) are most worried about 'postmodernism'. The two groups have in common a firm belief that science is objective. There are two problems with the science warriors' position. First, most of the people they label postmodernists are not: they do not use the ideas of postmodernism at all. Second, as Callon (1999) shows, the science warriors have not actually *read* the work of any of the postmodernists. Callon summarises the science warriors' argument as: 'are you willing to encourage these postmodernists and cognitive realists who corrupt our youth and bring decay to our civilisation?' (ibid.: 262).

Overall, then, none of the science warriors have actually read and understood any of the postmodernists. They have reacted violently to some postmodernists' use of some ideas from the natural sciences as metaphors (failed to recognise that they *are* metaphors), lumped those postmodernists in with the scholars of STIS, and created a panic. In many ways, the science wars are irrelevant to this book. I have dwelt on them for three reasons: first, STIS is an area that fascinates me not only for its own ideas but because it is so stubbornly impervious to feminism; second, because the sweeping together of everything disliked under a label of 'pomo' is equivalent to sweeping together everything under a label of 'feminism'; and third, because the science warriors' attacks on pomo received such massive press coverage (articles in the quality press, major reviews in the *New York Review of Books*, *Times Literary Supplement*, etc.) whereas the feminist attacks on pomo received no coverage at all in the general media.

143

This manic 'defence' of objectivity in science is only relevant to this book insofar as the confusion of postmodernism and feminism means that there has been a climate resistant to arguments from activists who wish to attract more women to science (Whyte, 1985), retain them in science (e.g. Glover, 2000; Rees, 2001), change the focus of scientific research (Lederman and Bartsch, 2001; Wyer et al., 2001), and even develop 'women-friendly' science (e.g. Mayberry et al., 2001). Indeed, as Donna Haraway (1988) pointed out, if women adopted a postmodern position, and believed that science was *only* rhetoric it absolved them from any need to grasp post-Newtonian physics. Adopting the strongest possible social constructivist position about science allowed women to slump back from mistressing 'hard' scientific ideas, rationalising: 'They're just texts anyway, so let the boys have them back' (1988: 597).

feminists against pomo

Lyon (1999: 80) argues that: 'Feminists frequently hesitate before the brink of full postmodernism.' Sceptical and hesitant feminists have not been slow to point out that the leading exponents of postmodernism were men. Many of the scholars who have argued that postmodernism renders extant research outdated, outmoded and passé are middle-class, white men in secure jobs in industrialised countries. Thus Fox-Genovese has commented: 'Surely it is no coincidence that the Western white male elite proclaimed the death of the subject at precisely the moment at which it might have had to share that status with the women and peoples of other races and classes who were beginning to challenge its supremacy' (1986: 134).

Fox-Genovese is an African-American woman. She has pointed out that the origins of postmodernism lie in Paris after 1945 among white men (Lévi-Strauss, Lacan, Foucault, Derrida, Lyotard) who are or were misogynist, sexist, and, in Foucault's case, gay. A similar point is made by Somer Brodribb (1992: 7–8) when she states 'postmodernism is the cultural capital of late patriarchy.' For those feminists hostile to postmodernism, its intellectual origins are inherently anti-women: 'postmodern theory's misogynist and very specific historical origins among post World War II Parisian Intellectuals – from Lévi-Strauss and Lacan to Foucault and Derrida – require excessive intellectual modification and machinations to include women' (Hoff, 1994: 151).

The debate about whether women can be *flâneurs*, or have to be *flâneuses*, if there can be such people, is particularly relevant here. Elizabeth Wilson (2001) explains the idea of the *flâneur* as follows. The *flâneur* arrived as an archetype with the urban revolution of the late eighteenth century. He was a creature of Paris in the opening decade of the 1800s: a symbol of a modern city. The *flâneur* walked, loitered, lurked and observed the city: its people, its buildings, its spectacle. He has no occupation, unless he is an artist gathering material for a novel, an epic or a painting. The urban lower classes are an object of amusement, cafés and restaurants allow time to spend pleasurably, window shopping is a regular pastime, while gossip, fashion and developments in the arts are a diversion. Wilson summarises the ideas of Walter Benjamin, and Siegfried Kracauer, who developed sociological analyses of the idea. The *flâneur* is an onlooker, a watcher, an observer, and particularly a male whose gaze both objectifies women and embodies modernity. Joseph Mitchell's (1993) story of Joe Gould and his (mythical) Oral History of New York can be seen as the story of a *flâneur*: Gould wandered New York for 35 years claiming that he was writing a modern equivalent of Gibbon's *Decline and Fall*. As Wilson points

144

out, during the 1980s as sociological interest in consumption and in the postmodern city with its culture and tourism economics of signs and space (Lash and Urry, 1994) grew, so too did interest in the *flâneur*. Tester's (1994a) edited collection marked the arrival of the concept in British sociology.

After Tester's collection appeared, the idea of the *flâneur* became embroiled in a debate about whether there could be such men in the Bluewater Mall or at Euro Disney. Could there be *flâneurs* not in cities but in postmodern consumer centres? Such debates are not relevant to this book. However, alongside that discussion, Janet Wolff (1985, 1990, 1994) a sociologist of art and culture had argued that although there was, in theory, a *flâneuse* (that is, the word had, in the nineteenth-century Larousse *Encyclopaedia*, a feminine form), in fact, only men could actually behave as *flâneurs*. There was no way that women could use the city in the ways that men could. A woman strolling in the Paris of 1807 was liable to be branded a harlot, not a fine fellow or an artist gathering material. Wolff illustrated her claims with case studies of women painters, contrasted with males from the same artistic movement. Tester himself avoided the issue: 'The question of the gender specificity of *flânerie* is very much an area for debate' (1994b: 19).

Elizabeth Wilson (2001) stresses that the essential quality of the *flâneur* is that he takes possession of the city by his gaze: he is the embodied male gaze. The male *flâneur* observes women, and exercises a seigniorial gaze upon them. This gaze is theoretically similar to the petrification of the Medusa's head, in Lacan's work, which fixes women permanently 'in the stasis of otherness' (Wilson, 2001: 82). If one accepts this link between Benjamin's *flâneur* and Lacan's Medusa head, then the concept of the *flâneur* is 'just' another sexy sociological idea that turns out to be a male-only idea; a theory that is really a male game, another concept which sounds analytically powerful but actually excludes women. The debate between Wolff and Wilson reveals the problems attendant on trying to harness postmodern ideas such as the Medusa gaze to feminist ends.

It is debates such as this – and, as Wilson (2001: 83) comments 'Debates among feminists seem often to begin as differences of emphasis and end as polarised antagonisms' – which have divided feminist sociologists over postmodernism. There are intellectual doubts and the feeling that postmodernism undermines the potential for radical social change. Gordon summarises the tension: 'we find an irreconcilable difference between feminism's commitment to mass, systematic social change for women, and those strains of postmodernism that find all modern "revolutions" suspect' (1993: 109).

Among the women anxious that postmodernism will destroy feminism and mounting a vigorous attack upon it is Brodribb (1992) who

145

reaches rhetorical heights which leave the majority of us gasping. Her opponents – those feminists who wish to become postmodernists, or adapt postmodernism to their own ends – are called 'ragpickers in the bins of male ideas' (1992: xxiii). The violence of the debate, and hence the anxieties underlying it, can be seen in a highly-charged debate in *Women's History Review* (vol. 5, no. 1, pp. 19–24) between Hoff (1994, 1996), Kent (1996) and Ramazanoglu (1996). Mascia-Lees et al. (1989) argued that in Anthropology postmodernism was predominantly about men appropriating insights from feminism (and Marxism) to create a 'prestige discourse' for their own career advancement. Marjorie Wolf (1992) makes similar claims. Singleton (1996) discusses the uneasy relationship between feminism and postmodernism in the sociology of science.

Felski offers a neat summary of the two opposed positions on the coming of postmodernism:

> For some it is a narrative of progress, as feminism sheds its essentialisms and universalisms to achieve a more sophisticated stage of theoretical consciousness. For others it is a narrative of the fall, as feminism is lured from its true goals by internecine squabbles and the spurious prestige of French avant-garde thought. (2000: 71)

146

Dorothy Smith (1999: 97–8) has two main objections to postmodernism. She argues that, first, postmodernism has imported the 'universalised subject of knowledge' while it repudiates it: 'The unitary subject of modernity is rejected only to be multiplied as subjects constituted in diverse and fragmented discourses' (ibid.: 98). Second, by prioritising language/discourse, postmodernism drives a wedge between the specific local practices of people's everynight/everyday lives and the language/discourse which the postmodernist studies. For Smith, this imprisons the sociologist in 'a phenomenal world in which nothing ever happens' (ibid.: 98) and prevents her from studying the world 'in which people are active' (ibid.: 98). Smith goes on to argue that the postmodernist feminist position is antithetical to *sociology*: it denies the 'possibility of discovery' (ibid.: 109).

Many of the contributors to the collection edited by Bell and Klein (1996), defending radical feminism, argued that the biggest danger is from postmodernism. The editors include a 'po-mo quiz' ridiculing postmodernism (Bell and Klein, 1996: 558–61). A section of their volume is devoted to criticisms of postmodernism, including a reprint of Joan Hoff (1994), Barbara Christian's (1996) 'The race for theory', and Christine Delphy's (1996) 'French feminism: an imperialist invention'. The editors summarise their position on postmodernism as follows. 'The post-modern turn is apolitical, ahistorical, irresponsible, and self-contradictory; it takes the "heat off patriarchy"' (Bell and Klein, 1996:

xix). Overall, therefore, feminists have been deeply divided in their responses to postmodernism. Lined up against Brodribb, Smith and Delphy are some very distinguished feminists, to whom we now turn.

feminists for pomo

As Flax points out, much feminist scholarship has been 'critical of the contents' of the Enlightenment dream, yet simultaneously 'unable to abandon them' (1993: 447). For Flax, postmodernism is particularly threatening for feminism because 'Three of the discourses feminists have attempted to adapt to our own purposes, liberal political theory, Marxism, and empirical social science, express some form of this Enlightenment dream' (1993: 448). For Flax this is not a proper feminist response. Because the Enlightenment was a male cosmology feminists must abandon it, to create their own. Flax is confident that the insights of postmodernism will set women free from a childlike state in which we wait for 'higher authorities' to rescue us, clinging to a naïve myth of 'sisterhood'. Similarly, Patti Lather argues: 'The essence of the postmodern argument is that the dualisms which continue to dominate Western thought are inadequate for understanding a world of multiple causes and effects interacting in complex and non-linear ways, all of which are rooted in a limitless array of historical and cultural specificities' (1991: 21). Since 1991 she has developed her postmodernist feminism in, for example, Lather (2001). Jane Flax (1990, 1993) argues that: 'Postmodern philosophers seek to throw into radical doubt beliefs ... derived from the Enlightenment' (1990: 41). She lists among the beliefs thrown into doubt: the existence of a stable self, reason, an objective foundation for knowledge, and universalism. As she forcefully expresses this: 'The meanings – or even existence – of concepts essential to all forms of Enlightenment metanarrative (reason, history, science, self, knowledge, power, gender, and the inherent superiority of Western culture) have been subjected to increasingly corrosive attacks' (1993: 450).

147

Judith Butler (1990, 1999) is one of the best-known exponents of postmodern feminism or feminist postmodernism. Butler (1990, 1999) published *Gender Trouble*, an influential book both in establishing queer theory and in disseminating the ideas of poststructuralism (a.k.a. postmodernism) among American feminist writers. Butler originally wrote *Gender Trouble* to challenge the anti-lesbian biases she saw in the assumptions in feminism that all women were heterosexual. She drew on French poststructuralism and applied it to American theories of gender and the 'political predicaments of feminism' (1999: ix). She wanted to carry out a 'feminist reformulation' (ibid.: ix) of postmodernism, instead she found herself celebrated as an advocate of postmodernism. By 1999 when her second edition appeared, the book had been translated into several languages (but not French), and postmodernism had transmuted and spread into many fields. Butler is not, of course, a sociologist, but a scholar in humanities: in the sphere of postmodernism, however, the distinctions between sociology, cultural studies, and the humanities are not hard and fast.

Maggie Maclure (2000), an educational researcher, is certain that feminists must swim in the postmodern tide:

> Feminism cannnot afford to keep its distance [from pomo]. It is all the more urgent that feminists engage in deconstructive play, in order to defend women's writing, and the specificity of women's voices, from erasure. But the status, and the possibility of such play with always be problematic in a discursive space where play is always already defined as the pastime of male theoretical cross-dressers. (ibid.: 63)

Sandra Harding (2000) is perhaps the most famous feminist to adopt a postmodern position, arguing that it has the most intellectual power of any feminist perspective yet devised. None of the feminist postmodernists in social science have adopted the philosophy naïvely or uncritically because they recognise that feminist modernism sets out a tough agenda. Linda Nicholson (1999: 113) describes the task as follows: 'How can we combine a postmodernist incredulity towards metanarratives with the social-critical power of feminism?'

My own position on postmodernism is ambivalent. I am totally opposed to adopting French theory merely because it is exotic, fashionable, and mystifying. I am equally opposed to rejecting French theories merely because they are exotic, fashionable and mystifying. It is not clear why some of the theorists have been seized on and valorised (especially Foucault in sociology), while others are left in French obscurity. For feminists, I see no alternative but to engage with postmodernism and its implications. Ignoring it, or feigning incomprehension, will leave feminism dying, like a beached whale. Active engagement with the postmodernists is essential.

The arguments of Fox-Genovese about white men discovering the death of the subject just as they were being forced to share the prestige of being the subject with women, non-whites, and other former 'outcasts' are clearly correct. The parallels with the vogue for Freud in the early part of the twentieth century are striking. The intelligentsia after the First World War were enthusiastic about Freudian ideas: they were progressive for thinking about shell shock; they were complex and demanding; they came from Vienna, a city with a great intellectual pedigree; they were new; they were a paradigm shift; *and* because of their concern with sexuality, they shocked older people and conservatives rigid. They were, therefore, perfect for a post-war generation. Conveniently for intellectual men, and for some women 'too young' for

First Wave feminism who felt out of tune with its Puritanism and purity crusading (see Delamont, 1989a and 1992a), Freudianism provided a 'modern' reason for rejecting First Wave feminism and all its works. Vicinus (1985) explores this in some detail.

In the final section of this chapter I want to explore the main consequence of postmodernism for the majority of sociologists and anthropologists: the consequences for what 'counts' as academic writing. Amanda Cross's (1981: 148) heroine Kate Fransler spoke of the new forms possible to women in making fictions of female destiny.

FICTION(S)

One movement which has frequently been embraced by sociologists who are sympathetic to postmodernism, and has been conflated with postmodernism by its opponents, is the playfulness, especially in the presentation of 'results'. For obvious reasons postmodern sociologists never use quantitative methods: their philosophical stance demands qualitative ones. Many enthusiasts for postmodernism are also keen on textual innovation. It is possible – even likely – that postmodern work will be written in an innovative and stylistically self-conscious way. The postmodern work is likely to be couched in terms of an open, 'messy' text, rather than a monograph or paper that conforms to all the conventions of scholarly factual writing. This text may well incorporate a mixture of different literary styles and genres. It may, for instance, include highly impressionistic, introspective and autobiographical passages of prose which are transgressive of the normal canons of academic discourse. Feminist sociologists and anthropologists have been particularly keen on challenging and transgressing the orthodoxies of academic writing. They have been delighted that personal, autobiographical and emotional texts are publishable in 2002, in ways unthinkable in 1962, or even 1982.

Since the Enlightenment, rhetoric – once a respected and canonical discipline – had been relegated to the margins of intellectual life. With the rise of modern science, rhetoric became a marginalised, even despised activity. It contrasted with the rational and factual status ascribed to science, having connotations of sophistry and persuasion. In recent years, however, there has been a growing movement to rehabilitate rhetoric, not least in the recognition that the 'sciences' and other factual enterprises are themselves inescapably rhetorical in character. The natural sciences, economics, history, among many other domains, have been shown to deploy their own rhetorical conventions – not least in their characteristic literary conventions. Such analyses have the consequence of demystifying those conventions. For instance, they can

149

show how scholars convey their own authoritative status; how they persuade their readers through the use of metaphors and other figures of speech; how they use examples and other illustrative materials to build plausible arguments.

One of the consequences of the literary and rhetorical turn is an enhanced awareness of the social processes involved in analysis. In the collection edited by Sanjek (1990), anthropologists reflected upon field-notes – how they are constructed, used and managed. We come to understand that fieldnotes are not a closed, completed, final text: rather, they are indeterminate, subject to reading, rereading, coding, recording, interpreting, reinterpreting. The literary turn has encouraged (or insisted) on the revisiting, or reopening, of ethnographer's accounts and analyses of their fieldwork. Wolf (1992), for example, revisited her fieldnotes, her journal, and a short story she had written while she was doing fieldwork in a Taiwanese village.

Different kinds of prose may be interspersed with poetry, resulting in a more promiscuous mix of styles and genres. Such experimental writing will serve a number of purposes. It subverts the smooth surface of the text in order to disrupt the monologic style in which the ethnographer/observer occupies the sole vantage-point, and from whose standpoint the entire account is provided. The kaleidoscopic presentation of different textual styles and fragments thus allows the writer and the reader to shift from one perspective to another. Couched in such innovative ways, the ethnographer may well be seeking to 'evoke' a social setting and social action. The writing may, therefore, be impressionistic in character. Moreover, the evocative text is evaluated in terms of its connotative or affective quality as much as, or more than, its denotative precision.

Moreover, there will be a multiplicity of 'voices'. The ethnographic text under the auspices of postmodernism aspires to be a polyvocal one. That is, in addition to the voice of the ethnographer/author, there will be the voices of social actors. Their experiences will not always, perhaps never, be filtered through the interpretative framework of the author. Rather, the text will reproduce the actors' own perspectives and experiences. This may include extended biographical and autobiographical accounts, extended dialogues between the researcher and informants, and other 'documents of life'. Typically, there is an emphasis on the kinds of narratives or stories through which social actors construct their own and others' experiences.

The ethnographer will be visible or audibly present in the text. Her or his own feelings, actions and reactions will be inscribed in the text. The mechanics of the research as well as its emotional content will be integral to its reportage. The postmodern text will be imbued with the work of research, which will not therefore be relegated or marginalised to a methodological appendix or an autobiographical confessional entirely divorced from the 'real' work of analysis and reportage. Indeed, some postmodern ethnographic texts may have the air of a 'confessional' throughout. The presence of the researcher reflects the principle of reflexivity. Reflexivity has a range of meanings in this context, but its most general sense, it captures the extent to which the researcher is inescapably a part of the social world that she or he is investigating. The researcher cannot wish away her or his presence or the fact that the social world under investigation is, in principle, being negotiated or co-produced with its members through the transactions of research. The reflexive ethnography is thus permeated with the presence and work of the ethnographer. Moreover, the postmodern ethnographer exhibits multiple identities, refracted through the variety of social relationships and transactions that constitute 'the field' of exploration. There are, therefore, multiple selves or identities associated with the ethnographer under the rubric of postmodernism, just as social actors in general are portrayed as fragmentary and fractile. The researcher may indeed become so much a part of the enterprise that she or he becomes not merely an observer or an interrogator, but the subject-matter of the research itself. The term 'auto-ethnography' is currently used to connote a wider range of issues than this alone, but among the practitioners of auto-ethnography are those who use introspection, memory, autobiography and other constructions of 'self' as the subject-matter of their own research. The genres of research text here blur with those of biographical work.

151

voice and polyvocality

The representational practices and devices alluded to relate closely to the analytic strategy of evoking multiple 'voices' in the reconstruction of social realities. If research dissolves the privilege of the observer/author, then it also implies that there should be multiple voices identifiable in the analysis. This goes well beyond the perfectly ordinary practice of quoting informants or including extracts from fieldnotes in order to illustrate ethnographic texts. The polyvocal text – and hence the analytic strategy that underlies it – does not subordinate the voices and press them into the service of a single narrative. Rather, there are multiple and shifting narratives. The point of view of the 'analysis' is a shifting one. There is no single implied narrator occupying a privileged interpretative position. A relatively early example of such a text is Krieger's (1983) account of a lesbian community. Krieger, as author/analyst, constructs a collage or palimpsest of narratives, juxtaposed in the style of stream-of-consciousness literary work. Her analysis of the community is implicit in those textual arrangements, which are not superseded or supplemented by a dominant authorial commentary. The expression of voices has become a major preoccupation of many qualitative researchers in recent years, and to some extent, the force of polyvocality has become blunted: in some contexts it can seem to mean little more than 'letting the informants speak for themselves', with little or no theoretical sophistication. On the other hand, it can give rise to complex and dense representations (see Atkinson, 1999, for a review of different kinds of recent contribution). Equally, the celebration of voices can allow the author to find her or his 'voice' in a way that differs from the canons of conventional academic writing: it provides permission for first-person narratives that insert the author in her or his texts, rather than suppressing the personal in the analytic.

autoethnography

Reflexivity and first-person narratives lead directly to the possibilities of autoethnography. The term itself has several connotations. Here we will focus briefly on analyses that are based substantially or even exclusively on the writer's personal experiences, memories and actions. This, therefore, moves the personal from the marginal notes of the confessional tale to occupy the central place of sociological or anthropological analysis. Autoethnography and autobiography can be virtually indistinguishable. The resulting accounts can be highly charged emotionally for the author and reader alike. Tillmann-Healy (1996), for instance, has written a highly personalised account of her own experience of bulimia, while in the same anthology Ronai (1996) writes a moving account of her 'mentally retarded' mother. Latta (1999) did her PhD on the narratives of five women writers who, like her, had writer's block. She reflects on how postmodern theory paralysed and silenced her, on how her father explained Marxism to her and the members of his trade union, and why she chose her thesis topic. Reed-Danahay's (1997) collection, and her overview (2001) showcase these developments.

Because of the feminist mantra 'the personal is political', autoethnography fits very well into feminist sociology, whether or not its inscribers enjoy playing with postmodernism.

CONCLUSION

The freedom provided by postmodernism to write in innovative ways, and the vogue for polyvocality are probably the most important aspects of postmodernism for sociology as a whole, and therefore for feminist sociology. If the disputes over postmodernist feminism can be resolved, the long-term legacy of textual freedom will be liberating for all of feminist sociology.

nine

prerogatives usurped?

conclusions

A manda Cross's (1981: 102) heroine, Kate Fansler, tells her friend
Sylvia: 'Men are always writing books about murdering women –
it's one of their favourite fantasies: revenge for having their prerogatives
usurped: sexual prerogatives, political prerogatives, social prerogatives
....' In this book I have displayed some of the wide range of empirical, methodological and theoretical materials that feminist sociologists have produced in the past, and in the 30 years since the current,
Third Wave, of feminism arose. I have criticised many male sociologists
for their failure to read, and then to cite, that material. I have shown
that the malestream has largely ignored a genderquake in sociology
although a few men are very disturbed about it, and a larger minority
of men are excited by it. The many topics where our knowledge is defi-
cient have been mentioned, alongside the areas where feminist sociology
has made a difference. Tributes to the ground-breaking work of giants,
such as Dorothy Smith, have been paid. In this brief conclusion we
return to Burminster, and to our heroines, Eowyn and Sophonisba.

In Chapter 2, Burminster in 2002 was presented as a university
department much changed by feminist sociology. It was, of course, a
very exaggerated vignette: no real department in Britain has seven professors, of whom three are women, nor does any insist that one-third
of items on reading lists have female authors or that all students write
about feminist or queer methods in one of their essays for a core course.
As the book was being completed, departments of gender studies, and
of sociology, were being merged and even closed. Feminist sociology in
Britain may be cut down, or even cut out altogether in the twenty-first
century: it is too soon to know.

To end the book on a reflexive and positive note, let us end the book
with Eowyn and Sophonisba. It is 2003 – and it is a rainy night in
Georgia. The American Sociological Association (ASA) is having its
annual conference, accompanied by the Society for the Study of Social
Problems (SSSP) and the Society for the Study of Symbolic Interaction

(SSSI). Eowyn and Sophonisba are in the Buckhead Diner. Sophonisba has come to the ASA because her book on Jane Addams is being launched, and most of its sales will be in the USA and because of the centenary celebrations for Marion McLean. She is not an ASA member and has never been to an ASA conference before. Eowyn is a regular at ASA, but has not been to Atlanta before. The Buckhead Diner is an upmarket restaurant: furnished like a classic American diner it serves modern eclectic food. Both women have given their papers, and are celebrating that the hardest part of the meeting is over:

> **Eowyn:** Atlanta is *just* like it is in a Kathy Trocheck detective story: everything really is called Peachtree Boulevard, or Crescent, or Avenue: but it is far too hot and too humid for me. I will be glad to get back to Glasgow.
>
> **Sophonisba:** Which is Kathy Trocheck? – the series with the woman who runs a house-cleaning service?
>
> **Eowyn:** Yes - I will lend you the one I found today when I have read it – her heroine, Callahan Garrity, is fun. I've enjoyed ASA but I'm ready to get home.
>
> **Sophonisba:** Me too – did you get into the publishers' exhibits today?
>
> **Eowyn:** Yes: awesome. And I'll never get used to the armed guards on the door or the Encyclopaedia Britannica having a stall. There's a useful looking series we should buy for the Library: The Gender Lens series from AltaMira. And did you *see* all those Chicago University Press titles?
>
> **Sophonisba:** Is Sara Delamont's book out? Is it there?
>
> **Eowyn:** Yes – though no one in America is going to take any notice of a British book, are they? It could be what we need – I asked for an inspection copy before we left home.
>
> **Sophonisba:** Let's hope we both like it. Oh here's our salads.

I, as the real author, hope you, the reader, like it. To be optimistic, and end with an even more positive note, let us conclude with words from Pierre Bourdieu and Ulrich Beck. These two giants of sociology offer uplift. Bourdieu argues that: 'masculine domination no longer imposes itself with the transparency of something taken for granted. Thanks, in particular, to the immense critical effort of the feminist movement ... it now appears as something to be avoided, excused or justified' (2001: 88).

Similarly radical in its recognition of the genderquake, we should end this chapter and the book with a comment on gender equality from Ulrich Beck, which addresses both my central themes: 'A society in which men and women were really equal ... would without doubt be a new modernity' (1994: 27).

appendix one
a critique of the orthodox histories of sociology

The history of sociology, as taught a century after it began in different industrialising countries, prioritises various scholars, but they are all men. Not only the three giants, Marx, Weber and Durkheim, but the supporting cast, are routinely presented as all-male. So, for example, two British scholars, Giddens (1971) and Hawthorn (1976) wrote histories of sociology, before the feminist sociologies had become prominent, which are only about founding fathers. Burford Rhea's (1981) American compilation *The Future of the Sociological Classics* covers Hobbes, Tönnies, Vico, Pareto, Simmel, Weber, Marx, Durkheim, Mead and Freud. Raymond Aron's (1965, 1967) French books *Main Currents in Sociological Thought* cover Comte, Montesquieu, Marx, Tocqueville, Pareto, Weber and Durkheim. German histories of sociology are similarly structured. In the history of sociology as written in the 1960s, 1970s and 1980s, students are taught that the founders of the discipline are all men, overwhelmingly *European* men. They are Italian, French, German or Austrian, rather than British or American.

The maleness of the key scholars in the orthodox history of sociology is reinforced to novices by the sex of the authors who write about it. Giddens, Hawthorn, Rhea, and Aron are men. To offer a few examples of works that figure on student reading lists we can scrutinise Bottomore and Nisbet (1978a), Lee and Newby (1983), Collins (1994a, 1994b) and the series of short volumes in Oxford University Press's 'Past Masters' series, each of which introduce one key thinker. First, Bottomore and Nisbet (1978a), an edited collection called *A History of Sociological Analysis*, intended for advanced students in sociology, rather than complete novices. It has 17 chapters by 19 authors, only one by a woman (writing jointly with a man). Most of the chapters cover movements or schools of thought, such as 'Structuralism'. These are written by experts on the leading historical figures in that tradition, and these leading historical figures are all men.

So all the scholars discussed in the chapters on positivism, functionalism, and structuralism are men. Furthermore, the authors of those chapters do not comment on their decision to characterise those schools of thought as being all-male. A novice reader cannot know whether there were any women, or that there were not, in that 'school'.

The male editors have not, themselves, challenged the 'founding fathers' idea of sociology, because although there is room for 17 intellectual movements, feminism was not one of them. Having decided not to include feminism as a sociological movement or school, the editors did not 'police' their contributors to thread feminist ideas throughout the 17 chapters either. The subject index has one entry on gender, directing the reader to a section in the chapter on stratification. Feminism is not an entry. Sexism is not an entry. Women is not an entry. The chapters on, for example, criticisms of positivism and on functionalism fail to address feminist critiques of these theoretical positions, although by the mid-1970s there were plenty of such criticisms around which could have been cited. In 703 pages of text, four pages deal with feminist sociology. The chapter on 'German Sociology in the time of Max Weber' (a man) is written by Freund (a man), ignores Helene and Marianne Weber and fails to cite feminist critiques of Weberian sociology. Alan Dawe (1978: 362) does mention Marianne Weber, but only as her husband's eulogist. The chapter by Wilbert Moore (1978) on functionalism is about Durkheim, Hobbes, Spencer, Parsons, Kingsley Davis, G.P. Murdock, Merton, Levy, Bales, Shils, and Smelser. Again, there are, apparently no women functionalists worth mentioning, nor are any feminist critiques of functionalism discussed. Bottomore and Nisbet (1978a) is a typical book on the history of the subject, designed for advanced students and collegial consultation, which showed no recognition of feminist ideas. Bottomore and Nisbet therefore uphold the founding fathers, malestream, history of sociology in four ways: (1) they recruit male authors; (2) they commission chapters on male scholars; (3) they omit to commission any chapter(s) on feminism or feminist sociologies; and (4) they do not require their contributors to include women sociologists in their chapters, or to address feminist critiques of the material they are presenting.

Similar exclusionary practices characterise the authors and editors of texts used for introductory courses. A high quality introductory text, Lee and Newby (1983) offered Tönnies, Marx, Weber, Durkheim and a group they called evolutionists (Locke, Comte, Spencer, Morgan, Darwin and Veblen). Feminism appears as a critique of the various theories, but there are no founding mothers. A novice would be left thinking that the subject was created by men between 1770 and 1970, since when a few 'feminists' have criticised some of the ideas.

Randall Collins (1994a, 1994b) catalogues four sociological traditions in a textbook with an accompanying reader. He distinguishes a 'conflict' tradition (Marx and Weber) from a Durkheimian one, plus a rational utilitarian and a microinteractionist tradition. In the accompanying reader, the conflict tradition is epitomised by Marx, Engels, Weber, Dahrendorf, Lenski and Collins himself (all men). The Reactional/Utilitarian section contains papers by Homans, March and Simon, Schelling, Olson, and Coleman (all men).

The Microinteractionist tradition is illustrated by the work of Goffman, Meehan, Wood, Blumer, Mead, and Cooley (all men). In the Durkheimian portion of the book are contributions by Durkheim, Hubert, Mauss, Lévi-Strauss, Goffman, Hagstrom (all men) and Mary Douglas. In Collins's text (1994a) there are some discussions of women and of feminism, but they are not indexed, and a novice would not learn of the breadth and depth of female participation or feminist ideas in the discipline. Collins originally published his text in 1988, and while he has altered it for the 1994a version, it remains marooned in an all-male world.

An alternative to the single text is the series of single volumes introducing concepts or individual authors. The Oxford University Press series 'Past Masters', which had published 67 titles by 1991, included six sociologists (loosely defined) Engels, Hobbes, Locke, Marx, Mill and Vico, with one more to come (Durkheim). All these men were written about by men. There were no female 'Past Masters' of sociology, and no sociological women authors. Again a novice could not find out whether there were any founding mothers. The Fontana series, 'Modern Masters', edited by Frank Kermode, had reached 37 titles by 1980, covering figures in the arts and social sciences. All the 'masters' were men: no woman was considered a modern master. Three of the authors were women.

157

Subsequently Routledge had a series of short volumes called 'Key Sociologists'. In 1987 it had 14 titles, 11 of which featured a single sociologist. Three covered a 'school': 'Marx and Marxism', 'The Frankfurt School' and 'The Ethnomethodologists'. The 11 individuals featured were all men (Weber, Durkheim, Parsons, Freud, Mills, Simmel, Mannheim, Foucault, Goffman, Habermas and Merton). No woman was featured in the three books on 'Schools' either. For example, Sharrock and Anderson (1986) treat ethnomethodology as a largely male specialism, focusing on Cicourel, Sacks and Garfinkel. Gail Jefferson is the only woman important enough to be indexed. A few other women are cited, but not discussed as scholars (Candace West, Mary Rogers, Karin Knorr-Cetina). All the authors of all the books in the series up to 1986 were men. Subsequently Bourdieu was added to the series.

The 1980s saw a growth in feminist sociology which might lead one to expect that volumes equivalent to the Bottomore and Nisbet (1978a) produced in the 1980s and 1990s would show change. However, this is not the case. In 1987 Giddens and Turner edited a volume called *Social Theory and Modern Sociology*. It has 12 chapters, by 12 men. Feminism is not a social theory, although there is a whole chapter on ethnomethodology. The index gives one reference for 'feminists' which directs the reader to Miliband on class analysis and his brief discussion of feminist critiques of such analyses. There is no index entry for gender. Entries on 'sexism' and 'women' send the reader to the same three pages as 'feminists'. So, in 403 pages, there are three on feminist sociology. The Giddens and Turner volume was part of a Polity Press series 'Social and Political Theory'. By 1987 it had 36 other volumes published and 11 'forthcoming'. Among the 47 were six with a woman author, and Bob Connell's *Gender and Power*. Three of the forthcoming books were to be by women. The Polity list included, in 1987, two of the most distinguished feminist sociologists in Britain (Sylvia Walby, Michèle Barrett). Yet, Giddens and Turner did not include Feminism as a theory in their compilation.

Anderson et al. (1987) edited *Classic Disputes in Sociology*. It has eight chapters by men, and the classic debates were about space, official statistics, laws and explanations, the individual and society, the Protestant work ethic, class, capitalism, and the transition from rural to urban society. The editors pointed out that Marx, Durkheim and Weber 'loom large in nearly every chapter' (ibid.: x). The index does not include feminism, sexism or women. There are index entries for 'gender' (five of them) but none of the single page citations leads to a sustained analysis of gender. So the 'classic disputes' as seen in 1987 in Britain are not touched by feminist sociology at all.

In 1988 Smelser edited an American *Handbook of Sociology*. There are 22 chapters by 33 authors, in four sections. Nine of the authors are women. The four sections focus on theory and method; inequalities; institutions and organisations; and change. Theory and method has all male authors, so does social process and change. In the theory and method section, Feminism is not discussed as a theory or a method. The index references to 'Feminism' and 'Feminist theory' send the reader to the empirical chapter on 'Gender and sex roles'. There are 38 index entries for gender, which send the reader to the Gender chapter, or those on work or on medicine. None of the 'gender' entries refers to a theory or methods chapter. Sexism is not an index term. There are 12 index entries for women, all to empirical chapters on work, health, or the chapter on gender. Overall, therefore, although there are women authors in the handbook, the impact of feminism is ghettoised and absent from the high status sections.

These compilations from the late 1980s show feminist ideas still absent, or ghettoised. Feminist sociology had not been 'mainstreamed' at all. Individual British theorists show a similar pattern. Craib's (1997) *Classical Social Theory* is only about men, and does not cover feminist ideas. In 1995 Barry Barnes published *The Elements of Social Theory*. Here he identified 'those fundamental theories and ideas in social theory that currently possess the most plausibility' (1995: vii). That is, these were the theories Barnes felt should be trusted, and used in future research. His chapters deal with Individualism, Functionalism, Interactionism and Knowledge in a section called Traditions; and then, in a section called 'Social formations and social processes', with status groups, social movements, social classes and administrative hierarchies. Feminism, gender, sexism and women are not indexed. There is no discussion at all of any issue raised by feminist sociology in the previous 20 years. Mary Douglas is the only woman cited, and her ideas are not discussed.

The same year John Scott produced his *Sociological Theory* (1995). Scott announces that 'Theory is fundamental to the whole sociological enterprise' (ibid.: xii). His book does not index feminism or sexism or women. There are index entries for 'gender divisions' and for 'gendered character of theory'. The latter takes the reader to a half-page on Mary Wollstonecraft. There are no citations to Barbara Adam, Michèle Barrett, Sylvia Walby, or Dorothy Smith. The discussion of the Chicago School of Sociology ignores Deegan (1988) whose feminist analysis of that tradition was the focus of Chapter 3. When Scott moves to more contemporary theories, the pattern continues. So his chapter on postmodernism ignores Butler, Flax and Lather. Scott's chapter on structuralism ignores Mary Douglas who is probably the most widely used structuralist theorist in the Anglophone world. Her ideas spread much further outside anthropology that those of Edmund Leach (Delamont, 1989b). Bauman's (2000) *Liquid Modernity* makes no mention of feminism, and has only six women in the bibliography.

Despite 30 years of feminist critiques of the orthodox history of the discipline, the recent accounts share with those written in the 1960s an adherence to a simplistic and uncritical all-male grand narrative.

159

appendix two
the autobiographical narratives

This appendix lists the locations of the 23 American 'silverback' narratives analysed in Chapter 7, and the 22 female narratives discussed throughout the book.

Scholar	Location of autobiography	Date published
George Homans	Annual Review of Sociology (ARS)	1986
Robert Merton	ARS	1987
David Riesman	ARS	1988
Amos Hawley	ARS	1992
Lewis Coser	ARS	1993
Peter Blau	ARS	1995
Seymour M. Lipset	ARS	1996
William J. Wilson	Riley	1988
Hubert Blalock	Riley	1988
William Sewell	Riley	1988
Dennis Wrong	Berger	1990
James Coleman	Berger	1990
Joseph Gusfield	Berger	1990
Dean MacCannell	Berger	1990
Andrew Greeley	Berger	1990
Herbert Gans	Berger	1990
Gary Marx	Berger	1990
Donald Cressey	Berger	1990
John Gagnon	Berger	1990
Nathan Glazer	Berger	1990
Reinhard Bendix	Berger	1990
Bennett Berger	Berger	1990
Erving Goffman	Verhoeven	1992
Total 23		

Table 1: *Autobiographical narratives of male sociologists analysed*

Scholar	Location of autobiography	Date published
Joan Acker	Laslett and Thorne	1997
Sarah Fenstermaker	L & T	1997
Evelyn N. Glenn	L & T	1997
Barbara Laslett	L & T	1997
Judith Stacey	L & T	1997
Barrie Thorne	L & T	1997
Arlene K. Daniels	Orlans and Wallace	1994
Arlie R. Hochschild	O & W	1994
Ruth Wallace	O & W	1994
Jackie Wiseman	O & W	1994
Suzanne Keller	Goetting and Fenstermaker	1995
Helen M. Hacker	G & F	1995
Lynda L. Holmstrom	G & F	1995
Judy Long	G & F	1995
Helen Z. Lopata	G & F	1995
Shulamit Reinharz	G & F	1995
Pamela A. Roby	G & F	1995
Coramae R. Mann	G & F	1995
Jessie Bernard	Berger	1990
Cynthia F. Epstein	Berger	1990
Alice S. Rossi	Berger	1990
Pepper Schwartz	Berger	1990

Total 22

161

Table 2: *Autobiographical narratives of female sociologists analysed*

bibliography

Abbott, A. (1999) *Department and Discipline: Chicago Sociology at One Hundred*. Chicago: University of Chicago Press.

Abbott, P. and Sapsford, R. (eds) (1987) *Women and Social Class*. London: Tavistock.

Acker, J. (1973) 'Women and social stratification', *American Journal of Sociology*, 78 (1): 174–83.

Acker, J. (1997) 'My life as a feminist sociologist', in B. Laslett and B. Thorne (eds), *Feminist Sociology*. New Brunswick, NJ: Rutgers University Press, pp. 28–47.

Acker, S. (1981) 'No woman's land', *Sociological Review*, 29 (1): 65–88.

Acker, S. (1994) 'No woman's land', in S. Acker, *Gendered Education*. Philadelphia: Open University Press, pp. 27–42.

Acker, S. and Warren-Piper, D. (eds) (1984) *Is Higher Education Fair to Women?* London: SRHE.

Adam, B. (1996) 'Feminist social theory needs time', in A. Coffey and J. Pilcher (eds), *Qualitative Research on Gender*. Aldershot: Ashgate, pp. 149–63.

Addams, J. (1895) *Hull-House Maps and Papers*. Boston: Thomas Y. Crowell.

Ahmed, S., Kilby, J., Lury, C., McNeil, M. and Skeggs, B. (eds) (2000) *Transformations*. London: Routledge.

Aisenberg, N. and Harrington, M. (1988) *Women of Academe: Outsiders in the Sacred Grove*. Amherst, MA: University of Massachusetts Press.

Albrow, M. (1997) *The Global Age*. Cambridge: Polity Press.

Allen, C. and Howard, J.A. (eds) (2000) *Provoking Feminisms*. Chicago: University of Chicago Press.

Allen, S. (2001) 'Peaks and troughs in British sociology', *Network*, 80: 1.

Alway, J. (1995) 'The trouble with gender: tales of the still-missing feminist revolution in sociological theory', *Sociological Theory*, 13 (3): 209–28.

Andermahr, S., Lovell, T. and Wolkowitz, C. (2000) *A Glossary of Feminist Theory*. London: Arnold.

Anderson, R.J., Hughes, J.A. and Sharrock, W.W. (eds) (1987) *Classic Disputes in Sociology*. London: Allen and Unwin.

Annandale, E. and Hunt, K. (eds) (2000) *Gender Inequalities and Health*. Buckingham: Open University Press.

Appignanesi, L. (1999) *The Dead of Winter*. London: Bantam.

Arber, S. and Ginn, J. (1991) *Gender and Later Life*. London: Sage.

Arber, S. and Ginn, J. (eds) (1995) *Connecting Gender and Ageing*. Buckingham: Open University Press.

Ardener, S. (ed.) (1975) *Perceiving Women*. London: Dent.

Ardener, S. (ed.) (1978) *Defining Female*. London: Croom Helm.

Ardener, S. (ed.) (1981) *Women and Space*. London: Croom Helm.

Ardener, S. (1985) 'The social anthropology of women and feminist anthropology', *Anthropology Today*, 1 (5): 24–6.

Arnot, M. (2001) 'Bernstein's sociology of pedagogy: female dialogues and feminist elaborations', in K. Weiler (ed.), *Feminist Engagements*. New York: Routledge. pp. 109–39.

Aron, R. (1965) *Main Currents in Sociological Thought*, volume I. Harmondsworth: Penguin.

Aron, R. (1967) *Main Currents in Sociological Thought*, volume II. Harmondsworth: Penguin.

Atkinson, P.A. (1983) 'The reproduction of professional community', in R. Dingwall and P. Lewis (eds), *The Sociology of Professions: Lawyers, Doctors and Others*. London: Macmillan, pp. 224–41.

Atkinson. P.A. (1985) *Language, Structure and Reproduction*. London: Tavistock.

Atkinson, P.A. (1995) 'From structuralism to discourse', in A. Sadovnik (ed.), *Knowledge and Pedagogy*. New York: Ablex, pp. 83–96.

Atkinson, P.A. (1999) 'Voiced and unvoiced', *Sociology*, 33 (1): 191–7.

Atkinson, P.A., Coffey, A. and Delamont, S. (1999) 'Ethnography: post, past and present', *Journal of Contemporary Ethnography*, 28 (5): 460–71.

Atkinson, P.A., Coffey, A. and Delamont, S. (2001) 'A debate about our canon', *Qualitative Research*, 1 (1): 5–22.

Atkinson, P.A. and Delamont, S. (1990) 'Professions and powerlessness', *Sociological Review*, 38 (1): 90–110.

Atkinson, P.A. and Housley, W. (2002) *Interactionism*. London: Sage.

Atkinson, P.A., Reid, M. and Sheldrake, P. (1977) 'Medical mystique', *Sociology of Work and Occupations*, 4 (3): 243–80.

Atkinson, P.A. and Silverman, D. (1997) 'Kundera's "Immortality": the interview society and the invention of the self', *Qualitative Inquiry*, 3 (3): 304–25.

Bailey, L. (1999) 'Refracted selves?', *Sociology*, 33 (2): 335–52.

Ball, S. (1980) *Beachside Comprehensive*. Cambridge: Cambridge University Press.

Banks, O. (1981) *Faces of Feminism*. Oxford: Martin Robertson.

Barker, D.L. and Allen, S. (eds) (1976) *Sexual Divisions and Society*. London: Tavistock.

Barker, P. (1993) *Regeneration*. Harmondsworth: Penguin.

Barker, P. (1994) *The Eye in the Door*. Harmondsworth: Penguin.

Barker, P. (1995) *The Ghost Road*. Harmondsworth: Penguin.

Barnes, B. (1995) *The Elements of Social Theory*. London: UCL Press.

Barrett, M. (1988) *Women's Oppression Today*. 2nd edition. London: Verso.

Barrett, M. (1992) 'Words and things', in M. Barrett and A. Phillips (eds), *Destabilizing Theory*. Cambridge: Polity Press, pp. 201–19.

Barrett, M. and Phillips, A. (eds) (1992) *Destabilizing Theory: Contemporary Feminist Debates*. Cambridge: Polity Press.

Bauman, Z. (2000) *Liquid Modernity*. Cambridge: Polity Press.

Baxter, J. and Western, M. (1998) 'Satisfaction with housework', *Sociology*, 32 (1): 101–20.

Beard, M. (2000) *The Invention of Jane Harrison*. Cambridge, MA: Harvard University Press.

Becher, T. (1989) *Academic Tribes and Territories*. Buckingham: Open University Press.

Becher, T. and Trowler, P.R. (2001) *Academic Tribes and Territories*, 2nd edition. Buckingham: Open University Press.

Beck, U. (1992) *Risk Society*. London: Sage.

Beck, U. (1994) 'The reinvention of politics', in U. Beck, A. Giddens and S. Lash (eds), *Reflexive Modernization*. Cambridge: Polity Press, pp. 1–55.

Beck, U. and Beck-Gernsheim, E. (1995) *The Normal Chaos of Love*. Cambridge: Polity Press.

Beck, U., Giddens, A. and Lash, S. (eds) (1994) *Reflexive Modernization*. Cambridge: Polity Press.

Behar, R. (1995) 'Introduction: out of exile', in R. Behar and D.A. Gordon (eds), *Women Writing Culture*. Berkeley, CA: University of California Press, pp. 1–29.

Behar, R. and Gordon, D.A. (eds) (1995) *Women Writing Culture*. Berkeley, CA: University of California Press.

Bell, D. and Klein, R. (eds) (1996) *Radically Speaking: Feminism Reclaimed*. London: Zed Books.

Bendelow, G., Carpenter, M., Vautier, C. and Williams, S. (eds) (2002) *Gender, Health and Healing*. London: Routledge.

Bendix, R. (1990) 'How I became an American sociologist', in B. Berger (ed.), *Authors of their Own Lives*. Berkeley, CA: University of California Press, pp. 452–71.

Benhabib, S. (1995) 'Feminism and postmodernism', in S. Benhabib, J. Butler, D. Cornell and N. Fraser (eds), *Feminist Contentions*. London: Routledge, pp. 17–34.

Berger, B. (ed.) (1990a) *Authors of their Own Lives*. Berkeley, CA: University of California Press.

Berger, B. (1990b) 'Looking for the interstices', in B. Berger (ed.), *Authors of their Own Lives*. Berkeley, CA: University of California Press, pp. 152–64.

Berghe, P.V. (1990) 'From the Popocatepetl to the Limpopo', in B. Berger (ed.), *Authors of their Own Lives*. Berkeley, CA: University of California Press, pp. 410–31.

Bernard, J. (1964) *Academic Women*. New York: New American Library.

Bernard, J. (1987) 'Re-viewing the impact of women's studies in sociology', in C. Farnham (ed.), *The Impact of Feminist Research in the Academy*. Bloomington, IN: Indiana University Press, pp. 193–216.

Bernard, L.L. and Bernard, J. (1943) *Origins of American Sociology*. New York: Thomas Y. Crowell.

Bernstein, B. (1971) 'On the classification and framing of educational knowledge', in M.F.D Young (ed.), *Knowledge and Control*. London: Macmillan, pp. 47–69.

Bernstein, B. (1975) 'Class and pedagogies', *Educational Studies*, 1 (1): 23–41.

Bird, E. (2001) 'Disciplining the interdisciplinary', *British Journal of the Sociology of Education*, 22 (4): 463–78.

Blackburn, R.M. and Mann, M. (1979) *The Working Class in the Labour Market*. London: Macmillan.

Blackstone, T. and Fulton, O. (1975) 'Sex discrimination among university teachers', *British Journal of Sociology*, 26 (3): 261–75.

Blau, P. (1995) 'A circuitous path to macrostructural theory', *Annual Review of Sociology*, 21: 1–19.

Bloor, M. (2001) 'The ethnography of health and medicine', in P.A. Atkinson, A. Coffey, S. Delamont, J. Lofland and L. Lofland (eds), *Handbook of Ethnography*. London: Sage, pp. 177–87.

Blumberg, D. (1966) *Florence Kelley: The Making of a Social Pioneer*. New York: Kelley.

Bochner, A. (2001) 'Narrative's virtues', *Qualitative Inquiry*, 7 (2): 131–57.

Bologh, R.W. (1990) *Love or Greatness*. London: Unwin Hyman.

Booth, M. (1919) 'The present day education of girls', *The Nineteenth Century and After*, 102 (August): 259–69.

Booth, M. (1927) *Youth and Sex*. London: Allen and Unwin.

Borneman, J. (1992) *Belonging in the Two Berlins*. Cambridge: Cambridge University Press.

Bottomore, T. (1978) 'Marxism and sociology', in T. Bottomore and R. Nisbet (eds), *A History of Sociological Analysis*. London: Heinemann, pp. 118–48.

Bottomore, T. and Nisbet, R. (eds) (1978a) *A History of Sociological Analysis*. London: Heinemann.

Bottomore, T. and Nisbet, R. (1978b) 'Structuralism', in T. Bottomore and R. Nisbet (eds), *A History of Sociological Analysis*. London: Heinemann, pp. 557–98.

Bourdieu, P. (1988) *Homo Academicus*. Cambridge: Polity Press.

Bourdieu, P. (2001) *Masculine Domination*. Cambridge: Polity Press.

Bowles, G. and Duelli-Klein, R. (eds) (1983) *Theories of Women's Studies*. London: Routledge.

Brack, D.C. (1995) 'Writing papers and stirring soup', in A. Goetting and S. Fenstermaker (eds), *Individual Voices, Collective Visions*. Philadelphia, PA: Temple University Press, pp. 23–36.

Bradley, H. (1997) *Fractured Identities*. Cambridge: Polity Press.

Braidotti, R. (2000) 'Comment on Felski's "The doxa of difference"', in C. Allen and J.A. Howard (eds), *Provoking Feminisms*. Chicago: University of Chicago Press, pp. 93–110.

Breugel, I. (1996) 'Whose myths are they anyway?', *British Journal of Sociology*, 47 (1): 175–7.

Brewer, J. (2000) *Ethnography*. Buckingham: Open University Press.

British Sociological Association (1977) *Sociology without Sexism: A Sourcebook*. London: BSA.

Britten, N. and Heath, A. (1983) 'Women, men and social class', in E. Gamarnikow et al. (eds), *Gender, Class and Work*. London: Heinemann, pp. 46–60.

Brodribb, S. (1992) *Nothing Matters*. Melbourne: Spinifex.

Brooks, A. (1997) *Academic Women*. Buckingham: Open University Press.

Brown, P. and Scase, R. (1994) *Higher Education and Corporate Realities*. London: UCL Press.

Brown, R. (1986) 'Researching women's issues – retrospect and prospect', *EOC Research Bulletin*, 10: 1–11.

Bryman, A. and Burgess, R.G. (eds) (1994) *Analysing Qualitative Data*. London: Routledge.

Buchan, J. (1919) *Mr Standfast*. London: Hodder and Stoughton.

Buchan, J. (1926) *The Dancing Floor*. London: Hodder and Stoughton.

Bucher, R. and Stelling, J.G. (1977) *Becoming Professional*. Beverly Hills, CA: Sage.

Bullock, A. and Stallybrass, O. (eds) (1977) *The Fontana Dictionary of Modern Thought*. London: Collins.

Bullock, A. and Trombley, S. (eds) (1999) *The New Fontana Dictionary of Modern Thought*, 3rd edition. London: HarperCollins.

Bulmer, M. (1984) *The Chicago School of Sociology*. Chicago: University of Chicago Press.

Bunch, C. (ed.) (1981) *Building Feminist Theory: Essays from 'Quest'*. New York: Longman.

Burgess, R.G. (ed.) (1985) *Field Methods in the Study of Education*. London: Falmer.

Burgoyne, C. and Morison, V. (1997) 'Money in remarriage', *Sociological Review*, 45 (3): 363–96.

Burgoyne, J. and Clark, D. (1983) 'You are what you eat', in A. Murcott (ed.), *The Sociology of Food and Eating*. Aldershot: Gower, pp. 152–63..

Burke, J.L. (1993) *In the Electronic Mist with the Confederate Dead*. London: Phoenix.

165

Burke, J.L. (1998) *Sunset Limited*. London: Orion.

Busfield, J. (1974) 'Ideologies and reproduction', in M. Richards (ed.), *The Integration of a Child into a Social World*. Cambridge: Cambridge University Press, pp. 11–36.

Butler, J. (1990) *Gender Trouble*. London: Routledge.

Butler, J. (1999) *Gender Trouble*, 2nd edn. London: Routledge.

Butler, J. and Scott, J. (eds) (1992) *Feminists Theorize the Political*. London: Routledge.

Callan, H. and Ardener, S. (eds) (1984) *The Incorporated Wife*. London: Croom Helm.

Callon, M. (1999) 'Whose imposture?', *Social Studies of Science*, 29 (2): 261–86.

Caplan, P.J. (1993) *Lifting a Ton of Feathers*. Toronto: University of Toronto Press.

Carey, J. (1975) *Sociology and Public Affairs: The Chicago School*. Beverly Hills, CA: Sage.

Cavan, S. (1994) 'Becoming an ethnographer', in K.P.M. Orlans and R.A. Wallace (eds), *Gender and the Academic Experience*. Lincoln, NE: University of Nebraska Press, pp. 57–70.

Cavendish, R. (1982) *Women on the Line*. London: Routledge and Kegan Paul.

Chafetz. J.A. (1988) *Feminist Sociology: An Overview of Contemporary Theories*. Itasca, IL: Peacock.

Chafetz, J.S. (1997) 'Feminist theory and sociology', *Annual Review of Sociology*, 23: 97–120.

Chaff, S. (ed.) (1977) *Women and Medicine: An Annotated Bibliography*. Lanham, MA: Scarecrow Press.

Charles, N. and Davies, C.A. (1997) 'Contested communities', *Sociological Review*, 45 (3): 416–37.

Charles, N. and Kerr, M. (1986) 'Food for feminist thought', *Sociological Review*, 34 (3): 537–72.

Charles, N. and Kerr, M. (1988) *Women, Food and Families*. Manchester: Manchester University Press.

Cheal, D. (1987) '"Showing them you love them": gift giving and the dialectic of intimacy', *Sociological Review*, 35 (1): 150–69.

Chodorow, N. (1978) *The Reproduction of Mothering*. Berkeley, CA: University of California Press.

Chodorow, N. (1987) *Feminism and Psychoanalytic Theory*. Cambridge: Polity Press.

Christian, B. (1996) 'The race for theory', in D. Bell and R. Klein (eds), *Radically Speaking*. London: Zed Books, pp. 311–20.

Chubin, D. (1974) 'Sociological manpower and womanpower', *American Sociologist*, 9 (2): 83–92.

Clark, V., Garner, S.N., Higonnet, M. and Katrak, K.H. (eds) (1996) *Anti-feminism in the Academy*. New York: Routledge.

Clegg, S. (1985) 'Feminist methodology', *Quality and Quantity*, 19 (1): 83–97.

Clifford, J. and Marcus, G. (eds) (1986) *Writing Culture: the Poetics and Politics of Ethnography*. Berkeley, CA: University of California Press.

Cockburn, C. (1983) *Brothers*. London: Pluto Press.

Coffey, A. (1999) *The Ethnographic Self*. London: Sage.

Coffey, A. and Delamont, S. (2000) *Feminism and the Classroom Teacher*. London: Falmer.

Cohen, L. and Manion, L. (1980) *Research Methods in Education*. London: Croom Helm.

Cohen, L. and Manion, L. (1985) *Research Methods in Education*, 2nd edition. London: Routledge.

Cohen, L. and Manion, L. (1989) *Research Methods in Education*, 3rd edition. London: Routledge.

Cohen, L. and Manion, L. (1995) *Research Methods in Education*, 4th edition. London: Routledge.

Cohen, L., Manion, L. and Morrison, K. (2000) *Research Methods in Education*, 5th edition. London: Routledge.

Cole, J.R. (1979) *Fair Science? Women in the Scientific Community*. New York: Free Press.

Cole, J.R. and Cole, S. (1973) *Social Stratification in Science*. Chicago: University of Chicago Press.

Coleman, J.S. (1990) 'Columbia in the 1950s', in B. Berger (ed.), *Authors of their Own Lives*. Berkeley, CA: University of California Press, pp. 75–103.

Collins, H. (1985) *Changing Order*. London: Sage.

Collins, H.M. (1999) 'The science police', *Social Studies of Science*, 29 (2): 287–94.

Collins, H.M. and Pinch, T. (1993) *The Golem*. Cambridge: Cambridge University Press.

Collins, H.M. and Pinch, T. (1998) *The Golem at Large*. Cambridge: Cambridge University Press.

Collins, P.H. (2000) 'Comment on Hekman's "Truth and method: feminist standpoint theory revisited": where's the power?', in C. Allen and J. Howard (eds), *Provoking Feminisms*. Chicago: University of Chicago Press, pp. 43–9.

Collins, R. (1994a) *Four Sociological Traditions*. Oxford: Oxford University Press.

Collins, R. (1994b) *Four Sociological Traditions: Selected Readings*. Oxford: Oxford University Press.

Connell, R.W. (1971) *The Child's Construction of Politics*. Sydney: Allen and Unwin.

Connell, R.W. (1985) *Teachers' Work*. Sydney: Allen and Unwin.

Connell, R.W. (1987) *Gender and Power*. Cambridge: Polity Press.

Connell, R.W. (1995) *Masculinities*. Cambridge: Polity Press.

Connell, R.W. (1997) 'Long and winding road', in B. Laslett and B. Thorne (eds), *Feminist Sociology: Life Histories of a Movement*. New Brunswick, NJ: Rutgers University Press, pp. 151–64.

Connell, R.W. (2000a) *The Men and the Boys*. Cambridge: Polity Press.

Connell, R.W. (2000b) 'Comment on Hawkeworth's "Confounding Gender": re-structuring gender', in C. Allen and J.A. Howard (eds), *Provoking Feminisms*. Chicago: The University of Chicago Press, pp. 194–8.

Coppock, V., Haydon, D. and Richter, I. (eds) (1995) *The Illusions of Post Feminism*. London: Taylor and Francis.

Cordasco, F. (ed.) (1970) *The School and the Social Order*. Scranton, PA: Intext.

Coser, L. (1978) 'American trends', in T. Bottomore and R. Nisbet (eds), *A History of Sociological Analysis*. London: Heinemann, pp, 287–320.

Coser, L. (1993) 'A sociologist's atypical life', *Annual Review of Sociology*, 19: 1–15. (Palo Alto, CA: Annual Reviews Inc.)

Costin, L. (1983) *Two Sisters for Social Justice: a Biography of Edith and Grace Abbott*. Urbana, IL: University of Illinois Press.

Couch, C. (1997) 'Forming the unformable', *Symbolic Interaction*, 20 (2): 101–6.

Coxon, A.P.M. and Jones, C.L. (1978) *The Images of Occupational Prestige*. London: Macmillan.

Coxon, A.P.M. and Jones, C.L. (1979a) *Class and Hierarchy*. London: Macmillan.

Coxon, A.P.M. and Jones, C. (1979b) *Measurement and Meanings*. London: Macmillan.

Coxon, A.P.M., Davies, P.M. and Jones, C.L. (1986) *Images of Social Stratification: Occupational Structures and Class*. London: Sage.

Craib, I. (1992) *Modern Social Theory*. Brighton: Harvester Wheatsheaf.

Craib, I. (1997) *Classical Social Theory*. London: Oxford University Press.

167

Cressey, D.R. (1990) 'Learning and living', in B. Berger (ed.), *Authors of their Own Lives*. Berkeley, CA: University of California Press, pp. 235–9.

Crompton, R. (1987) 'Gender, status and professionalism', *Sociology*, 21 (4): 413–28.

Crompton, R. (2000) 'The gendered restructuring of the middle classes: employment and caring', in R. Crompton, F. Devine, M. Savage and J. Scott (eds), *Renewing Class Analysis*. Oxford: Blackwell, pp. 165–83.

Crompton, R., Devine, F., Savage, M. and Scott, J. (eds) (2000) *Renewing Class Analysis*. Oxford: Blackwell.

Crompton, R. and Mann, M. (eds) (1986) *Gender and Stratification*. Cambridge: Polity Press.

Crompton, R. and Sanderson, K. (1989) *Gendered Jobs and Social Change*. London: Unwin Hyman.

Crompton, R. and Scott, J. (2000) 'Introduction: the state of class analysis', in R. Crompton, F. Devine, M. Savage and J. Scott (eds), *Renewing Class Analysis*. Oxford: Blackwell, pp. 1–15.

Cross, A. (1981) *A Death in the Faculty*. London: Gollancz.

Cross, A. (1984) *Sweet Death, Kind Death*. London: Gollancz.

Dane, C. ([1917] 1995) *Regiment of Women*. London: Heinemann. Reprinted in 1995 by Virago, London.

Daniels, A.K. (1994) 'When we were all boys together', in K.P.M. Orlans and R.A. Wallace (eds), *Gender and the Academic Experience*. Lincoln, NE: University of Nebraska Press, pp. 27–44.

Daniels, A.K. (1999) 'Finding one's footing in the profession', *Contemporary Sociology*, 28 (3): 259–62.

Darden, D. (1997) 'How I fit into the history of the SSSI since I was never in the basement with any of these people', *Symbolic Interaction*, 20 (2): 97–100.

Datnow, A. (1998) *The Gender Politics of Educational Change*. London: Falmer.

Davidson, J. (1997) *Courtesans and Fishcakes*. London: HarperCollins.

Davis, J. (1994) 'What's wrong with sociology?', *Sociological Forum*, 9: 179–97.

Dawe, A. (1978) 'Themes of social action', in T. Bottomore and R. Nisbet (eds), *A History of Sociological Analysis*. London: Heinemann, pp. 362–417.

Deacon, D. (1997) 'Brave new Sociology?', in B. Laslett and B. Thorne (eds), *Feminist Sociology: Life Histories of a Movement*. New Brunswick, NJ: Rutgers University Press, pp. 165–93.

Deegan, M.J. (1988) *Jane Addams and the Men of the Chicago School*. New Brunswick, NJ: Transaction Press.

Deegan, M.J. (1995) 'The second sex and the Chicago School', in G.A. Fine (ed.), *A Second Chicago School?* Chicago: University of Chicago Press, pp. 322–64.

Deegan, M.J. (1996) '"Dear love, dear love": feminist pragmatism and the Chicago female world of love and ritual', *Gender and Society*, 10 (5): 590–607.

Deegan, M.J. (2001) 'The Chicago School of ethnography', in P.A. Atkinson, A. Coffey, S. Delamont, J. Lofland and L. Lofland (eds), *Handbook of Ethnography*. London: Sage, pp. 11–25.

Deegan, M.J. and Hill, M. (eds) (1987) *Women and Symbolic Interactionism*. Boston: Allen and Unwin.

Deem, R. (1986) *All Work and No Play?* Buckingham: Open University Press.

Deem, R. (1996) 'Border territories', *British Journal of the Sociology of Education*, 17 (1): 5–20.

Deem, R. and Gilroy, S. (1998) 'Physical activity, lifelong learning and empowerment', *Sport, Education and Society*, 3 (1): 89–104.

Delamont. S. (1972) 'Fallen Engels?', *New Edinburgh Review*, 18: 16–19.

Delamont, S. (1976) *Interaction in the Classroom*. London: Methuen.

Delamont, S.(1978a) 'The contradictions in ladies' education', in S. Delamont and L. Duffin (eds), *The Nineteenth Century Woman*. London: Croom Helm, pp. 134–63.

Delamont, S. (1978b) 'The domestic ideology and women's education', in S. Delamont and L. Duffin (eds), *The Nineteenth Century Woman*. London: Croom Helm, pp. 164–87.

Delamont, S. (1980) *The Sociology of Women: An Introduction*. London: Allen and Unwin.

Delamont, S. (1983) 'Salmon, chicken, cake and tears', in A. Murcott (ed.), *Essays on the Sociology of Food*. Farnborough: Gower, pp. 141–51.

Delamont, S. (1987a) 'Three blind spots?', *Social Studies of Science*, 17 (1): 163–70.

Delamont, S. (1987b) 'Clean baths and dirty women: pollution beliefs on a gynaecology ward', in N. McKeganey and S. Cunningham-Burley (eds), *Enter the Sociologist*. Aldershot: Avebury, pp. 127–43.

Delamont, S. (1989a) 'Citation and social mobility research', *Sociological Review*, 37 (2): 332–7.

Delamont, S. (1989b) *Knowledgeable Women*. London: Routledge.

Delamont, S. (1990) *Sex Roles and the School*, 2nd edition. London: Routledge.

Delamont, S. (1991) 'The Hit List and other horror stories', *Sociological Review*, 39 (2): 238–59.

Delamont, S. (1992a) 'Old fogies and intellectual women', *Women's History Review*, 1 (1): 39–61.

Delamont, S. (1992b) *Fieldwork in Educational Settings*. London: Falmer.

Delamont, S. (1993) 'Distant dangers and forgotten standards', *Women's History Review*, 2 (1): 233–52.

Delamont, S. (1994) *Appetites and Identities*. London: Routledge.

Delamont, S. (1995) 'Bernstein and the analysis of gender inequality', in A. Sadovnik (ed.), *Knowledge and Pedagogy*. New York: Ablex, pp. 323–36.

Delamont, S. (1996a) *A Woman's Place in Education*. Aldershot: Ashgate.

Delamont, S. (1996b) 'Murder after suffrage', in S. Delamont, *A Woman's Place in Education*. Aldershot: Ashgate, pp. 166–76.

Delamont, S. (1998) 'You need the leotard', *Sport, Education and Society*, 3 (1): 5–18.

Delamont, S. (1999) 'Gender and the discourse of derision', *Research Papers in Education*, 20 (3): 99–126.

Delamont, S. (2000a) 'The anomalous beasts', *Sociology*, 34 (1): 95–112.

Delamont, S. (2000b) 'Confessions of a ragpicker', in H. Hodkinson (ed.), *Feminism and Educational Research Methodologies*. Manchester: Manchester Metropolitan University, pp. 36–60.

Delamont, S. (2001) *Changing Women, Unchanged Men?* Buckingham: Open University Press.

Delamont, S. (2002a) *Fieldwork in Educational Settings*. 2nd edition. London: Falmer.

Delamont, S. (2002b) 'Hypatia's revenge?', *Social Studies of Science*, 32 (1): 167–94.

Delamont, S. (2003) 'Planning enlightenment, planning dignity', in G. Walford (ed.), forthcoming.

Delamont, S. and Atkinson, P.A. (1995) *Fighting Familiarity*. Cresskill, NJ: Hampton.

Delamont, S., Atkinson, P.A. and Coffey, A. (2000a) 'The twilight years? Educational ethnography and the five moments model', *Qualitative Studies in Education*, 13 (3): 223–38.

Delamont, S., Atkinson, P.A. and Parry, O. (1997) 'Critical mass and pedagogic continuity', *British Journal of the Sociology of Education*, 18 (4): 533–50.

Delamont, S., Atkinson, P.A. and Parry, O. (2000) *The Doctoral Experience*. London: Falmer.

Delphy, C. (1996) 'French feminism: an imperialist invention', in D. Bell and R. Klein (eds), *Radically Speaking*. London: Zed Books, pp. 383–92.

Dench, G. (1994) *The Frog, the Prince and the Problem of Men*. London: Neanderthal Books.

Dench, G. (1996) *Transforming Men*. New Brunswick, NJ: Transaction Books.

Dennis, N. (1997) *The Invention of Permanent Poverty*. London: Civitas.

Dennis, N. and Erdos, G. (1993) *Families without Fatherhood*. London: Civitas.

Dennis, N. and Erdos, G. (2000) *Families without Fatherhood*, 3rd edition. London: Civitas.

Dennis, N., Henriques, F. and Slaughter, C. (1956) *Coal is our Life*. London: Routledge and Kegan Paul.

De Vault, M.L. (1997) 'A second generation story', in B. Laslett and B. Thorne (eds), *Feminist Sociology: Life Histories of a Movement*. New Brunswick, NJ: Rutgers University Press, pp. 257–74.

De Vault, M.L. (1999) *Liberating Method*. Philadelphia, PA: Temple University Press.

Dixon-Mueller, R. (1994) 'Accidental tourist', in K.P.M. Orlans and R.A. Wallace (eds), *Gender and the Academic Experience*. Lincoln, NE: University of Nebraska Press, pp. 201–18.

Dobash, R.E. and Dobash, R. (1992) *Women, Violence and Social Change*. London: Routledge.

Dobash, R.E. and Dobash, R. (eds) (1998) *Rethinking Violence against Women*. London: Sage.

Dobash, R.E. et al. (1977) 'Wifebeating', *Victimology*, 2 (3): 608–22.

Dominelli, L. (1986) ' The power of the powerless', *Sociological Review*, 34 (1), 65–92.

Douglas, M. (1966) *Purity and Danger*. London: Routledge and Kegan Paul.

Douglas, M. (1970) *Natural Symbols*. London: Barrie and Rockliff.

Douglas, M. (1982) *In the Active Voice*. London: Routledge and Kegan Paul.

Dube, L., Leacock, E. and Ardener, S. (eds) (1986) *Visibility and Power*. Delhi: Oxford University Press.

Du Bois, B. (1983) 'Passionate scholarship', in R. Duelli-Klein and G. Bowles (eds), *Theories of Women's Studies*. London: Routledge, pp. 105–16.

Duffin, L. (1978) 'Prisoners of progress', in S. Delamont and L. Duffin (eds), *The Nineteenth Century Woman*. London: Croom Helm, pp. 57–91.

Duncombe, J. and Marsden, D. (1995) 'Workaholics and whingeing women', *Sociological Review*, 43 (1): 150–69.

Eadie, J. (2001) 'Boy talk: social theory and its discontents', *Sociology*, 35 (2): 575–82.

Een, J.A.D. and Rosenberg-Dishman, M.B. (eds) (1978) *Women and Society: Citations 3001 to 6000, an Annotated Bibliography*. Beverly Hills, CA: Sage.

Eichler, M. (1988) *Nonsexist Research Methods: A Practical Guide*. Boston: Allen and Unwin.

Eldridge, J., MacInnes, J., Scott, S., Warhurst, C. and Witz, A. (eds) (2000) *For Sociology*. Durham, NC: Sociology Press.

England, P. (1999) 'The impact of feminist thought on sociology', *Contemporary Sociology*, 28 (3): 263–8.

Epstein, C. (1970) *Woman's Place*. Berkeley, CA: University of California Press.

Erickson, F. (1986) 'Qualitative methods in research on teaching', in M.C. Wittrock (ed.), *Handbook of Research on Teaching*, 3rd edition. New York: Macmillan, pp. 119–61.

Eskola, K. (1992) 'Women and the media-related intellectual public sphere', in N. Kauppi and P. Sulkunen (eds), *Vanguards of Modernity*. Jyvaskyla: University of Jyvaskyla Press, pp. 146–67.

170

Faris, R.E.L. (1967) *Chicago Sociology 1920–1932*. Chicago: University of Chicago Press.

Featherstone, K. and Donovan, J.L. (2002) 'Why don't they tell me straight, why allocate it?', *Social Science and Medicine*, 55: 709–19.

Featherstone, K. and Latimer, J. (2001) 'Review of Ann Oakley *Experiments in Knowing*', *Sociology of Health and Illness*, 223 (6): 868.

Felski, R. (2000) 'The doxa of difference', in C. Allen and J.A. Howard (eds), *Provoking Feminisms*. Chicago: University of Chicago Press, pp. 71–92.

Feminist Scholars in Sociology (1995) 'What's wrong is right: a response to the state of the discipline', *Sociological Forum*, 10 (3): 493–8.

Fenstermaker, S. (1997) 'Telling tales out of school', in B. Laslett and B. Thorne (eds), *Feminist Sociology: Life Histories of a Movement*. New Brunswick, NJ: Rutgers University Press, pp. 209–28.

Finch, J. (1984) 'A first-class environment?', *British Education Research Journal*, 10 (1): 3–18.

Finch, J. and Groves, D. (eds) (1983) *A Labour of Love?* London: Routledge and Kegan Paul.

Finch, J. and Mason, J. (1990) 'Divorce, marriage, and family obligations', *The Sociological Review*, 2: 219–46.

Finch, J. and Summerfield, P. (1991) 'Social reconstruction and the emergence of companionate marriage 1945–59', in D. Clark (ed.), *Marriage, Domestic Life and Social Change*. London: Routledge, pp. 7–32.

Fine, G.A. (ed.) (1995) *A Second Chicago School? The Development of a Postwar American Sociology*. Chicago: University of Chicago Press.

Fine, G.A. (2000) 'Review of Tomasi (ed.) "The Tradition of the Chicago School of Sociology"', *Contemporary Sociology*, 29 (4): 674–5.

Fine, M. (1999) *Disruptive Voices*. Ann Arbor, MI: University of Michigan Press.

Fischer, B. (1995) 'Marginality, migration and metamorphoses', in A. Goetting and S. Fenstermaker (eds), *Individual Voices, Collective Visions*. Philadelphia: Temple University Press, pp. 135–50.

Fish, V.K. (1981) 'Annie Marion Maclean: a neglected part of the Chicago School', *Journal of the History of Sociology*, 3: 43–62.

Fisher, B.M. and Strauss, A.L. (1978a) 'Interactionism', in T. Bottomore and R. Nisbet (eds), *A History of Sociological Analysis*. London: Heinemann, pp. 457–98.

Fisher, B.M. and Strauss, A.L. (1978b) 'The Chicago tradition and social change', *Symbolic Interaction*, 1 (1): 5–23.

Fisher, B.M. and Strauss, A.L. (1979a) 'George Herbert Mead and the Chicago tradition of sociology', part 1, *Symbolic Interaction*, 2 (1): 9–26.

Fisher, B.M. and Strauss, A.L. (1979b) 'George Herbert Mead and the Chicago tradition of sociology', part 2, *Symbolic Interaction*, 2 (2): 9–20.

Flax, J. (1990) 'Postmodernism and gender relations in feminist theory', in L. Nicholson (ed.), *Feminism/Postmodernism*. London: Routledge, pp. 39–62.

Flax, J. (1993) 'The end of innocence', in J. Butler and J.W. Scott (eds), *Feminists Theorise the Political*. New York: Routledge, pp. 445–63.

Fleck, L. (1979) *The Genesis and Development of a Scientific Fact*. Chicago: University of Chicago Press.

Fonow, M.M. and Cook, J.A. (eds) (1991) *Beyond Methodology*. Bloomington, IN: Indiana University Press.

Foucault, M. (1979) *Discipline and Punish*. New York: Vintage.

Fox-Genovese, E. (1986) 'The claims of a common culture', *Salmagundi*, 72 (Fall): 134–51.

Francis, B. and Skelton, C. (eds) (2001) *Investigating Gender*. Buckingham: Open University Press.

Frankenberg, R. (1957) *Village on the Border*. London: Cohen and West.

Frankenberg, R. (1966) *Communities in Britain*. Harmondsworth: Penguin.

Frankenberg, R. (1976) 'In the production of their lives: men (?) ... sex and gender in British community studies', in D.L. Barker and S. Allen (eds), *Sexual Divisions and Society*. London: Tavistock, pp. 25–51.

Frankenberg, R. (ed.) (1982) *Custom and Conflict in British Society*. Manchester: Manchester University Press.

Freedman, J. (2001) *Feminism*. Buckingham: Open University Press.

Freund, J. (1978) 'German sociology in the time of Max Weber', in T. Bottomore and R. Nisbet (eds), *A History of Sociological Analysis*. London: Heinemann, pp. 149–86.

Friedan, B. (1963) *The Feminine Mystique*. Harmondsworth: Penguin.

Gaston, J. (1978) *The Reward System in British and American Science*. New York: Wiley.

George, A. (1990) 'Social and cultural aspects of menstruation'. unpublished PhD thesis, University of Wales, Cardiff.

George, A. and Murcott, A. (1992) 'Monthly strategies for discretion', *Sociological Review*, 40 (1): 146–62.

Giddens, A. (1971) *Capitalism and Modern Social Theory*. Cambridge: Cambridge University Press.

Giddens, A. (1973) *The Class Structure of the Advanced Societies*. London: Heinemann.

Giddens, A, (1992) *The Transformation of Lunacy*. Cambridge: Polity.

Giddens, A. and Turner, J. (eds) (1987) *Social Theory and Modern Sociology*. Oxford: Basil Blackwell.

Gilbert, N. and Mulkay, M. (1984) *Opening Pandora's Box*. Cambridge: Cambridge University Press.

Gilbert, S. and Gubar, S. (1979) *The Madwoman in the Attic*. New Haven, CT: Yale University Press.

Gimlin, D. (1996) 'Pamela's Place: power and negotiation in the hair salon', *Gender and Society*, 10 (5): 505–26.

Gimenez, M. (1995) 'Sociologist by default', in A. Goetting and S. Fenstermaker (eds), *Individual Voices, Collective Visions*. Philadelphia. PA: Temple University Press, pp. 169–84.

Ginn, J., Arber, S., Brannen, J., Dale, A., Dex, S., Elias, P., Moss, P., Pahl, J., Roberts, C. and Rubery, J. (1996) 'Feminist fallacies: a reply to Hakim on women's employment', *British Journal of Sociology*, 47 (1): 167–74.

Glass, D.V. (ed.) (1954) *Social Mobility in Britain*. London: Routledge and Kegan Paul.

Glazer, N. (1990) 'From socialism to sociology', in B. Berger (ed.), *Authors of their Own Lives*. Berkeley, CA: University of California Press, pp. 190–210.

Glazer-Raymo, J. (1999) *Shattering the Myths*. Baltimore: Johns Hopkins University Press.

Glenn, B.N. (1997) 'Looking back in anger?', in B. Laslett and B. Thorne (eds), *Feminist Sociology: Life Histories of a Movement*. New Brunswick, NJ: Rutgers University Press, pp. 73–102.

Glover, J. (2000) *Women and Scientific Employment*. Basingstoke: Macmillan.

Goetting, A. and Fenstermaker, S. (eds) (1995) *Individual Voices, Collective Visions: Fifty Years of Women in Sociology*. Philadelphia, PA: Temple University Press.

Goffman, E. (1992) 'An interview with Erving Goffman, 1980', *Research on Language and Social Interaction*, 26 (3): 317–48.

Goldthorpe, J.H. (with Llewellyn, C. and Payne, C.) (1980) *Social Mobility and Class Structure in Modern Britain*. Oxford: Clarendon Press.

Goldthorpe, J.H. (1983) 'Women and class analysis: in defence of the conventional view', *Sociology*, 17 (4): 465–88.

Goldthorpe, J.H. (1984) 'Women and class analysis: a reply to the replies', *Sociology*, 18 (4): 491–9.

Goodrich, D.W. (1994) 'Varieties of sociological experience', in K.P.M. Orlans and R.A. Wallace (eds), *Gender and the Academic Experience*. Lincoln, NE: University of Nebraska Press, pp. 11–26.

Gordon, D.A. (1993) 'The unhappy relationship of feminism and postmodernism in anthropology', *Anthropological Quarterly*, 66 (3): 109–17.

Gordon, L. (1994) *Pitied But Not Entitled*. New York: Free Press.

Gordon, L.D. (1990) *Gender and Higher Education in the Progressive Era*. New Haven, CT: Yale University Press.

Gordon, T., Holland, J. and Lahelma, E. (2001) 'Ethnographic research in educational settings', in P.A. Atkinson, A. Coffey, S. Delamont, J. Lofland and L. Lofland (eds), *Handbook of Ethnography*. London: Sage, pp. 188–203.

Gould, S.J. (1998) *Questioning the Millennium*. London: Vintage.

Gouldner, A. (1971) *The Coming Crisis of Western Sociology*. London: Heinemann.

Graham, H. (1993) *Hardship and Health in Women's Lives*. London: Harvester Wheatsheaf.

Greeley, A. (1990) 'The crooked lines of God', in B. Berger (ed.), *Authors of their Own Lives*. Berkeley, CA: University of California Press, pp. 133–51.

Gross, P.R. and Levitt, N. (1994) *Higher Superstition*, 2nd edition. Baltimore, MD: Johns Hopkins University Press.

Gross, P.R., Levitt, N. and Lewis, M.W. (eds) (1996) 'The flight from science and reason', *Annals of the New York Academy of Sciences*, 775 (24 June).

Gubrium, J. and Holstein, J. (1995) 'Biographical work and new ethnography', in R. Josselson and A. Lieblich (eds), *Interpreting Experience: The Narrative Study of Lives*. Thousand Oaks, CA: Sage, pp. 45–58.

Gusfield, J. (1990) 'My life and soft times', in B. Berger (ed.), *Authors of their Own Lives*. Berkeley, CA: University of California Press, pp. 104–30.

Gusfield, J. (1995) 'Preface', in G.A. Fine (ed.), *A Second Chicago School?* Chicago: University of Chicago Press, pp. ix–xvi.

Haack, S. (1995) *Evidence and Inquiry*. Oxford: Blackwell.

Haavio-Mannila, E. (1992) 'Preface', in N. Kauppi and P. Sulkunen (eds), *Vanguards of Modernity: Society, Intellectuals and the University*. Jyvaskyla: University of Jyvaskyla. p. 5.

Hacker, H.M. (1995) 'Slouching toward sociology', in A. Goetting and S. Fenstermaker (eds), *Individual Voices, Collective Visions*. Philadelphia, PA: Temple University Press, pp. 233–50.

Hakim, C. (1995) 'Five feminist myths about women's employment', *British Journal of Sociology*, 46 (3): 429–55.

Hakim, C. (1996) *Key Issues in Women's Work*. London: Athlone.

Hall, E.J. (1995) 'Discovering gender', in A. Goetting and S. Fenstermaker (eds), *Individual Voices, Collective Visions*. Philadelphia, PA: Temple University Press, pp. 203–18.

Halsey, A.H. (1978) *Change in British Society*. Oxford: Oxford University Press.

Halsey, A.H. (1985) 'Provincials and professionals', in M. Bulmer (ed.), *Essays on the History of British Social Research*. Cambridge: Cambridge University Press, pp. 151–64.

173

Halsey, A.H., Heath, A. and Ridge, J.M. (1980) *Origins and Destinations*. Oxford: Clarendon Press.

Hamilton, R. (1978) *The Liberation of Women*. London: Allen and Unwin.

Hammersley, M. (1992) 'On feminist methodology', *Sociology*, 26 (2): 187–206.

Hammersley, M. (2000) *Taking Sides in Social Research*. London: Routledge.

Hammersley, M. (2001) 'A reply to partisan reviews', *British Journal of the Sociology of Education*, 22 (3): 417–22.

Hammersley, M. and Atkinson, P. (1995) *Ethnography*. 2nd edition. London: Routledge.

Hammersley, M. and Gomm, R. (1997) 'Bias in social research', *Sociological Research Online*, 2 (4): http://www.socresonline.org.uk/socresonline/2/4/7.html

Hammond, P. (ed.) (1964) *Sociologists at Work*. New York: Doubleday Anchor.

Hansen, J. (2000) 'There are two sexes, not one: Luce Irigaray', in K. Oliver (ed.), *French Feminism Reader*. Lanham, MD: Rowman and Littlefield, pp. 201–6.

Haraway, D. (1988) 'Situated knowledges', *Feminist Studies*, 14 (3): 575–97.

Harding, S. (1986) *The Science Question in Feminism*. Milton Keynes: Open University Press.

Harding, S. (ed.) (1987) *Feminism and Methodology*. Bloomington, ON: Indiana University Press.

Harding, S. (1991) *Whose Science? Whose Knowledge?* Ithaca, NY: Cornell University Press.

Harding, S. (2000) 'Comment on Hekman's "Truth and method: feminist standpoint theory revisited"', in C. Allen and J.A. Howard (eds), *Provoking Feminisms*. Chicago: University of Chicago Press, pp. 50–8.

Harding, S. and Hintikka, M. (eds) (1983) *Discovering Reality?* Dordrecht: Reidel/Kluwer.

Harding, S. and O'Barr, J.F. (eds) (1987) *Sex and Scientific Inquiry*. Chicago: University of Chicago Press.

Hargreaves, D. (1967) *Social Relations in a Secondary School*. London: Routledge and Kegan Paul.

Harrison, L. (1975) 'Cro-Magnon women in eclipse', *Science Teacher*, 12 (1): 25–38.

Hartley, S.F. (1994) 'Multiple roles, multiple selves', in K.P.M. Orlans and R.A. Wallace (eds), *Gender and the Academic Experience*. Lincoln, NE: University of Nebraska Press, pp. 113–24.

Hartmann, H. (1979) 'Capitalism, patriarchy and job segregation by sex', in Z.R. Eisenstein (ed.), *Capitalism, Patriarchy and the Case for Socialist Feminism*. New York: Monthly Review Press, pp. 206–47.

Hartmann, H. (1981) 'The unhappy marriage of Marxism and feminism', in L. Sargent (ed.), *Women and Revolution*. London: Pluto Press, pp. 1–41.

Hartsock, N.C.M. (1975) 'Fundamental feminism', *Quest*, 2 (2): 171–82.

Hartsock, N.C.M. (1981) 'Fundamental feminism', in C. Bunch (ed.), *Building Feminist Theory*. New York: Longman, pp. 32–43.

Hartsock, N.C.M. (2000) 'Comment on Hekman's "Truth and method: feminist standpoint theory revisited"', in C. Allen and J.A. Howard (eds), *Provoking Feminisms*. Chicago: University of Chicago Press, pp. 35–42.

Harvey, L. (1987) *Myths of the Chicago School*. Farnborough: Avebury.

Haste, H. (1994) *The Sexual Metaphor*. Cambridge, MA: Harvard University Press.

Havighurst, R.J. and Neugarten, B. (1967) *Society and Education*, 3rd edition. Boston: Allyn and Bacon.

Havighurst, R.J. and Neugarten, B. (1975) *Society and Education*, 4th edition. Boston: Allyn and Bacon.

174

Hawthorn, G. (1976) *Enlightenment and Despair*. Cambridge: Cambridge University Press.

Heath, A. (1981) *Social Mobility*. London: HarperCollins.

Heath, A. and Britten, N. (1983) 'Women's jobs do make a difference', *Sociology*, 18 (1): 475–90.

Heitlinger, A. (1979) *Women and State Socialism*. London: Macmillan.

Hekman, S. (2000) 'Truth and method: feminist standpoint theory revisited', in C. Allen and J.A. Howard (eds), *Provoking Feminisms*. Chicago: University of Chicago Press, pp. 9–34.

Henkel, M. (2000) *Academic Identities and Policy Change in Higher Education*. London: Jessica Kingsley.

Herbert, C. (1989) *Talking of Silence*. London: Falmer.

Hernandez, G. (1995) 'Multiple subjectives and strategic positionality', in R. Behar and D. Gordon (eds), *Women Writing Culture*. Berkeley, CA: University of California Press, pp. 148–66.

Hess, B. (1999) 'Biography as destiny', *Contemporary Sociology*, 28 (3): 286–8.

Hess, B.B. (1995) 'An accidental sociologist', in A. Goetting and S. Fenstermaker (eds), *Individual Voices, Collective Visions*. Philadelphia, PA: Temple University Press, pp. 37–50.

Hilton, G.L.S. (1991) 'Boys will be boys – won't they?', *Gender and Education*, 3 (3): 311–14.

Hirsch, M. and Keller, E.F. (eds) (1990) *Conflicts in Feminism*. New York: Routledge.

Hobbs, D. (2001) 'Ethnography and the study of deviance', in P.A. Atkinson, A. Coffey, S. Delamont, J. Lofland and L. Lofland (eds), *Handbook of Ethnography*. London: Sage, pp. 204–19.

Hochschild, A.R. (1994) 'Inside the clockwork of male careers', in K.P.M. Orlans and R.A. Wallace (eds), *Gender and the Academic Experience*. Lincoln, NE: University of Nebraska Press, pp. 125–40.

Hoff, J. (1994) 'Gender as a postmodern category of paralysis', *Women's History Review*, 3 (2): 149–68.

Hoff, J. (1996) 'A response to my critics', *Women's History Review*, 5 (1): 25–30.

Holland, J., Ramazanoglu, C., Sharpe, S. and Thomson, R. (1988) *The Male in the Head*. London: Tufnell Press.

Holly, L. (ed.) (1989) *Girls and Sexuality*. Milton Keynes: Open University Press.

Holmstrom, L.L. (1995) 'Working the third shift', in A. Goetting and S. Fenstermaker (eds), *Individual Voices, Collective Visions*. Philadelphia, PA: Temple University Press, pp. 251–70.

Holmwood, J. (1985) 'Feminism and epistemology', *Sociology*, 29 (3): 411–28.

Holtby, W. (1936) *Women and a Changing Civilisation*. London: John Lane.

hooks, b. (1981) *Ain't I a Woman?* Boston: South End.

hooks, b. (1990) *Yearning*. Toronto: Between-the-Lines Press.

Hope, K. (1984) *As Others See Us*. Cambridge: Cambridge University Press.

Hopper, E. (1981) *Social Mobility*. London: Blackwell.

Huber, J. (ed.) (1973) *Changing Women in a Changing Society*. Chicago: University of Chicago Press.

Huber, J. (1990) 'Macro–micro links in gender stratification', *American Sociological Review*, 55: 1–10.

Hughes, H. McG. (1961) *The Fantastic Lodge*. Greenwich, CT: Fawcett.

Humm, M. (1992) 'Introduction', in M. Humm (ed.), *Feminisms: a Reader*. Brighton: Harvester Wheatsheaf.

Hurston, Z.N. ([1935] 1990) *Mules and Men*. Philadelphia, PA: J.B. Lippincott. Reprinted in 1990 by Perennial Library, New York.

Hurston, Z.N. ([1938] 1990) *Tell My Horse*. Philadelphia, PA: J.B. Lippincott. Reprinted in 1990 by Perennial Library, New York.

Imber, J.B. (1999) 'Values, politics and science', *Contemporary Sociology*, 28 (3): 255–9.

Jackson, S. (2000) 'For a sociological feminism', in J. Eldridge, J. MacInnes, S. Scott, C. Warhurst and A. Witz (eds), *For Sociology*. Durham, NC: Sociology Press, pp. 92–106.

Jackson, S. and Scott, S. (eds) (1997) *Feminism and Sexuality: A Reader*. Edinburgh: Edinburgh University Press.

Jay, M. (1973)*The Dialectical Imagination*. London: Heinemann.

Jayaratne, T.E. (1983) 'The value of quantitative methodology for feminist research', in G. Bowles and R. Duelli-Klein (eds), *Theories of Women's Studies*. London: Routledge and Kegan Paul, pp. 140–61.

Jeffreys, S. (1985) *The Spinster and her Enemies*. London: Pandora.

Jeffreys, S. (ed.) (1987) *The Sexuality Debates*. London: Routledge.

Joeres, R.-E.B. and Laslett, B. (eds) (1996) *The Second Signs Reader*. Chicago: University of Chicago Press.

Johnson, B.D. (1972) 'Durkheim on women', in N. Glazer-Malbin and H.Y. Waehrer (eds), *Women in a Man-made World*. Chicago: Rand McNally, pp. 37–52.

Johnson, M. M. (1989) 'Feminism and the theories of Talcott Parsons', in R. Wallace (ed.), *Feminism and Sociological Theory*. Newbury Park, CA: Sage, pp. 101–18.

Johnson, T. (1972) *Professions and Power*. London: Macmillan.

Jones, I. (1974) 'A critique of Murdock and Phelps' "Mass Media and the Secondary School"', unpublished dissertation, School of Education, University of Leicester.

Judt, T. (1992) *Past Imperfect*. Berkeley, CA: University of California Press.

Kay, H. (1990) 'Constructing the epistemological gap', *Sociological Review*, 38 (2): 344–51.

Keller, E.F. (1983) *A Feeling for the Organism*. New York: W.E. Freeman.

Keller, E.F. (1985) *Reflections on Gender and Science*. New Haven, CT: Yale University Press.

Keller, S. (1995) 'Bridging worlds', in A. Goetting and S. Fenstermaker (eds), *Individual Voices, Collective Visions*. Philadelphia, PA: Temple University Press, pp. 151–68.

Kelley, F. ([1899] 1998) 'Aims and principles of the Consumers' League', *American Journal of Sociology*, 5: 289–304. Reprinted in P.M. Lengermann and J. Niebrugge-Brantley (eds) (1998) *The Women Founders*. Boston: McGraw-Hill, pp. 261–3.

Kellor, F. ([1900] 1998) 'Psychological and environmental study of women criminals', *American Journal of Sociology*, 5: 671–82. Reprinted in P.M. Lengermann and J. Niebrugge-Brantley (eds) (1998) *The Women Founders*. Boston: McGraw-Hill, pp. 263–5.

Kent, S.K. (1996) 'Mistrials and tribulations', *Women's History Review*, 5 (1): 9-18.

Keohane, N.O., Rosaldo, M.Z. and Gelpi, B.C. (eds) (1982) *Feminist Theory*. Brighton: Harvester.

Koertge, N. (ed.) (1998) *A House Built on Sand*. Oxford: Oxford University Press.

Kong, T.S.K., Mahoney, D. and Plummer, K. (2002) 'Queering the interview', in J.F. Gubrium and J.A. Holstein (eds), *Handbook of Interview Research*. London: Sage, pp. 239–58.

Krieger, S. (1983) *The Mirror Dance*. Philadelphia, PA: Temple University Press.

176

Krieger, S. (1997) 'Lesbian in academe', in B. Laslett and B. Thorne (eds), *Feminist Sociology: Life Histories of a Movement*. New Brunswick, NJ: Rutgers University Press, pp. 194–208.

Kuper, J. (ed.) (1987) *Key Thinkers: Past and Present*. London: Routledge and Kegan Paul.

Kurtz, L.R. (1984) *Evaluating Chicago Sociology*. Chicago: University of Chicago Press.

Lash, S. and Urry, J. (1994) *Economies of Signs and Space*. London: Sage.

Laslett, B. (1997) 'On finding a feminist voice', in B. Laslett and B. Thorne (eds), *Feminist Sociology: Life Histories of a Movement*. New Brunswick, NJ: Rutgers University Press, pp. 48–72.

Laslett, B. and Thorne, B. (eds) (1997) *Feminist Sociology: Life Histories of a Movement*. New Brunswick, NJ: Rutgers University Press.

Lather, P. (1991) *Getting Smart*. London: Routledge.

Lather, P. (2001) 'Postmodernism, post-structuralism and post (critical) ethnography', in P.A. Atkinson, A. Coffey, S. Delamont, J. Lofland and L. Lofland (eds), *Handbook of Ethnography*. London: Sage, pp. 477–92.

Latta, S. (1999) 'Which me is the me that got the PhD?', in J. Addison and S.J. McGee (eds), *Feminist Empirical Research*. Portsmouth, NH: Boynton/Cook, pp. 9–23.

LeCompte, M. (1998) 'Synonyms and sequences: the development of an intellectual autobiography', in K.B. de Marrais (ed.), *Inside Stories*. Mahwah, NJ: Lawrence Erlbaum, pp. 197–210.

Lederman, M. and Bartsch, I. (eds) (2001) *The Gender and Science Reader*. London: Routledge.

Lee, D. and Newby, H. (1983) *The Problem of Sociology*. London: Unwin Hyman.

Lees, S. (1986) *Losing Out*. London: Hutchinson.

Lemert, C.C. (ed.) (1981) *French Sociology*. New York: Columbia University Press.

Lengermann, P.M. and Niebrugge-Brantley, J. (eds) (1998) *The Women Founders: Sociology and Social Theory 1830–1930*. Boston: McGraw-Hill.

Leonard, D. (1980) *Sex and Generation*. London: Tavistock.

Leonard, D. and Adkins, L. (eds) (1996) *Sex in Question: French Materialist Feminism*. London: Taylor and Francis.

Lever, J. (1995) 'Reflections on a serendipitous and rocky career', in A. Goetting and S. Fenstermaker (eds), *Individual Voices, Collective Visions*. Philadelphia, PA: Temple University Press, pp. 87–108.

Lewis, C. and O'Brien, R. (eds) (1987) *Fatherhood Reassessed*. London: Sage.

Lewis, J. and Meredith, B. (1998) *Daughters Who Care*. London: Routledge.

Lichtenstein, R. and Sinclair, I. (1999) *Rodinsky's Room*. London: Granta.

Lightfoot, S.L. (1975) 'Sociologies of education', in M. Millman and R.M. Kanter (eds), *Another Voice*. New York: Anchor, pp. 106–43.

Lofland, L.H. (1975) 'The "thereness" of women', in M. Millman and R.M. Kanter (eds), *Another Voice*. New York: Anchor, pp. 144–70.

Lofland, L.H. (1983) 'Understanding urban life', *Urban Life*, 11 (4): 491–511.

Lofland, L.H. (1997) 'From "Our Gang" to "Society For": reminiscences of an organization in transition', *Symbolic Interaction*, 20 (2): 135–40.

Long, J. (1995) 'Paradigm lost', in A. Goetting and S. Fenstermaker (eds), *Individual Voices, Collective Visions*. Philadelphia, PA: Temple University Press, pp. 109–33.

Lopata, H.Z. (1995a) 'The life course of a sociologist', in A. Goetting and S. Fenstermaker (eds), *Individual Voices, Collective Visions*. Philadelphia, PA: Temple University Press, pp. 185–202.

Lopata, H.Z. (1995b) 'Postscript', in G.A. Fine (ed.), *A Second Chicago School?* Chicago: University of Chicago Press, pp. 365–84.

Lorber, J. (1975) 'Women and medical sociology', in M. Millman and R.B. Kanter (eds), *Another Voice*. New York: Anchor, pp. 75–105.

Lorber, J. (1984) *Women Physicians*. London: Tavistock.

Lorber, J. (2000) *Gender and the Social Construction of Illness*. Walnut Creek, CA: AltaMira.

Lorde, A. (1984) *Sister Outsider*. Trumansberg, NY: Crossing Press.

Lortie, D. (1968) *Schoolteacher*. Chicago: University of Chicago Press.

Lury, C. (1997) *Consumer Culture*. Cambridge: Polity Press.

Lutz, C. (1990) 'The erasure of women's writing in sociocultural anthropology', *American Ethnologist*, 17 (4): 611–27.

Lutz, C. (1995) 'The gender of theory', in R. Behar and D. Gordon (eds), *Women Writing Culture*. Berkeley, CA: University of California Press, pp. 249–66.

Lyon, D. (1999) *Postmodernity*, 2nd edition. Buckingham: Open University Press.

Lyotard, J-F. ([1979] 1984) *The Postmodern Condition*. English edition published in 1984, Minneapolis: University of Minnesota Press.

Mac an Ghaill, M. (1988) *Young, Gifted and Black*. Buckingham: Open University Press.

Mac an Ghaill, M. (1994) *The Making of Men*. Buckingham: Open University Press.

Mac an Ghaill, M. (ed.) (1996) *Understanding Masculinities*. Buckingham: Open University Press.

Mac an Ghaill, M. (1999) *Contemporary Racisms and Ethnicities*. Buckingham: Open University Press.

MacCannell, D. (1990) 'Working in other fields', in B. Berger (ed.), *Authors of their Own Lives*. Berkeley, CA: University of California Press, pp. 165–89.

Macdonald, S., Holden, P. and Ardener, S. (eds) (1987) *Images of Women in Peace and War*. London: Macmillan.

Macintyre, S. (1977) *Single and Pregnant*. London: Croom Helm.

Mackenzie, D. (1999) 'The Science Wars and the past's quiet voices', *Social Studies of Science*, 29 (2): 199–214.

Mackie, M. (1976) 'Professional women's collegial relations and productivity', *Sociology and Social Research*, 61 (3): 277–93.

MacLure, M. (2000) 'The repulsion of theory: women, writing, research', in H. Hodkinson (ed.), *Feminism and Educational Research*. Manchester: Manchester University Press, pp. 61–78.

Mahony, P. and Zmroczek, C. (1996) 'Working-class radical feminism', in D. Bell and R. Klein (eds), *Radically Speaking*. London: Zed Books, pp. 67–76.

Maines, D. (2000) *The Faultline of Consciousness*. New York: Aldine de Gruyter.

Mann, C.R. (1995) 'Seventeen white men and me', in A. Goetting and S. Fenstermaker (eds), *Individual Voices, Collective Visions*. Philadelphia, PA: Temple University Press, pp. 273–84.

Mansfield, P. and Collard, J. (1988) *The Beginning of the Rest of Your Life?* London: Macmillan.

Margolis, D.R. (1995) 'Isolation and the woman scholar', in A. Goetting and S. Fenstermaker (eds), *Individual Voices, Collective Visions*. Philadelphia, PA: Temple University Press, pp. 219–32.

Marks, E. and de Courtivron, I. (eds) (1981) *New French Feminisms*. Brighton: Harvester.

Marshall, G., Newby, H., Rose, D. and Vogler, C. (1988) *Social Class in Modern Britain*. London: Hutchinson.

Marshall, G., Swift, A. and Roberts, S. (1997) *Against the Odds? Social Class and Social Justice in Industrial Societies*. Oxford: Clarendon Press.

Martin, J.R. (1984) 'Philosophy, gender and education', in S. Acker et al. (eds), *Women and Education*. London: Kogan Page, pp. 31–9.

Martin, J.R. (1985) *Reclaiming a Conversation*. New Haven, CT: Yale University Press.

Mascia-Lees, F.E., Sharpe, P. and Cohen, C.B. (1989) 'The postmodern turn in anthropology', *Signs*, 15 (1): 7–23.

Matthews, F.H. (1977) *Quest for an American Sociology*. Montreal: McGill-Queen's University Press.

Mayberry, M., Subramaniam, B. and Weasel, L.H. (eds) (2001) *Feminist Science Studies: A New Generation*. New York: Routledge.

Maynard, Mary (1994) 'Methods, practice and epistemology', in M. Maynard and J. Purvis (eds), *Researching Women's Lives from a Feminist Perspective*. London: Taylor and Francis, pp. 10–26.

Maynard, M. (1995) 'Beyond the big three: the development of feminist theory into the 1990s', *Women's History Review*, 4 (3): 259–82.

Maynard, M. and Purvis, J. (eds) (1994) *Researching Women's Lives from a Feminist Perspective*. London: Taylor and Francis.

McDonald, L. (1994) *The Women Founders of the Social Sciences*. Ottawa: Carleton University Press.

McKie, L., Bowlby, S. and Gregory, S. (eds) (1999) *Gender, Power and the Household*. London: Macmillan.

McLean, A.M. ([1899] 1998) 'Two weeks in department stores', *American Journal of Sociology*, 4: 721–41. Reprinted in P.M. Lengermann and J. Niebrugge-Brantley (eds) (1998) *The Women Founders*. Boston: McGraw-Hill, pp. 259–61.

McLennan, G. (1985) 'Feminism, epistemology and postmodernism', *Sociology*, 29 (3): 391–410.

McRobbie, A. and Garber, J. (1975) 'Girls and subcultures', in S. Hall and T. Jefferson (eds), *Resistance through Rituals*. London: Hutchinson, pp. 209–22.

Metz, M.H. (1994) 'Running between the raindrops', in K.P.M. Orlans and R.A. Wallace (eds), *Gender and the Academic Experience*. Lincoln, NE: University of Nebraska Press, pp. 219–28.

Meyrink, G. ([1915] 1985) *The Golem*. Leipzig: K. Wolff. Reprinted in English in 1985 by Dedalus, Cambridge.

Mirza, H.S. (ed.) (1997) *Black British Feminism*. London: Routledge.

Mitchell, Joseph (1993) *Up in the Old Hotel*. New York: Vintage.

Mitchell, Juliet (1966) *Woman's Estate*. Harmondsworth: Penguin.

Mitchell, Juliet (1975) *Psychoanalysis and Feminism*. London: Allen and Unwin.

Moi, T. (1994) *Simone de Beauvoir*. Oxford: Blackwell.

Moravcsik, M. (1988) 'Some contextual problems of science indicators', in A.F.J. van Raan (ed.), *Handbook of Quantitative Studies of Science and Technology*. New York: Elsevier, pp. 1–30.

Morgan, D.H.J. (1975) *The Family and Social Theory*. London: Routledge and Kegan Paul.

Morgan, D.H.J. (1981) 'Men, masculinity and the process of sociological enquiry', in H. Roberts (ed.), *Doing Feminist Research*. London: Routledge, pp. 83–113.

Morgan, D.H.J. and Stanley, L. (eds) (1993) *Debates in Sociology*. Manchester: Manchester University Press.

Morley, L. (1999) *Organising Feminisms*. London: Macmillan.

Morley, L. and Walsh, V. (eds) (1995) *Feminist Academics*. London: Taylor and Francis.

Morrish, I. (1972) *The Sociology of Education*, 2nd edition. London: Allen and Unwin.

Muncy, R. (1991) *Creating a Female Dominion in American Reform 1890–1935*. New York: Oxford University Press.

179

Murcott, A. (ed.) (1983) *A Sociology of Food and Eating*. Aldershot: Gower.

Murcott, A. (ed.) (1998) *The Nation's Diet*. London: Longman.

Murdock, G. and Phelps, C. (1973) *Mass Media and the Secondary School*. London: Macmillan.

Murphy, E. and Dingwall, R. (2001) 'The ethics of ethnography', in P.A. Atkinson, A. Coffey, S. Delamont, J. Lofland and L. Lofland (eds), *Handbook of Ethnography*. London: Sage, pp. 339–51.

Nelson, C. and Olesen, V. (1977) 'Veil of illusion', *Catalyst*, 10/11: 8–36.

Nicholson, L. (1999) *The Play of Reason*. Buckingham: Open University Press.

Nicholson, L. J. (ed.) (1990) *Feminism/Postmodernism*. London: Routledge.

Nielsen, J. McC. (ed.) (1990) *Feminist Research Methods*. Boulder, CO: Westview Press.

Noble, D.F. (1992) *A World without Women?* New York: Oxford University Press.

Numbers, R. (1992) *The Creationists*. New York: A.A. Knopf.

Oakley, A. (1974) *The Sociology of Housework*. Oxford: Martin Robertson.

Oakley, A. (1979) *Becoming a Mother*. London: Martin Robertson.

Oakley, A. (1998a) 'Science, gender and women's liberation: an argument against post-modernism', *Women's Studies International Forum*, 31 (2): 133–46.

Oakley, A. (1998b) 'Gender, methodology and people's ways of knowing', *Sociology*, 32 (4): 707–31.

Olesen, V. (1994) 'Feminisms and models of qualitative research', in N.K. Denzin and Y.S. Lincoln (eds), *Handbook of Qualitative Research*. Thousand Oaks, CA: Sage, pp. 158–74.

Olesen, V. (2000) 'Feminisms and qualitative research at and into the Millennium', in N. Denzin and Y. Lincoln (eds), *Handbook of Qualitative Research*, 2nd edition. Thousand Oaks, CA: Sage, pp. 215–56.

Olesen, V. (2002) 'Resisting "fatal unclutteredness": conceptualising the sociology of health and illness into the Millennium', in G. Bendelow, M. Carpenter, C. Vautier and S. Williams (eds), *Gender, Health and Healing*. London: Routledge. pp. 254–66.

Oliver, K. (ed.) (2000a) *French Feminism Reader*. Lanham, MD: Rowman and Littlefield.

Oliver, K. (2000b) 'Maternity, feminism, and language: Julie Kristeva', in K. Oliver (ed.), *French Feminism Reader*. Lanham, MD: Rowman and Littlefield, pp. 153–8.

ONS (1998) *Social Trends*. London: ONS.

Orlans, K.P.M. (1994) 'Gold and blue in California', in K.P.M. Orlans and R.A. Wallace (eds), *Gender and the Academic Experience*. Lincoln, NE: University of Nebraska Press, pp. 71–84.

Orlans, K.P.M. and Wallace, R.A. (eds) (1994) *Gender and the Academic Experience: Berkeley Women Sociologists*. Lincoln, NE: University of Nebraska Press.

Paechter, C. (1998) *Educating the Other*. Buckingham: Open University Press.

Pahl, J. (ed.) (1985) *Private Violence and Public Policy*. London: Routledge.

Pahl, J. (1990) *Money and Marriage*. London: Macmillan.

Pahl, J. (2000) 'Social polarisation in the electronic economy', in R. Crompton, F. Devine, M. Savage and J. Scott (eds), *Renewing Class Analysis*. Oxford: Blackwell, pp. 87–106.

Pahl, R. (1996) *After Success: Fin-de-siècle Anxiety and Identity*. Cambridge: Polity Press.

Parker, R. (1982) *Looking for Rachel Wallace*. London: Keyhole Crime.

Parker, R. (1985) *A Catskill Eagle*. Harmondsworth: Penguin.

Parkin, F. (1979) *Marxism and Class Theory: a Bourgeois Critique*. London: Tavistock.

Parsons, D.L. (2000) *Streetwalking the Metropolis*. Oxford: Oxford University Press.

Payne, G. (1987a) *Mobility and Change in Modern Society*. London: Macmillan.

Payne, G. (1987b) *Employment and Opportunity*. London: Macmillan.

Payne, G. and Abbott, P. (eds) (1990) *The Social Mobility of Women*. London: Taylor and Francis.

Pearson, D. (2000) Unpublished material supplied by the author.

Peshkin, A. (1986) *God's Choice*. Chicago: University of Chicago Press.

Phoenix, A., Woollet, A. and Lloyd, E. (eds) (1991) *Motherhood*. London: Sage.

Pilcher, J. (1998) *Women of their Time*. Aldershot: Ashgate.

Pilcher, J. (1999) *Women in Contemporary Britain*. London: Routledge.

Pilcher, J. and Wagg, S. (eds) (1996) *Thatcher's Children*. London: Falmer.

Platt, J. (1995) 'Research methods and the Second Chicago School', in G.A. Fine (ed.), *A Second Chicago School?* Chicago: University of Chicago Press, pp. 82–107.

Prather, J.E. (1995) 'Acquiring an academic room of one's own', in A. Goetting and S. Fenstermaker (eds), *Individual Voices, Collective Visions*. Philadelphia, PA: Temple University Press, pp. 69–86.

Pratt, M.L. (1986) 'Fieldwork in common places', in J. Clifford and G. Marcus (eds), *Writing Culture*. Berkeley, CA: University of California Press, pp. 27–50.

Presser, H.B. (1994) 'The personal is political and professional', in K.P.M. Orlans and R.A. Wallace (eds), *Gender and the Academic Experience*. Lincoln, NE: University of Nebraska Press, pp. 141–56.

Pugsley, L. (1998) 'Throwing your brains at it', *International Studies in the Sociology of Education*, 8 (1): 71–90.

Purdue, D., Durrschmidt, J., Jowers, P. and O'Doherty, R. (1997) 'DIY culture and extended milieux', *Sociological Review*, 45 (4): 645–667.

Rahkonen, K. and Roos, J.P. (1992) 'The field of intellectuals', in N. Kauppi and P. Sulkunen (eds), *Vanguards of Modernity*. Jyvaskyla: University of Jyvaskyla Press, pp. 107–28.

Ramazanoglu, C. (1996) 'Unravelling postmodern paralysis', *Women's History Review*, 5 (1): 19–24.

Rapaport, R. and Rapaport, R. (1976) *Dual Career Families*. Harmondsworth: Penguin.

Raushenbush, W. (1979) *Robert E. Park: Biography of a Sociologist*. Durham, NC: Duke University Press.

Reed-Danahay, D. (ed.) (1997) *Auto/Ethnography*. Oxford: Berg.

Reed-Danahay, D. (2001) 'Autobiography, intimacy and ethnography', in P.A. Atkinson, A. Coffey, S. Delamont, J. Lofland and L. Lofland (eds), *Handbook of Ethnography*. London: Sage, pp. 407–25.

Rees, T. (2001) 'Mainstreaming gender equality in science in the European Union: the ETAN Report', *Gender and Education*, 13 (3): 243–60.

Reinharz, S. (1995) 'Marginality, motherhood, and method', in A. Goetting and S. Fenstermaker (eds), *Individual Voices, Collective Visions*. Philadelphia, PA: Temple University Press, pp. 285–302.

Rendel, M. (1980) 'How many women academics 1912–1976?', in R. Deem (ed.), *Schooling for Women's Work*. London: Routledge and Kegan Paul, pp. 142–61.

Reskin, B. (1978) 'Sex differentiation and the social organisation of science', in J. Gaston (ed.), *The Sociology of Science*. San Francisco: Jossey-Bass, pp. 6–37.

Rhea, B. (ed.) (1981) *The Future of the Sociological Classics*. London: Allen and Unwin.

Richardson, C.J. (1977) *Contemporary Social Mobility*. London: Frances Pinter.

Richardson, D. (1996) 'Misguided, dangerous and wrong', in D. Bell and R. Klein (eds), *Radically Speaking*. London: Zed Books, pp. 143–54.

Riesman, D. (1988) 'On discovering and teaching sociology', *Annual Review of Sociology*, 14: 1–24.

Riley, M.W. (ed.) (1988) *Sociological Lives*. Newbury Park, CA: Sage.

181

Riley, M.W. (1990) 'The influence of sociological lives: personal reflections', *Annual Review of Sociology*, 16: 1–25.

Ripellino, A.M. (1995) *Magic Prague*. Harmondsworth: Penguin.

Risman, B.J. and Tomaskovic-Devey, D. (1999) 'Editor's note', *Contemporary Sociology*, 28 (3): vii–viii.

Roberts, H. (ed.) (1981) *Doing Feminist Research*. London: Routledge.

Roberts, H. (1986) 'The social classification of women', *EOC Research Bulletin*, 10, 47–70.

Roberts, H. (1993) 'The women and class debate', in D. Morgan and L. Stanley (eds), *Debates in Sociology*. Manchester: Manchester University Press. pp. 72–90.

Roby, P.A. (1995) 'Becoming an active, feminist, academic', in A. Goetting and S. Fenstermaker (eds), *Individual Voices, Collective Visions*. Philadelphia, PA: Temple University Press, pp. 319–42.

Rock, P. (1979) *The Making of Symbolic Interactionism*. London: Macmillan.

Rock, P. (2001) 'Symbolic interactionism and ethnography', in P.A. Atkinson, A. Coffey, S. Delamont, J. Lofland and L. Lofland (eds), *Handbook of Ethnography*. London: Sage, pp. 26–38.

Roman, L.G. (1992) 'The political significance of other ways of narrating ethnography', in M.D. LeCompte, W.L. Millroy and J. Preissle (eds), *The Handbook of Qualitative Research in Education*. San Diego: Academic Press, pp. 555–94.

Ronai, C.R. (1996) 'My mother is mentally retarded', in C. Ellis and A.P. Bochner (eds), *Composing Ethnography*. Walnut Creek, CA: AltaMira, pp. 109–31.

Rose, H. (1983) 'Hand, brain and heart: towards a feminist epistemology for the natural sciences', *Signs*, 9 (1): 73–96.

Rose, H. (1994) *Love, Power and Knowledge*. Cambridge: Polity Press.

Rose, S. (1986) *Keeping Them out of the Hands of Satan*. New York: Routledge.

Rosenberg, M.B. and Bergstrom, L.V. (eds) (1975) *Women and Society: a Critical Review of the Literature with a Selected, Annotated Bibliography*. London: Sage.

Rosenberg, R. (1982) *Beyond Separate Spheres: Intellectual Roots of Modern Feminism*. New Haven, CT: Yale University Press.

Roseneil, L. (1995) 'The coming of age of feminist sociology', *British Journal of Sociology*, 46 (2): 191–205.

Rossi, A. (1984) 'Gender and parenthood', *American Sociological Review*, 49 (1): 1–19.

Rossiter, M. (1982) *Women Scientists in America: Struggles and Strategies to 1940*. Baltimore, MD: Johns Hopkins University Press.

Rossiter, M. (1995) *Women Scientists in America: Before Affirmative Action 1940–1972*. Baltimore, MD: Johns Hopkins University Press.

Roth, G. (1990) 'Partisanship and scholarship', in B. Berger (ed.), *Authors of their Own Lives*. Berkeley, CA: University of California Press, pp. 383–409.

Rubin, L.B. (1994) 'An unanticipated life', in K.P.M. Orlans and R.A. Wallace (eds), *Gender and the Academic Experience*. Lincoln, NE: University of Nebraska Press, pp. 229–48.

Sanjek, R. (ed.) (1990) *Fieldnotes*. Ithaca, NY: Cornell University Press.

Savage, M. (2000) *Class Analysis and Social Transformation*. Buckingham: Open University Press.

Sayers, J. (1991) *Mothering Psychoanalysis*. London: Hamish Hamilton.

Sayers, J., Evans, M. and Redclift, N. (eds) (1987) *Engels Revisited: New Feminist Essays*. London: Tavistock.

Scanlon, J. (1998) 'Educating the living, remembering the dead: the Montreal massacre as metaphor', in G. Cohee et al. (eds), *The Feminist Teacher Anthology*. New York: Teachers College Press, pp. 224–33.

Schiebinger, L. (1989) *The Mind Has No Sex?* Cambridge, MA: Harvard University Press.

Schiebinger, L. (1993) *Nature's Body*. Boston: Beacon.

Schiebinger, L. (1999) *Has Feminism Changed Science?* Cambridge, MA: Harvard University Press.

Schwendinger, J. and Schwendinger, H. (1971) 'Sociology's founding fathers: sexists to a man', *Journal of Marriage and the Family*, 33 (4): 708–800.

Schwendinger, J. and Schwendinger, H. (1974) *The Sociologists of the Chair*. New York: Basic Books.

Scott, H. (1974) *Does Socialism Liberate Women?* Boston: Beacon Press.

Scott, J. (1995) *Sociological Theory: Contemporary Debates*. Aldershot: Edward Elgar.

Scott, J. (1997) 'Changing households in Britain', *Sociological Review*, 45 (4): 591–620.

Scott, S. and Morgan, D.H.J. (eds) (1993) *Body Matters*. London: Falmer.

Sharrock, W. and Anderson, J. (1986) *The Ethnomethodologists*. London: Tavistock.

Sherman, J.A. and Beck, E.T. (eds) (1979) *The Prism of Sex: Essays in the Sociology of Knowledge*. Madison, WI: University of Wisconsin Press.

Showalter, E. (1996) *Hystories: Hysterical Epidemics and Modern Culture*. London: Picador.

Singleton, V. (1996) 'Feminism, sociology of scientific knowledge and postmodernism', *Social Studies of Science*, 26 (2): 445–64.

Skeggs, B. (1988) 'Gender reproduction and further education', *British Journal of the Sociology of Education*, 9 (2): 131–49.

Sklar, K.K. (1973) *Catharine Beecher*. New Haven, CT: Yale University Press.

Sklar, K.K. (1995) *Florence Kelley and the Nation's Work*. New Haven, CT: Yale University Press.

Smart, C. (1976) *Women, Crime and Criminology*. London: Routledge and Kegan Paul.

Smelser, N. (ed.) (1988) *Handbook of Sociology*. London: Sage.

Smith, D. (1988) *The Chicago School*. London: Macmillan.

Smith, D. (1972) 'Women, the family and corporate capitalism', unpublished paper presented to the Canadian Anthropological and Sociological Association.

Smith, D. (1973) 'Women, the family and corporate capitalism', in M. Stephenson (ed.), *Women in Canada*. Don Mills, ON: General Publishing Co. pp. 14–48.

Smith, D. (1975) 'An analysis of ideological structures and how women are excluded', *Canadian Review of Sociology and Anthropology*, 12, 4, 1, 335.

Smith, D. (1977) 'Women and corporate capitalism', in M. Stephenson (ed.), *Women in Canada*, revised expanded edition. Don Mills, ON: General Publishing Co, pp. 14–48.

Smith, D. (1978) 'K is mentally ill', *Sociology*, 12 (1): 25–53.

Smith, D. (1979) 'A sociology for women', in J.A. Sherman and E.T. Beck (eds), *The Prism of Sex*. Madison, WI: University of Wisconsin Press, pp. 135–84.

Smith, D. (1987) *The Everyday World as Problematic: a Feminist Sociology*. Boston: Northeastern University Press.

Smith, D. (1989) 'Sociological theory: methods of writing patriarchy', in R.A. Wallace (ed.), *Feminism and Sociological Theory*. Newbury Park, CA: Sage, pp. 34–64.

Smith, D. (1990) *The Conceptual Practices of Power*. Toronto: University of Toronto Press.

Smith, D. (1994) 'A Berkeley education', in K.P.M. Orlans and R.A. Wallace (eds), *Gender and the Academic Experience*. Lincoln, NE: University of Nebraska Press, pp. 45–56.

Smith, D. (1999) *Writing the Social: Critique, Theory, and Investigations*. Toronto: University of Toronto Press.

Smith, D. (2000) 'Comment on Hekman's "Truth and method: feminist standpoint theory revisited"', in C. Allen and J.A. Howard (eds), *Provoking Feminisms*. London: Routledge, pp. 59–65.

Smith, D. and David, S. (eds) (1975) *Women Look at Psychiatry*. Vancouver: Press Gang.

Smith, L.S. (1978) 'Sexist assumptions and female delinquency', in C. Smart and B. Smart (eds), *Women, Sexuality and Social Control*. London: Routledge and Kegan Paul, pp. 74–86.

Snow, C.P. (1934) *The Search*. London: Gollancz.

Sokal, A. and Bricmont, J. (1997) *Impostures Intellectuelles*. Paris: Odile Jacob.

Sonnert, G. and Holton, G. (1995) *Gender Differences in Science Careers*. New Brunswick, NJ: Rutgers University Press.

Spencer, M. (1994) 'On the way to the forum', in K.P.M. Orlans and R.A. Wallace (eds), *Gender and the Academic Experience*. Lincoln, NE: University of Nebraska Press, pp. 157–72.

Spender, D. (1983) *Feminist Theorists: Three Centuries of Key Women Thinkers*. New York: Pantheon.

Spivak, G. (1988) 'Can the Subaltern speak?', in C. Nelson and L. Grossberg (eds), *Marxism and the Interpretation of Culture*. Urbana, IL: University of Illinois Press, pp. 271–313.

Stacey, J. (1997) 'Disloyal to the disciplines', in B. Laslett and B. Thorne (eds), *Feminist Sociology: Life Histories of a Movement*. New Brunswick, NJ: Rutgers University Press, pp. 126–50.

Stacey, J. and Thorne, B. (1985) 'The missing feminist revolution in sociology', *Social Problems*, 32: 301–16.

Stacey, M. (2002) 'Concluding comments', in G. Bendelow, M. Carpenter, C. Vautier and S. Williams (eds), *Gender, Health and Healing*. London: Routledge, pp. 267–83.

Stacey, M., Batstone, E., Bell, C. and Murcott, A. (1975) *Power, Persistence and Change*. London: Routledge.

Stanley, L. (ed.) (1992) *The Auto/biographical I*. Manchester: Manchester University Press.

Stanley, L. (1996) 'The mother of invention: necessity, writing and representatives', *Feminism and Psychology*, 6 (1): 45–52.

Stanley, L. (2000) 'Children of our time', in H. Hodkinson (ed.), *Feminism and Educational Research Methodologies*. Manchester: Manchester Metropolitan University, pp. 5–35.

Stanley, L. (2001) 'Mass-observation's fieldwork methods', in P.A. Atkinson, A. Coffey, S. Delamont, J. Lofland and L. Lofland (eds), *Handbook of Ethnography*. London: Sage, pp. 92–108.

Stanley, L. and Wise, S. (1979) 'Feminist research, feminist consciousness and experience of sexism', *Women's Studies International Quarterly*, 2 (4): 359–74.

Stanley, L. and Wise, S. (1983) *Breaking Out*. London: Routledge.

Stanley, L. and Wise, S. (1993) *Breaking Out Again*. London: Routledge.

Stanton, D.C. and Stewart, A.J. (eds) (1995) *Feminisms in the Academy*. Ann Arbor, MI: University of Michigan Press.

Stanworth, M. (1981) *Gender and Schooling*. London: Women's Research and Resources Centre.

Stanworth, M. (1983) 'Women and class analysis', *Sociology*, 18 (2): 159–70.

Statham, A., Richardson, L. and Cook, J.A. (1991) *Gender and University Teaching*. Albany, NY: SUNY Press.

Stephenson, M. (ed.) (1973) *Women in Canada*. Don Mills, ON: General Publishing Co.

184

Stephenson, M. (ed.) (1977a) *Women in Canada*, revised expanded edition. Don Mills, ON: General Publishing Co.

Stephenson, M. (1977b) 'Women, the family and corporate capitalism', in M. Stephenson (ed.), *Women in Canada*, revised expanded edition. Don Mills, ON: General Publishing Co, pp. 14–16.

Stewart, A., Prandy, K. and Blackburn, R.M. (1980) *Social Stratification and Occupations*. London: Macmillan.

Stewart, C. (1990) *Demons and the Devil*. Princeton, NJ: Princeton University Press.

Storace, C. (1996) *Dinner with Persephone*. London: Granta.

Sullivan, O. (1997) 'Time waits for no (wo)man', *Sociology*, 31 (2): 221–40.

Sullivan, P. (1999) 'Response to MacKenzie', *Social Studies of Science*, 29 (2): 215–22.

Taft, J. ([1913] 1987) 'The woman movement and social consciousness'. Reprinted in M.J. Deegan and M. Hill (eds), *Women and Symbolic Interactionism*. Boston: Allen and Unwin, pp. 19–50.

Talbot, M. ([1910] 1998) *The Education of Women*. Chicago: University of Chicago Press. Extract reprinted in P.M. Lengermann and J. Niebrugge-Brantley (eds) (1998) *The Women Founders*. Boston: McGraw-Hill, pp. 269–71.

Talbot, M. (1936) *More than Lore*. Chicago: University of Chicago Press.

Tan, M.G. (1994) 'Indonesian odyssey', in K.P.M. Orlans and R.A. Wallace (eds), *Gender and the Academic Experience*. Lincoln, NE: University of Nebraska Press, pp. 85–94.

Taraborrelli, P. (1993) 'Becoming a carer', in N. Gilbert (ed.), *Researching Social Life*. London: Sage, pp. 172–86.

Tescione, S.M. (1998) 'A woman's name: implications for publication, citation and tenure', *Educational Researcher*, 27 (8): 38–42.

Tester, K. (ed.) (1994a) *The Flâneur*. London: Routledge.

Tester, K. (1994b) 'Introduction', in K. Tester (ed.), *The Flâneur*. London: Routledge, pp. 1–21.

Tey, J. (1946) *Miss Pym Disposes*. London: Peter Davies.

Thomas, R. (1986) 'Classification of women's occupations', *EOC Research Bulletin*, 10., 28–46.

Thorne, B. (1997) 'Brandeis as a generative institution', in B. Laslett and B. Thorne (eds), *Feminist Sociology: Life Histories of a Movement*. New Brunswick, NJ: Rutgers University Press, pp. 103–25.

Thorne, B., Kramarae, C. and Henley, N. (1983) *Language, Gender and Society*. Rowley, MA: Newbury House.

Tierney, W.G. (1993) 'Self and identity in a postmodern world', in D. McLaughlin and W.G. Tierney (eds), *Naming Silenced Lives*. New York: Routledge, pp. 119–34.

Tierney, W.G. and Dilley, P. (1998) 'Constructing knowledge', in W.F. Pinar (ed.), *Queer Theory in Education*. Mahwah, NJ: Erlbaum, pp. 49–71.

Tierney, W.G. and Dilley, P. (2002) 'Interviewing in education', in J.F. Gubrium and J.A. Holstein (eds), *Handbook of Interview Research*. London: Sage, pp. 453–72.

Tillmann-Healy, L.M. (1996) 'A secret life in a culture of thinness', in C. Ellis and A. Bochner (eds), *Composing Ethnography*. Walnut Creek, CA: AltaMira, pp. 76–108.

Tiryakian, E.A. (1978) 'Emile Durkheim', in T. Bottomore and R. Nisbet (eds), *A History of Sociological Analysis*. London: Heinemann, pp. 187–236.

Tomasi, L. (ed.) (1998) *The Tradition of the Chicago School of Sociology*. Aldershot: Ashgate.

Tooley, J. (1998) *Educational Research: An OFSTED Critique*. London: OFSTED.

Tuchman, G. (1995) 'Kaddish and renewal', in A. Goetting and S. Fenstermaker (eds), *Individual Voices, Collective Visions*. Philadelphia, PA: Temple University Press, pp. 303–18.

185

Urban Life (1983) Special issue on the Chicago School, *Urban Life,* 11 (4).

Valentine, G. (1999) 'Eating in', *Sociological Review*, 47 (3): 491–524.

Verhoeven, J. (1992) 'Backstage with Erving Goffman', *Research on Language and Social Interaction*, 26 (3): 307–16.

Vicinus, M. (1985) *Independent Women*. London: Virago.

Vogler, C. (1998) 'Money in the household', *Sociological Review*, 46 (4): 687–713.

Vogler, C. and Pahl, J. (1994) 'Money, power and inequality within marriage', *Sociological Review*, 42 (2): 263–88.

Wade, L.C. (1977) 'Julia Lathrop', in E.T. James et al. (eds), *Notable American Women*, volume 2. Cambridge, MA: Harvard University Press, pp. 370–2.

Walby, S. (1990) *Theorising Patriarchy*. Oxford: Blackwell.

Walby, S. (1992) 'Post-post-modernism? Theorizing social complexity', in M. Barrett and A. Phillips (eds), *Destabilising Theory*. Cambridge: Polity Press, pp. 31–52.

Walby, S. (1997) *Gender Transformations*. London: Routledge.

Walker, S. and Barton, L. (eds) (1983) *Gender, Class and Education*. Brighton: Falmer.

Walkowitz, J.R. (1992) *City of Dreadful Delight: Narratives of Danger in Late-Victorian London*. London: Virago.

Wallace, R. (ed.) (1989) *Feminism and Sociological Theory*. Newbury Park, CA: Sage.

Wallace, R.A. (1994) 'Transformation from sacred to secular', in K.P.M. Orlans and R.A. Wallace (eds), *Gender and the Academic Experience*. Lincoln, NE: University of Nebraska Press, pp. 99–112.

Ward, K.B. and Grant, L. (1985) 'The feminist critique and a decade of published research in sociology journals', *Sociological Quarterly*, 26 (2): 139–57.

Warde, A., Martens, L. and Olsen, W. (1999) 'Consumption and the problem of variety', *Sociology*, 33 (1): 105–28.

Wartenberg, H.S. (1995) 'Obstacles and opportunities en route to a career in sociology', in A. Goetting and S. Fenstermaker (eds), *Individual Voices, Collective Visions*. Philadelphia, PA: Temple University Press, pp. 51–67.

Waters, K. (1996) '(Re) turning to the modern', in D. Bell and R. Klein (eds), *Radically Speaking*. London: Zed Books, pp. 280–96.

Watson, C. (1971) *Snobbery with Violence*. London: Eyre and Spottiswood.

Watson, G.L. (ed.) (1990a) *Feminism and Women's Issues: an Annotated Bibliography and Research Guide*, volume I. New York: Garland.

Watson, G.L. (ed.) (1990b) *Feminism and Women's Issues: An Annotated Bibliography and Research Guide*, volume II. New York: Garland.

Weedon, C. (1987) *Feminist Practice and Poststructuralist Theory*. Oxford: Blackwell.

Weiler, K. (ed.) (2001) *Feminist Engagements: Reading, Resisting and Revisioning Male Theorists in Education and Cultural Studies*. New York: Routledge.

Weiner, G. (1994) *Feminisms in Education*. Buckingham: Open University Press.

Whitford, M. (1991) *Luce Irigaray: Philosophy in the Feminine*. London: Routledge.

Whittier, N. (1999) 'The academic is political is personal', *Contemporary Sociology*, 28 (3): 285–6.

Whyte, J. (1985) *Girls into Science and Technology*. London: Routledge and Kegan Paul.

Williams, G., Blackstone, T. and Metcalf, D. (1974) *The Academic Labour Market*. Amsterdam: Elsevier.

Willmott, P. (1985) 'The Institute of Community Studies', in M. Bulmer (ed.), *Essays on the History of British Social Research*. Cambridge: Cambridge University Press, pp. 137–50.

Wilson, D. (1978) 'Sexual codes and conduct', in C. Smart and B. Smart (eds), *Women, Sexuality and Social Control*. London: Routledge and Kegan Paul, pp. 65–73.

Wilson, E. (1991) *The Sphinx in the City: Urban Life, the Control of Disorder, and Women*. London: Virago.

Wilson, E. (2001) *The Contradictions of Culture*. London: Sage.

Wipper, A. (1994) 'A sociological venture', in K.P.M. Orlans and R.A. Wallace (eds), *Gender and the Academic Experience*. Lincoln, NE: University of Nebraska Press, pp. 173–82.

Wiseman, J.P. (1994) 'New perspectives, new freedoms', in K.P.M. Orlans and R.A. Wallace (eds), *Gender and the Academic Experience*. Lincoln, NE: University of Nebraska Press, pp. 183–200.

Wittig, M. (1992) *The Straight Mind and Other Essays*. Hemel Hempstead: Harvester Wheatsheaf.

Witz, A. (1992) *Professions and Patriarchy*. London: Routledge.

Wolf, M. (1992) *The Thrice Told Tale*. Stanford, CA: Stanford University Press.

Wolff, J. (1985) 'The invisible flâneuse', *Theory, Culture and Society*, 2 (3): 37–48.

Wolff, J. (1993) *Feminine Sentences* Cambridge: Polity

Wolff, J. (1994) 'The artist and the flâneur', in K. Tester (ed.), *The Flâneur*. London: Routledge, pp. 111-37.

Woodhead, C. (1998) 'Academia gone to seed', *New Statesman*, 20 March: 51–2.

Woods, P. (1996) *Researching the Art of Teaching*. London: Routledge.

Worsley, P. (ed.) (1970) *Introducing Sociology*. Harmondsworth: Penguin.

Worsley, P. (ed.) (1977) *Introducing Sociology*, 2nd edition. Harmondsworth: Penguin.

Worsley, P. (ed.) (1987) *The New Introducing Sociology*, 3rd edition. Harmondsworth: Penguin.

Wyer, M., Barbercheck, M., Giesman, D., Orun Ozturk, H. and Wayne, M. (eds) (2001) *Women, Science and Technology: A Reader in Feminist Science Studies*. New York: Routledge.

Yair, G. (2001) 'Ex cathedra', *Sociology*, 35 (2): 477–500.

Yeo, E.J. (ed.) (1997) *Mary Wollstonecraft and 200 Years of Feminisms*. London: Rivers Oram.

Young, M. and Willmott, P. (1975) *The Symmetrical Family*. Harmondsworth: Penguin.

Zuckerman, H. (1977) *Scientific Elite*. New York: Free Press.

Zuckerman, H., Cole, J.R. and Bruer, J.T. (eds) (1991) *The Outer Circle*. New York: W.W. Norton.

index